History of the Church in Ukraine
Rev. George Fedoriw, S.Th.D.

A MILLENNIUM OF CHRISTIANITY IN UKRAINE
PROJECT

Rev. George Fedoriw, S.Th.D.

History of the Church in Ukraine*

Publishers

"ST. SOPHIA" RELIGIOUS ASSOCIATION
OF UKRAINIAN CATHOLICS IN CANADA
85 Lakeshore Road, St. Catharines
Ontario L2N 2T6

* The views expressed in this book are solely those of the author.

Rev. George Fedoriw, S.Th.D.

History of the Church in Ukraine

Translated by Petro Krawchuk

Toronto, 1983

Canadian Cataloguing in Publication Data

Fedoriv, IUriĭ, 1907 —
    History of the Church in Ukraine

Translation of: Istoriia Tserkvy v Ukraïni
Bibliography: p.
ISBN 0-9691657-0-6

1. Christianity — Ukraine — History.
I. St. Sophia Religious Association of Ukrainian
    Catholics in Canada
II. Title.

BR937.U4F413 1984   209'.47'71   C84-090048-1

Preface

The evangelic rule, which teaches eternal and unchanging laws, is the only road to the transformation of a person into a being filled with love and respect for his neighbour, for his nation and for mankind in general. The Church teaches a person obedience, discipline, organization, and the subordination of one's own interests to the common needs, the temporal to the eternal, and the materialistic to the spiritual.

In this way, the Church, along with her primary purpose of bringing souls to eternal bliss, also makes possible a wise and just arrangement of one's life on this earth. The Church helps to form good and honest citizens, self-giving and honorable members of society, and directs a person's natural talents to the highest goals.

The Church develops literature and art, occupies herself with charitable works, spreads education and knowledge, improves the school system, takes care of the sick, the orphans, the old, prisoners, widows etc. In this light, the Church has an unusually important and responsible place in society.

The Church is neither a building nor a collection of priests and bishops. Rather, she is the community of believers, united in the true faith under the guidance of the teaching authority of the Church established by Jesus Christ.

For this reason, believers in the Church should realize their living organic bond to this Church, and their calling to be actual members of this mystical body, to care for her and to regard her destiny, her joy and her affliction as their own.

Each person who is a member of the Church should be familiar with her past, her history and development, her periods of growth and decline, her mistakes and how these mistakes could have been avoided and how they could be eliminated in the future.

Ukrainian children although they are a small part of the Christian Church, are the future bearers of Ukrainian traditions and culture. The fate of the Ukrainian Church rests with them - whether she is to develop or wither or decay, grow or decline, bring peace and love to her nation or squabbles and disorder. For this reason, Ukrainian children should carefully study the past of their Mother Church as well as her present, they should love their Church, realize her importance and her eternal and timely mission and make all possible effort to help Christ's Church grow among Ukrainians, so that she may spread and carefully observe the commandments of her Founder - for God's glory, for the salvation of human souls, and for the good of Ukrainian people.

Introduction

Pre-christian Beliefs in the Ukraine.

History teaches that every nation, regardless of its stage of cultural development, has some sort of religion. This religion serves to give the nation an explanation for the mysteries of life and the surrounding powers of nature and to provide a certain order of interaction among people.

Each ancient nation had its own religion before embracing Christianity. The more developed nations such as the Egyptians, the Romans, the Greeks, and the Persians, had the more developed religions, with a hierarchical order of greater and lesser gods, while the less developed nations had more primitive religions. Many factors influenced the formation of a religious complex, for example the character of the ancient country's proximity to other religions, social relations, and in a significant way even the natural setting of the country.

In what did the Ukrainian ancestors believe before they accepted Christianity? Christianity was probably filtering into Ukraine long before its official establishment in the tenth century, but we have no definite record of this. Up until that time, the general belief of Ukrainian ancestors was pagan, in that they believed in different natural powers and the imaginary gods whom these powers of nature represented. Since the natural environment setting of Ukraine is gentle, sunny, and rich, so too its gods were gentle. Generally speaking, they neither helped nor hindered anyone very much. This was the oldest form of religious belief in the Ukraine. Only later, under the influence of other religions, mainly the Iranian, did a differentiation between good and hostile gods set in.

The greatest god in the ancient religion of those who dwelt in the Ukraine was "Svaroh", god of the heavens, who controlled the destiny of the whole world. In the period of the formation of the nation in the IX century, primacy was taken by the terrible god "Perun". The fight for life against the elements of nature and vicious neighbours demanded effort and sacrifice. Therefore the early Ukrainian ancestors determined that a god who controlled great power and whom one had to respect should take precedence. The greatest power, which could not be understood, was that of thunder and lightning and Perun became its personification. All the other gods, both greater and lesser, had to obey and yield to him.

Dazhboh was the sun-god, on whom depended life and harvests. Veles had charge of beasts - not a very honorable position, but an important one, since cattle constituted wealth. The wind-god was Striboh and the god of the subterranean fires was Cora, the latter probably of Greek origin. Thus each natural power had its own god. Besides the gods, there were also goddesses. Lada was the goddess of beauty and love. Spring symbolized the mystery of life, the secret powers which gave life to flowers and greenery and fed and beautified the earth and after the winter's sleep. Clouds gave rain and so fulfilled an essential need of the people. The only figure among the greater gods which filled the people with fear was Marena, the goddess of death.

Besides these greater gods, there were also the lesser ones. In this group were the house demons, the woodland spirits, the field demons, the water deities, the water nymphs and many more.

The house demons looked after houses, the home fires, the households; they brought luck but could also bring misfortune to anyone who offended them. The woodland spirits took on different forms, chiefly those of forest animals and would often do mischief to people. It was better not to meet these spirits. The field demons had a useful function - to guard the fields. They danced in the fields, meadows, and hayfields and could change into all sorts of birds. The water deities stayed in the streams, lakes and swamps, watched the fishes, and wooed the nymphs. Nymphs were women or girls who had died an unusual death. They were weary of the world and so they took on a human likeness and wandered like real people through forests, along streams and lakes, and showed themselves to people, especially youths. The water nymphs were dead children as well. Like the nymphs, they could also take on a human likeness, but their bodies were transparent from the back and their insides were visible.

Each of these gods and deities had his own specialty and his own special talents, and each was generally helpful. Under the influence of the eastern Pagan religions, the notion of the existence of hostile gods other than these kindly or indifferent gods was adopted by the Ukrainian ancestors. Just at the beginning of the formation of the nation, the god Div, of night and fear in the night, came to the fore. He always appeared as the soothsayer bringing news of great misfortune, as the ominous spirit of night and the dark world. Subject to him were a whole group of evil deities of lesser rank - devils, demons, fiends, and possibly witches, vampires and other horrors.

Recognizing these gods, our ancestors preferred to live with them in peace and harmony, so they evolved certain modes of behaviour towards the gods. They normally prayed to their gods near water, near a stream or a well, or under trees. Prayer in these places was most pleasing to the gods. In contrast with Greek or Roman practice, no temples were put up, nor were these gods very capricious. Instead, chapels or statues were built to which sacrifices of animals or plants were brought. There was no separate caste of magicians or priests and only seldom is there any mention of such functions. Perhaps those magicians who are mentioned were in the service of a foreign cult. The function of priest was carried out by the eldest male in the family, either the father or the grandfather.

The whole year was divided into ritual cycles. As soon as the snow had melted, processions to the nymphs took place and the dead were remembered. The belief was that this was the time when the nymphs and water nymphs came out of the water to breathe some fresh air. Bread was left for the nourishment of the nymphs, and entertainment - music with drums and zithers and dancing - was provided so that they wouldn't be sad. Each family took the opportunity to remember its dead. They believed that only the body

7

dies, while the soul lives on. The soul lives either in the same place as did the body before death, or it goes to paradise. When someone was being buried, he was given food and such things as was believed would be of use to him in the other world. Sometimes even drinks were included.

When spring blossomed in all her beauty, she was also greeted with songs and dances. The approach of the summer sun was celebrated by the Kupalo feast. Kupalo had some connection with the harvest or crops (corresponding to the Greeks' Demeter and the Romans' Ceres). This was when nature put forth its greatest beauty and many wondrous things occurred; ferns, whose flowers had miraculous power began to bloom. On this eve, people gathered near streams, burned bonfires, sang, played games, and danced. Also at this time young people took the opportunity to socialize.

In the winter, the feast of the Koliada took place. This was the feast of the shortest day of the year, when the sun turned from the autumn season to the winter. At this feast the dead were again remembered - parents, grandparents and great-grandparents. The feast began with a sacred supper, to which ghosts were invited as well, so that they could come and be merry with live people. The Koliada feast went on for two weeks of good times until Shchedry Vechir. Members of families would visit one another, feast, and sing Koliada - Shchedry Vechir carols. In these carols they glorified the gods, kings and heroes, sang of military compaigns, and finally sang to the honor of their host and to each other's good health.

Pagan religions evolved throughout long centuries. Within the religions, there are observable influences of other neighbouring religions, stratification of cultures, historical changes and so on, all these having an effect on the people's view of the world and all their beliefs.

What is striking in the religion of the Ukrainian forefathers is that in it is reflected a regular cycle of life throughout the whole year. Entering the spring season, the people considered it necessary to remember their dead ancestors, whose souls remained near the family hearth. This tight bond between the living and the dead shows their belief in the immortal should, despite the fact that they understood this immortality in their own way. In the spring, the time of the awakening of nature, the blooming of life, the exuberance of nature, the freshness of the wind, one had to make manifest one's gladness, enter into the spirit of nature, and emulate her hospitality, her readiness for action and her creative power. This was the beginning of a time of work, joyful, profitable work which is the basis, the essence of life. And since life itself is a mystery, all these accompanying customs have an unusual, mysterious character.

With the introduction of Christianity, many elements of the ancient pagan religions were adapted to the needs of the Church and the demands of the new faith. The ancient pagan feasts were replaced with Christian feasts, the pagan cycle with the Christian. Still with us today are many of the ancient customs, customs which do not conflict with Christian teaching but vigorously remind us of the efforts of our forefathers to discover the eternal laws and to realize them in their lives.

The First Era

From the beginnings of Christianity in the Rus-Ukraine to the decline of Kiev (1240)

1. St. Andrew the First-Called Apostle in the Hills of Kiev.

Historical Facts.
It is not known exactly when the word of God's grace first sounded in the Ukrainian territories. Perhaps this was in the early period of Christianity. There is preserved from ancient times an oral tradition that the Apostle St. Andrew, the first disciple of Christ the Saviour, had already proclaimed God's word or truth among the Ukrainian ancestors. In keeping with the traditions of the early Church, after the Apostles' baptism with the Holy Spirit, St. Andrew the Apostle immediately left to proclaim Christ's message among the nations of Asia Minor, Georgia, Scythia, Macedonia and Greece. The information that the Apostle Andrew stayed in the territories of Ukraine is found in Eusebius, who first began the writing of the history of the Christian Church at about the beginning of the fourth century, as well as in the writings of other ancient authors. At that time Eusebius had better sources on the beginnings of Christianity and the missionary activity of the Apostles than we have today. For this reason the legend about Saint Andrew and his teachings in the hills of Kiev is today not without foundation.

St. Andrew in the mountains of Kiev.
In the Tale of Bygone Years, the chronicler tells of the Apostle Andrew's coming from Synopa, a small town in Asia Minor, to Corsunia at Crimea. Corsunia, which at that time was called Kherson, was largely populated by Greek-colonists and constituted an important trade center. Traders came here from Asia Minor, Greece, Scythia and other northern countries. Having found out in Corsunia about the trade route "from the Varangians to the Greeks" that is, the Dnieper, Saint Andrew - writes the chronicler Nestor - travelled up the Dnieper and came to the present site of Kiev. Here he stayed the night, and upon rising in the morning, he turned to his followers and pointing to the hills of Kiev he announced, "Do you see those hills? Look, for God's grace will shine on those hills and a great city with many churches will rise in that place!" After this prophecy he went up the hills, blessed them and erected a cross, the first cross on the Ukrainian lands.

A critique of the oral tradition about St. Andrew.
Historians do not give credence to this oral tradition, believing that it is a product of the times when Christianity began to flourish on a large scale in Ukraine. So as not to be a "lesser" among nations, historians say that the chronicler thought it worthwhile to have an Apostle as the first announcer of God's word in Rus-Ukraine. This very conjecture of the annalist was re-

peated and upheld by the Synod in Kiev, at a very uncomfortable time for the Ukrainian Church. The Synod stated that "Ukraine is in no way lesser than any other Eastern nations, since an Apostle preached on her territories as well".

Indeed, a complete denial of the preaching of St. Andrew in these lands is not altogether justified. Even though we have no reliable source materials, written documents, or other convincing proofs, there is at least a kernel of truth hidden in the legend about St. Andrew. The afore-mentioned historian Eusebius and others of his contemporaries, like Theooret, Hippolit and Origen, described the missionary activity of St. Andrew in sufficient detail, and they had at that time better information about the spread of Christianity. Their assertions could be based on either documentary materials about which we know nothing, or at least on a living Christian tradition which was then still fresh. The nation cultivated and kept this tradition as its great treasure, and the tradition has been preserved to the present time.

As has already been mentioned, Corsunia, or Kherson, was a very important city for trade. Traders, came here from Asia Minor, Persia, Greece, Rome, Scythia, and other northern lands. The Apostle Andrew preached Christ's teaching for close to forty years; in that time he probably visited many cities and countries. He couldn't therefore, have passed up such an important center as Corsunia, out of which his teachings of joy could spread throughout various nations. Today Corsunia belongs to the Ukraine and for this reason, we would assign special importance to the assertions of the first Ukrainian Church historian. We should preserve and prolong this tradition and not dispute it.

In one old handwritten book dating from perhaps the 16th century, another oral tradition has been preserved which is similar to the one written by the chronicler Nestor. It is narrated there that when the Apostle Andrew was proclaiming the word of God in Pontia, an angel appeared to him and said, "Andrew, go to the land of Rus. It is necessary that you teach the people there." St. Andrew, having heard the angel's voice, left Pontia and departed for the "land of Rus" in the north. Here he loudly proclaimed Christ in villages and cities and taught many people to believe in Christ's teaching. From there the Apostle Saint set off for Greece in the south. This oral tradition is interesting in that it is a variant of that tradtion recorded by the chronicler.

The cult of St. Andrew in the Ukrainian nation.

In Byzantium it was also believed that St. Andrew the Apostle had preached in the Ukrainian lands. In the 11th century, the Byzantine Emperor, Michael III Duka, wrote to king Vsevolod of Kiev that the same disciples of Christ had proclaimed Christianity in both countries, that is, in Greece and in Rus. The name of the Apostle Andrew has always been honored in the Ukrainian tradition. We know that king Vsevolod erected a church to St. Andrew in Kiev in 1086; a few years later he built another church in Pereyaslav, and also named it after St. Andrew.

10

The cult of St. Andrew was observed in the Ukrainian Church from the very beginnings of its existence. In his name churches and monastries were built, kings took his name, and the nation collected many oral traditions and devout songs and surrounded him with a large following. The feast of St. Andrew the First - Called Apostle is celebrated on the 13th of December in the Ukrainian Church.

2. The Spread of Christianity among the Slavs.

Christianity among the Slavs.

Among the Slavic nations, Christianity spread and was established at approximately the same time as in Ukraine. It did not arrive suddenly, spontaneously, but filtered in from both centers of Christian culture over many long years. Of course, the nations which were in immediate proximity to either Byzantium or Rome had an easier and better opportunity to acquaint themselves with the new faith than did the Slavic nations living farther to the north.

On the territory which is populated today by the Slavic nations, Christianity may have appeared in early times, perhaps even in apostolic times. Our legend about St. Andrew, for example, mentions that he preached the gospel in Macedonia as well. There are later records to the effect that Christianity was also widespread in the territories of present day Bulgaria. From the end of the third century, we have an interesting and valuable document recording the life of Demetrius Solunsky, who died a martyr's death under Diocletian, and this is a sign that already in that time there were church-communities of Slavs. While it is true that the Slavic colonies did not reach the present land of Ukraine when the Slavs entered the present-day territories in the 5th century, they certainly meshed with the Christian element which had populated these countries.

Okhrida, an ancient Christian center.

Bulgaria was Christianized in 864, during the reign of Boris. This means that Christianity was officially established, but this is no proof that Christianity did not previously exist here. It is known that as early as the fourth century there was an episcopate at Okhrida, and that the first Okhridian bishop was St. Zosym (c. 430). From there, obviously, Chrsitianity could spread to those Slavs living on the river plain of the Danube.

It would be worth our knowing somewhat more about the beginnings of Bulgarian Christianity because among historians the view prevails that the Ukrainian Church accepted its first hierarchy not from the Greeks, that is, Byzantium, but from Okhrida, from the Bulgarians.

Okhrida is an ancient city mentioned as early as the third century B.C. In early Christian times, this city was going through an age of growth and fame, decline and fall. In the sixth century it was destroyed by an earthquake and the emperor Justinian, who was himself from that district, rebuilt it and made it an important religious center. It was Justinian (527-565) who began taking pains to procure from the Pope patriarchal rights for Okhrida. However his efforts were without success and only later Okhrida obtained extended powers from Pope Vigilius. In that century the Avars destroyed Okhryda and it declined for a full two centuries. Only in the ninth century, after the conversion of the Bulgarians, did this seat grow once more; it became the seat of the Bulgarian hierarchs.

Christianity among the Bulgarians.

The history of the conversion of the Bulgarians has some parallels with the beginning of Christianity in Ukraine. King Boris, no matter how zealous a neophyte he was and how he drove men with "fire and sword" to Christ, nevertheless understood very well that in embracing Christianity from Byzantium, he was at the same time falling into a political dependence on the Byzantine emperors. To prevent this, he demanded a hierarchy for his church independent of patriarch Photius. In other words, he wanted a separate patriarch for her. But the situation with Photius was not amicable. A few years after his conversion, Boris broke ties with Byzantium and turned to Pope Nicholas I with the same requests. The Pope replied with promises, sent his bishops and priests, but was in no hurry to ordain a patriarch. Nor was his successor Pope Hadrian in any hurry either. For this reason Boris abandoned Rome, sent away the Latin priests and bishops and again turned to Byzantium in 870. This time the Bulgarians were given an archbishop and a few bishops. Even so, dependence in church matters continued, with the liturgical language being Greek. Only in the time of Simeon, the successor of King Boris, was begun the change of liturgical language to Bulgarian, or old Church-Slavonic. The Greeks taught that there was but the one greatest ruler on earth - the Byzantine emperor, heir to the glory of the honored Rome. Simeon, so as to compare favorably in worthiness with the emperor, accepted the title of Czar and furthered an unyielding campaign towards the independence of his Church. The campaign continued until the middle of the tenth century and only then with the consent of the emperor, patriarch Damian was ordained for the Bulgarian Church. He was the first hierarch of the Bulgarian Church. However, the Greeks did not wish to call his successors patriarchs, even though they did not refuse them the rights of autocephaly, that is, independent governing of their own Church.

This Bulgarian conflict and oscillation between Rome and Byzantium is very instructive for us. In many ways it reminds us of and explains similar occurrences in the Ukraine after the introduction of Christianity.

One must keep in mind that the Byzantine emperors had a big say in the affairs of the Church. For this reason the submission of a foreign Church to the Byzantine patriarch could bring with it a political dependence as well. Understandable, no ruler of a newly Christianized country wished this on himself. This is why the Bulgarian kings defended the jurisdiction of their hierarchies so stubbornly and unwaveringly. There is no doubt that the situation was understood in Ukraine and that this may have been one reason why Princess Olga sought ties with the western Christian world at some distance from the boundaries of her kingdom, or why Prince Sviatoslav did not rush to Christianize his kingdom.

Christianity among the Serbs and the Croatians.

A similar history unfolded with other Slavic nations. Emperor Heracles christianized the Serbs and the Croatians, not primarily to save their souls but to create out of them a hindrance to the Avars, who continuously menaced the northern provinces of the empire. The Serbs and Croatians settled in the Balkans sometime at the end of the sixth century and slowly began to embrace Christianity. Nevertheless, Christianity did not take strong root here, for when the division from the Byzantine empire came in 827, the dominant worship was again pagan. Only at the end of the 9th century, when the Serbs and Croatians returned once again to the fold of the Byzantine empire, did Christianity take precedence. Western rulers also took care of the Serbs and the Croatians. Charles the Great, having occupied Panonia and Croatia, immediately sent them his missionaries. This rivalry between East and West for the possession of souls Christianized in their own manner resulted in a division of the Slavs into those under the sphere of influence of Rome and those under the sphere of Byzantium. Dogmatic disputes did not play a role here as yet. The main question was that of political reckonings.

The Luzians.

In the last quarter of the eighth century, one of the westernmost Slavic races, the Luzians, were baptized; falling under the cultural influence of mighty Carolingian empire, they dissolved and disappeared in the Germanic sea.

The Moravians.

The Moravians were also temporarily under the influence of the Franconian empire; by the beginning of the 9th century they had formed a great and strong nation. After the coming of the Frankish legionaries came the Germanic missionaries, but their work was unsuccessful in that the Moravian Prince, Rostislav, accepted Christianity in the Eastern rite in 863.

The Czechs.

The same happened with the Czechs. At the very beginning of the 9th century, they too fell into dependance on their western neighbors. Of course western missionaries came here as well, but again their efforts went unrewarded. This was because, following Christianity like a shadow, was a world wide, insatiable hegemony. Usually all people, whether Christian or pagan, love freedom. In 874 the Czech Prince Bozhyvoy was baptized in the eastern rite, together with his wife St. Ludmyla, on the occasion of a visit to the great Moravian Prince Sviatopolk. However, his son, under the pressure of his Western neighbors, was soon compelled to acknowledge as higher the Germanic authority; hand-in-hand came a Latinization of the Church. Latinization was not readily accepted and notwithstanding the efforts of Ger-

13

manic bishops and missionaries, liturgies of the Eastern rite and in old Church Slavonic language persisted until the second half of the eleventh century. Only then did the Latinization push away the traces of the self-sacrificing work of the brothers St. Cyril and St. Methodius.

Poland.

Christianity was filtering through to Poland from the Southern Slavs, the Moravians and the Czechs. There is no doubt that the first semination of Christianity came here from the east. But Poland, in a similar situation to Czechia, was neighbored by a Germanic empire with an agressive Germanic spirituality. Under the rule of Otto I, Poland fell into a feudal dependence on the Germanic empire. The Christianization of Poland began at that time, or, as some historians say, the reversion to the Latin Church began.

In 965 the Polish Prince, Mecheslav I, married Princess Dubravka of Czechia; a year later he was baptized and decreed that the nation should be baptized. Although a few episcopates sprang up immediately and in 1000 even an arche-episcopate was established in Gnezno, paganism held its own here for a long time until Casimir I, in the middle of the 11th century, pacified the pagans with a firm hand and made possible the development of Christianity. The organization of parish life, that is, definitely ordered forms of church life, appeared only as late as the end of the 13th or the beginning of the 14th century. Whether there were in Poland any bishops of the Eastern rite is not exactly known. Some historians speculate that there were, but a careful hand erased all traces of them. What knowledge remains is that the first bishops of Poland were German, Jordan and Unger, bishops of the Recognition and that the first archbishop of Gnezny was the Czech Radym-Gavdensi, the brother of St. Edelbert, who suffered a martyr's death in 997 during his missionary work in Prussia.

As we see from this short overview, the Christianity of the Southern and the Western Slavs was not embraced spontaneously. The main factors which slowed the spread of Christianity were, above all else, political; no matter how good and pious the emperors were they never forgot to take the opportunity inherent in the baptism of pagans to gain some political benefit for their own empires.

3. The Enlighteners of the Slavs - The Brothers St. Cyril and St. Methodius

The Slavic nations.

The spread of Christianity among the Slavic nations on a larger scale began in the middle of the 9th century. At this time there was a great service rendered by two brothers - Saints Cyril and Methodius. Their apostolic activity and zeal in the spreading of the gospel was such that historians often compare them with St. Paul the Apostle. Were it not for their taking a stand, perhaps Christianity would have come to the Slavs far later.

Who were these great preachers of the gospel?

The Origins of Cyril and Methodius.

Cyril and Methodius came from a well-known family from the city of Solunia, where their father was a highly-placed empire official. They were perhaps of Greek descent, though in one Czech chronicle of the 13th century Methodius is called a "Rusyn". There is little probability that they were "Rusyn", and the given place in the Czech chronicle has Methodius in mind as one who gave the initiative and who spread the "Rusyn" rite, that is the Eastern rite with a living Slavic language understood by all being used in the liturgy. Of this rite in the 13th century Czechia there was not a trace left, which is why the chronicler unfortunately recalls the "Rusyn" Methodius.

The Education of the Apostles to the Slavs.

The brothers Cyril and Methodius received a good education in Constantinople at the emperor's court and brilliant careers were open for them. Methodius even spent some time in service to the empire but soon left this to be tonsured into monkhood. His younger brother, Cyril, also entered the monastery at an early age. Because he distinguished himself with his exceptional talents, he was almost forcibly transferred to Constantinople, ordained a priest, and set up as the librarian at St. Sophia's. He was the most obvious choice among his contemporaries for the job. A person of deep intellect, unusual memory, and with an exemplary meekness, he was a man of apostolic life. He was one of the greatest linguists of his time. According to sources which have reached us, Cyril knew not only Greek but also Slavonic, Latin, Hebrew, Arabic and Croatian. When we realize that in ancient times it was not as easy to study foreign languages as it is today, we begin to know what colossal talents he must have possessed. He knew the Slavonic language as well as he did his own. At Solunia there were many Slavs, so he had a good opportunity to study this language from an early age.

In a work about his life written by one of Methodius' pupils, it is recounted that in Solunia there once arrived a foreign grammarian. When Cyril found out about this (he was then still Constantine because he took on the name Cyril only when entering the monastery) he ran up to the grammarian and begged him to teach him the foreigh grammar. When the grammarian refused, Cyril told him, with tears in his eyes, that he would give all the wealth which was coming to him from his father if only the grammarian would teach him, for he loved knowledge so much.

The Mission Among the Khozars.

In 858 a delegation came to Constantinople from the Khozars, who had their kingdom on the Caspian sea. The Khozars asked the emperor to send them Christian preachers, because they too wanted to learn the Christian faith. Cyril and Methodius were commissioned for this mission. Missions were not easy in those times. Besides the difficulties of the long journey, missionaries were often martyred while preaching the gospel. But the brothers gladly accepted the commission. His biographer relates that Cyril said, "I'll gladly go on foot and barefoot, without anything which the Lord did not want His followers to carry. I'll go gladly for the Christian faith, for is there anything sweeter for me on this earth then to live and die for the Holy Trinity?"

Their mission among the Khozars lasted about three years. Returning from the Khozars, the brothers stopped at Corsunia and there discovered the relics of St. Clement, Pope of Rome, who had been sent there at the beginning of the second century and died there a martyr.

After arriving in Constantinople, the brothers did not rest there for long. In 863, the Moravian Prince Rostyslav sent a delegation to the emperor Michael and requested missionary preachers of the word of God. The brothers prepared themselves well for this mission. They knew that just preaching would have no lasting success.

To fix a faith firmly and to help spread it, the nation must be brought the gospels and the other Biblical books and liturgical services in an understandable language. For this reason, as tradition tells us, Cyril provided himself with or discovered an alphabet for Slavonic and translated into this language the Holy Bible and the liturgical services which were then in use in the Greek Church.

A difficult task awaited Cyril and Methodius on their arrival in Moravia. Earlier, German missionaries had tried to institute Christianity here, but without success. The people did not understand nor trust the missions for these usually brought along political subjugation with them. Establishing themselves in Moravia, Cyril and Methodius began their self-sacrificing work. Along with their pupils, they criss-crossed the country back and forth. God's word, proclaimed in an understandable language, fell on good soil; the people gathered around them and soon Christian communities began to spring up in this great empire, which stretched past Cracow in the north, past the Carpthians in the east and up to the Stryj river.

The success of their work did not please the German bishops and missionaries and the latter sent denunciations to Rome. Cyril and Methodius were accused of unlawfully bringing the Slavic language into the liturgy and this was comparable to heresy. Pope Nicholas I called the brothers to Rome for trial. When they arrived, Pope Nicholas had already died. His successor, Pope Hadrian II, welcomed them warmly. He recognized their apostolic pains as profitable, rejected the accusations of the German bishops, accepted the translation of the holy books as a work pleasing to God and the Slavic language as worthy for liturgy.

The generous apostleship of the younger brother, Cyril, ended in Rome. Here he became ill and in a short time, died, on the fourth of February, 869. The Pope ordained Methodius bishop and, on the request of the Moravian Prince Rostislav, created a separate church province out of the countries of the brother-Saints' missionary activity, independent of the neighboring German bishops. This was a great success for the missionary activity of the brothers.

16

The Imprisonment of Methodius.

Methodius returned to Moravia to continue the work. In the meantime Rostislav had fallen victim of a conspiracy, his successor being Sviatopolk, a nephew of Rostislav and a confederate of the Germans. Taking advantage of the opportunity, the German bishops imprisoned Methodius, disregarding the fact the Pope had praised his work. Under unusually severe conditions, this saintly man sat imprisoned for two and a half years and only at the demand and threat of Pope John VIII was he released, the Pope giving him the rank of archbishop. But this did not resolve the problem and the Salzburgian and Passavian bishops did not cease their accusations.

Soon they again accused Methodius before the Pope, saying that he did not recognize the Pope. Again Methodius had to travel to Rome and again the charges proved groundless.

Returning, he worked unceasingly, organizing new church communities. Now the territory of his activity increased still further, for after the baptism of the Czech Prince Bozhivoy, Czechia also belonged to Methodius' archepiscopate. But his strength was failing. He died on the 6th of April 885 and was buried in Velegrad, his archiepiscopal capital and the capital of Moravia at the time.

The cult of the brother-Saints began very early in Ukraine. Their feast is celebrated on the 19th of July, by the Ukrainian Church, which honors the God-wisened Cyril and Methodius as teachers of the word of God and enlighteners of the Slavic countries equal to the apostles.

The Significance of Missionary Activity.

One cannot write a history of the Church, in particular of the Ukrainian Church, without mentioning the great champions of the propagation of Christ's gospel. No missionary of the Eastern or the Western Church contributed more to the spreading of Christianity or had a greater influence on the future development of the Christian, especially the Slavic Christian world, as did the brother-Saints.

It is not known how events in the Eastern Church would have unfolded, what face Eastern Christianity would have had, had there not been their contribution in an understandable language, an input for Christ and not for this or that political power. It is not their fault that the Slavic world did not completely understand their intentions and commands but throughout many years often also tried to make the Church a means for earthly ends. Against this background, the figures of the brother-Saints stand out to yet more brilliance and they will always remain, for Slavs or goodwill and Christians in general, teachers and examples of apostolic zeal for the truth of Christ.

The Missionary Activity of the brother-Saints and Ukraine.

The Cyril - Methodian missionary activity has a special interest for us. The pre-Carpatian lands of the Ukraine today belonged in the 870's at the time of Sviatopolk to the Moravian Empire. There is much evidence that as

17

early as that time, Christianity was known in the western parts of the Ukraine. This knowledge had been brought here by followers of Cyril and Methodius, whose work was supported by Prince Sviatopolk because he preferred to have Christianized eastern neighbors and not pagans who troubled the eastern boundaries of his empire.

Christianity of the Eastern rite, of Cyril-Methodian origin, was spread (and in all probability had its own bishop) in the provinces of the upper Vistula river, reaching past Cracow, and about this there is no doubt in historical study. There it fell under the influence of the Latinizing work of the western missionaries and the political pressure of the German emperors.

Especially after the official Christening of Poland during the reign of Mecheslav I, there was an increase in freedom of motion for the western influences. The long-established Christianity of the Eastern rite, with liturgical services in Church Slavonic, a language detested and not understood by the western missionaries, was slowly squeezed out, its traces swept away, and the new orientation was to the western world and to western Christian culture.

4. Christianity in the Ukraine before Volodimir the Great Prehistoric Traces.

Prehistoric Traces.

Archeological finds in the Ukraine indicate that the lands of the Ukraine were populated very early - many thousands of years before Christ. In Kiev, for example, there have been found traces of human habitation which archeologists place at fifteen centuries before the coming of Christ. These are very important historical testimonies. They indicate that already at this ancient date, in the place of the present Kiev, there lived people, and these populations had no break in continuity until today. From the earliest times to the present there are continuous records of populations and their way of life. This seems to show that Kiev is a very ancient city - much older than is witnessed by recorded history.

The Waterways.

The Dnipro made a very comfortable water route, especially to the south; hence communication with southern countries could take place many centuries before Christ. On the southern banks of the Black Sea and in Crimea there were Greek colonies, whose members doubtless came into contact with their northern neighbors.

Nevertheless, as has already been mentioned, no information about the ancient traces of Christianity is available besides legends. The reason for this is that from ancient times the lands of the Ukraine drew different nomads who destroyed all traces of material and spiritual culture. Thus we are forced to speculate on or interpolate conclusions from intermediary proofs about the ancient times.

One of these proofs would be the fact that in Constantinople there was a separate district where the Slavs lived, both settlers and passing traders, long before the beginnings of Ukrainian history. In other words, communication between the Ukrainian ancestors and Greeks took place from very ancient times, and if so, it could not have been a matter of no concern to traders what faith was professed by the people with whom they associated.

The First Bishops.
At the Council of Nicea in 325, bishop Theophilus was the representative of the Christian community at Bosphorus. Somewhat later, also in the fourth century, another interesting figure was the Gothic bishop, Ulfila, who translated the Holy Sciptures into Gothic. This Ulfila, or Ulfilas, took part in the Council of Constantinople. It is true that Christianity did not long survive among the Visigoths, and it is unknown how it was spread, but certain information about Christianity could have filtered northward from here as well.

In the 9th century, Christianity spread among many Slavic nations. The greatest part in this spread was of course played by the untiring work of the Slavic Apostles Cyril and Methodius. The spread certainly took place on the Ukrainian territories as well. All the requirements were present. The Ukrainian ancestors were slowly organizing a country and developing economic ties somewhat later the Holy Scripture appeared in an understood language and Christianization of neighboring Slavic countries was proceeding. All this created fertile ground for the spread of Christianity in the Ukrainian lands. There was also no caste of priests who might have successfully stemmed the tide of Christianization.

Christian Influences among the Ukrainians.
At the time of Askold and Dyr in Kiev, Christianity was not a novelty. On Askold's buriel mound, a church was built; this is undeniable proof that he was a Christian, since nobody would have built a church on the grave of a pagan. Also if the Prince was a Christian, there must have been Christians among his soldiers.

There is yet another proof that Christianity was practiced among the Ukrainian ancestors in the middle of the 9th century. The Greek patriarch, Photius, in his circular to the other eastern patriarchs, mentioned that he had sent a bishop and a missionary to Kiev in Rus. Some historians assert that it was not Photius but his predecessor, St. Ignatius, who sent the missionaries. In any case, it is important only that such a mission indeed existed. In sending a bishop, the patriarch must have known that there were a significant number of Christians among whom this bishop was to organize or build a Church. The reason why this Church was not at once confirmed may have been the fact that the Ukrainian ancestors often fought with the Greeks. Peaceful and good relations alternated with wars. Not having a supply of missionaries and fresh blood, the new church organization had no prospect for success or spread.

Christianity at the time of Prince Ihor.

From the agreements Prince Ihor reached with the Greeks, we know about Christianity in the Ukraine at the time of his reign. This Prince, as the chronicler narrates, made two military campaigns against the Greeks. After the second campaign, Ihor drew up an agreement with the Greeks, guaranteeing the agreement with a pledge. From the text of the pledge, we see that there were Christians even among Ihor's soldiers.

The pledge reads:

".. . and whosoever of the Rus side dares to overstep this agreement, if he be a Christian let him accept the vengeance of God the Almighty and condemnation to eternal perdition in this and in the next world, and may those who are unbaptized have help neither from God nor from Perun. Let their shields not protect them but let them die by their own swords, arrows, and their other armaments. Let them be slaves in this life and the life to come . . ."

This is a very significant record.It shows there must have been many Christians. Christians are mentioned first in the pledge, and even in the section which directs itself to the pagans, there is mention made of God, in whom even the pagans believed, with the plea that this God will not give aid to breakers of the pledge. In a later section of the agreement, mention is made of the church of St. Illya in Kiev.

". . . and we, as many of us are Christians swore by the church of St. Illya, in the synodal church by the Holy Cross . . ."

The Church Community in Kiev.

Reference to the church of St. Illya leads us to believe that there was already an organized Christian community in the Ukraine. The word "synodal" may mean either that it was a bishop's church or that it was a principal church, that is, besides this church, there were others.

Prince Ihor himself was not a Christian, for he makes his pledge in the pagan tradition. But his is also an interesting fact. It shows that even though the Prince himself did not belong to the Christian community, nevertheless he respected the faith of his Christian comrades-in-arms or at least tolerated it and did not forbid its spread.

In general, we must assert that among the Slavic nations, who had neither a rich nor a developed mythology, Christianity was much more readily accepted than among those nations which had such a mythology. Also there was no separate class of pagan priests among the Ukrainian ancestors, as there were in other nations. These pagan priests tenaciously defended their own interests, and for this reason they fought Christianity.

5. St. Olga the Great.

The Baptism of Princess Olga.

After the death of Ihor, his wife, Princess Olga, took charge of the empire because Ihor's son, Sviatoslav, was still too young. She was the first among the rulers of the Ukraine who was certainly a Christian. The Chronicler describes her baptism in 955. According to this narrative, in that year, Princess Olga set out for Constantinople, received her education there in the Christian faith, and was baptized. The patriarch himself was to baptize her. Our chronicler recounts that emperor Constantine was so enchanted with her beauty and wisdom that he wanted to marry her. But perhaps he was not to the Princess liking, for she determined to trick him. She asked the emperor to be her godfather at the baptism. He, understandably, agreed, and when he renewed his plea, after the baptism Olga reminded him that in keeping with the Christian law, a godparent may not marry his own godchild. In this way our chronicler hoped to show how intelligent the Princess was.

In the records of the baptism of Princess Olga, there are a few unclear matters. The Greek emperor then was Constantine Porphyrogenitus (912 - 959), who wrote the book, "On the Administration of the Empire". In this book he also mentions the arrival of Princess Olga, describes in detail all the ceremonies of her welcome, but says nothing about her baptism. From this historians make the deduction that Olga had perhaps already been baptized earlier.

There was a tradition at the emperor's court that pagans were not allowed to eat at the emperor's table but had to eat at a separate table and not with the emperor and his retinue. Olga sat at the emperor's table, together with his family, and the emperor did not treat her as a pagan.

If Princess Olga was baptized in Constantinople a short while after her arrival, it seems odd that the emperor made no mention of such an important event in his book. The absence of such a note may be explained either by the theory that Olga was baptized while still in Kiev immediately before her trip or even earlier, or by the theory that the emperor Constantine wrote another book just about her baptism but that this book has not survived. If he did write such a book, he would obviously not need to mention the baptism of our Princess in the aforementioned book.

The Retinue of Princess Olga.

Interesting are the notes of other chroniclers in connection with this journey of Princess Olga to Constantinople. They recount that the retinue of the Princess was made up of 18 women, her consorts from her court, 22 messengers, 42 traders, 12 translators and Gregory, a priest. The presence of a priest would indicate that she was already a Christian and that the priest was her spiritual adivsor.

Western chroniclers also note this journey of Princess Olga to Constantinople and record that Olga set out to Constantinople where she was baptized by patriarch Poliotus. Such a patriarch really existed and managed the

Byzantine patriarchate between 956 and 970. From this it would seem that the Princess was baptized no sooner than 956 and no later thatn 957, because in that year, on the 9th of September, she left Constantinople.

Where and when this baptism took place is difficult to determine. Taking into consideration all the given facts, we would like to believe that the Princess really was baptized in Constantinople. The statements of the chronicler and the western chroniclers had to be founded on some concrete sources. This was not the only goal of her visit. She must have had other goals and plans about which the chronicler obviously knew nothing. We can speculate about this from the fact that, after her return, relations with Constantinople cooled off significantly, meaning that the mission had failed and that Olga had not achieved all she had intended, in spite of the fact that she had carefully thought out what she was to do.

On the occasion of such an unusual event as the baptism of a ruler of a foreign country, the opportunity should have been open to the profitable resolution of other matters, matters with an empire - wide significance. But notwithstanding for a moment the full majesty of the event of the turning to Christianity of the ruler of a great and mighty empire, Emperor Constantine did not sympathize with Olga's plans. Because of this there arose in her a sense of injured pride. When in the next year the emperor's messengers came to Kiev, Olga received them very coldly. A change had occurred in the relations between Kiev and Constantinople. Olga diverted her attention in another direction.

An Attempt at Ties with the West.

In 959, writes the German chronicler Ditmar, bishop of Merzburg, in his "Chronicle", Olga, the ruler of Rus, sent messengers to the German emperor Otto I with the request that bishops and priests be sent to Rus. Otto passed this matter on to the bishop of Bremen, Adaldag, and the latter obtained a bishop in Frankfurt, Libusius, a monk of the monastery of St. Alban, for Rus. However, Libusius did not get to Rus. He died either that same year or at the beginning of the next. In his place another candidate was ordained, Edelbert, a monk from the monastery of St. Maximin in Trieri. He came to Rus in 962 and stayed in Kiev, but his mission was unsuccessful. After his return to Germany, Edelbert complained that he had been poorly received in Kiev.

The Ukrainian chronicles do not mention these ties with the West. Perhaps they are not mentioned because the chronicler was writing his chronicle at a time when there was a complete separation between the Eastern and Western Churches; therefore, he did not wish to mention that the Ukrainian Church had, at its inception, ties with the Latin Church. It is also possible that in the original writings of the chronicle such a reference existed and was only left out later by its copiers.

Having became a Christian, Princess Olga wished to convert her son, Sviatoslav, to Christianity as well. Doubtless he knew of his mother's new faith, but he still belonged to that caste of warriors whose ideal was war, campaigns and unmerciful treatment of the vanquished. The Christian religion, on the other hand, preached love of neighbor, kindness, and restraint from the world's lures. When his mother urged him to be baptized, Sviatoslav replied, "How can I accept this law? My retinue would laugh at me". The exhortation of his mother had no effect and Sviatoslav remained a pagan.

Princess Olga died in 969. The chronicler relates that she was buried in the Christian way, with a priest attending. The Church entered her in the roster of Saints and remembers her on the 24th of July, praising God that "He glorified Olga the Wise in Rus".

6. The Apostolic Co-Equal, Prince Volodimir the Great

After the death of Olga, Sviatoslav led a campaign against the Bulgarians. Besides his adventurous spirit, he had good political sense. Because the southern regions of the Ukraine were in constant peril from the Pecheneg nomads who broke the link with Byzantium, Sviatoslav decided to move his capitol to Pereyaslavets on the Danube. However his campaign was unsuccessful. Sviatoslav, beaten by the Greeks, was returning to the Ukraine when he was ambushed by the Pechenegs near the foot of the Dnipro and died in battle.

His three sons, Yaropolk, Oleh and Volodimir inherited his empire. Yaropolk reigned in Kiev, Oleh in Ovruch (in Polisya) and the youngest, Volodimir in Novhorod. For a while the brothers lived peacefully, but after a few years, quarrels sprang up among them.

First of all, Yaropolk waged war on his brother Oleh and took his share. Volodimir, fearing that the same would happen to him, fled to the Varangians, enlisted their support, and started a war with Yaropolk. Yarolpolk lost the war and in 980, Volodimir took the throne at Kiev as the sole ruler of a huge empire. At that time he was 21 years old (Volodimir was born in 959). He had the same spirit as his father.

The Pagan Background of Prince Volodimir the Great.
The first years of his reign were marked by an upswing of paganism. It is also possible that one reason for the war between Volodimir and Yaropolk was that both Yaropolk and Oleh were, in all probability, Christians, but Volodimir, who was the son of a different mother, grew up a pagan. His older brothers grew up in the emperor's court and a strong influence on them could have been their grandmother, Princess Olga. Volodimir was only ten when Princess Olga died, so she could not have had much of an influence on him. Hence it is no surprise that with his taking the throne, paganism took precedence. Volodimir revivified the pagan cult, began setting up statues of pagan gods, bringing them sacrifices, and leading a merry life.

But from his father, besides his adventurous spirit, he also inherited the wisdom of a statesman. After his stormy younger years, a noticeable change took place in him. He came to understand that to rule such a large kingdom was impossible without some kind of unifying power, without a central idea which could place his nation on an even footing with the other great civilized nations of Europe. Such an idea was Christianity.

The Eastern Roman Empire with its seat in Byzantium was at that time the symbol of culture, knowledge, brilliance and fame. Already during the life of Volodimir, a second imperial center, the Roman Empire of the German Nation (962) had sprung up, with German emperors as successors of the ancient might of Rome. Of course, Volodimir knew of this. His grandmother Olga had been sending messengers there at the time of the formation of this empire.

Christianizing Plans.

Volodimir's kingdom compared favorably in territory with the Greek empire. Thus instead of making further conquests, Volodimir turned his attention to the consolidation of the kingdom. This is precisely where one should seek the origin of his Christianizing plans.

There are few sources on the Christianization of the Ukraine remaining. Of the Ukrainian sources, the Primary Chronicle, the literary work of the monk Yakiw under the title "Praise to the Great Prince Volodimir" and a Greek priest's "Life of Volodimir" are extensively involved with this matter. Much material may also be found in foreign writings, for example, those of the German chronicler Ditmar, the Italian Damiani, the Greeks Cedrin and Zonar, and many more.

An interesting account about the considerations of Volodimir as to which faith to accept is given by the Ukrainian chronicler. The chronicler, who was recording these events in the beginning of the 12th century, makes it seem as if Volodimir thought about which faith to accept for a long time. He finally decided on Christianity and the chronicler points out why exactly he chose Christianity and why from Byzantium.

Thus he relates how in 986 the Bulgarians (from above the Volga), who were Muslims, came to Volodimir. They praised him for his wisdom and his statesman's ability and advised him to accept their faith. But the Mohammedan faith didn't interest Volodimir and he sent them away empty-handed. Later the Germans came and exalted their own faith - Christianity of the Western rite. Volodimir didn't like the fact that the Germans charged one to fast and to lead a strict life. Later came the Jews with whome Volodimir finished quickly, and finally the Greeks came.

The Ukrainian Prince must have been very patient, because, according to the chronicler, the Greeks gave him a long lesson, beginning with the creation of the world and ending with a description of the Last Judgement and he listened carefully to this teaching.

The Choice of Faith.

The next year (987), continues the chronicler, Volodimir gathered together his noblemen and had a council with them as to which faith to accept. The nobleman advised Volodimir to send envoys to different countries so that they could observe the faith of each nation in action. Having travelled through the different countries, the envoys decided that the best faith was that which they recognized in Constantinople. There they liked the beauty of the Christian churches and the grandeur of the liturgy. Finally they added that if the "Greek law" had not been good, his grandmother Olga, who had been wiser than anyone else, would not have accepted it. Seemingly this convinced Volodimir and he decided to receive Christianity from Constantinople. In this narrative of the chronicler there is obviously much that is fantasy. He is trying to show how carefully Volodimir sought the true faith, how he studied the faiths of different nations, and why he finally chose to receive Christianity in Greece. But behind this idealized history is hidden a certain set of historical events. Volodimir was primarily a ruler, a statesman - not a philosopher. So political motives played a large part here. What profit would there have been for him to make ties with the Bulgarians or the Khozars (who practiced the Jewish faith), who did not play an important political role at that time. The mightiest empire at the time was the Byzantine court. This is what may have induced Volodimir to form strong, good-neighborly relations with his neighbor in the south.

But the Byzantine emperors thought very highly of themselves. They did not accept foreign rulers as their equals. They believed that there was but one emperor in the world - the Byzantine emperor. All others must be subject to him. For this reason it was not suitable for Volodimir to form relations through an entreating legation. He decided to form relations in another, less peaceful way. He decided to tame the Byzantine pride and talk down to it from the heights of his power.

The Campaign against Corsunia.

In the following year (988), Volodimir led a military campaign against Crimea and occupied Corsunia (then called Kherson), one of the most important Greek centers of trade. This was an annoying wound to the proud Byzantium, but this was not the final goal of Volodimir's campaign. His goal was to become related to the Byzantine emperor's family by marriage.

The Greek emperors, Basil and Constantine, two brothers who ruled the empire together, saw no other course in this situation but to let their sister Anna become Volodimir's wife. They set the condition that Volodimir be baptized. There was no difficulty with this. Volodimir was ready for it.

The chronicler's narrative, insofar as it refers to the campaign against Corsunia and the negotiations with the emperors, must be accepted as true and authentic. The matter discussed is the historical fact of the occupation of Corsunia, with historical personages. That the goal of Volodimir was not simply some sort of military adventure is borne out by the fact that Volodimir returned Corsunia to the Greeks after he had married their Princess.

His plan and approach to the acceptance of Christianity lead one to surmise that he was a proud ruler who wished to speak with the Byzantine emperors on an equal footing.

The Baptism of Volodimir.

He accepted Christianity not as a vassal, not as a ruler of a lower category, but as a sovereign and mighty warrior. He accepted it in full awareness; possibly he had even already learned about the Christian religion. He accepted it because he saw in it a cementing power for his kingdom and the greatest truth in human life.

Whether Volodimir was baptized in Corsunia or in another city (Vasylkiv) or in Kiev is not known exactly and about this historians are divided. There is even the view that Volodimir was baptized before the campaign to Corsunia in 986. However one should be ready to believe that Volodimir really was baptized in Corsunia. The chronicle even names the church, St. Basil's, where he was baptized and points out the palace where he lived and where princess Anna lived. Some Greek sources move the year of baptism ahead to 989 but we can accept as a sufficiently probable date the year 988 for the baptism of Prince Volodimir and the Christianization of the nation.

7. The Christening of Rus-Ukraine

The Destruction of Pagan Gods.

The Christening of the Ukrainian nation began in that same year (988). Having married Princess Anna, Volodimir, according to the chronicler, took with him from Corsunia the priest Anastasius and other Corsunian priests, relics of saints (popes Clement and Titus), and church icons and vessels, and set off for Kiev. Once in Kiev, Volodimir first settled accounts with his old gods. He gave orders that the idols of the gods be removed and that the idol of the main pagan god, Perun, be dragged through the streets of the city and beaten with clubs - so that everyone could see and know that the pagan gods have no power.

Having destroyed the pagan gods, Volodimir sent out criers throughout the city who announced to all that the Prince wanted all to be baptized. This is the order which the Prince gave the Kievans:

> "and whosoever does not come tomorrow to the river, rich or poor, pilgrim or worker - will be my emeny".

One must allow that the Christening of the Kievans did not take place immediately after the arrival of Volodimir in Kiev. While Christianity was already known of in the Ukraine, nevertheless the general populace knew very little about the truths of the Christian faith - if anything at all. For this reason, the priests, which Volodimir had brought with him from Corsunia, preached and taught the people the new faith, and they especially explained the importance of the sacrament of Baptism.

Having prepared the nation in this way, it was now feasible to approach mass baptisms. This took place without difficulty. The chronicler relates that the people even came with joy to be baptized, saying that "if this were not good (that is, the new faith), then neither the king nor the nobles would have accepted it". The actual event of the baptism is described in great detail in the chronicle. "In heaven there was great joy and in the kingdom of Satan - great sadness". The Prince was glad and praised God, who gave the nation the grace to see the true God, the same one who is professed by other Christian nations.

The spread of Christianity.

Of course, Christianity did not at once spread throughout a large kingdom in the period of the year. It spread gradually and slowly. Also, there was not an adequate number of priests to serve the whole nation in a short time. Volodimir took care of this as well. Sending his sons to the lands he was giving them, he fervently charged them to encourage the spread of the faith. He himself built churches, primarily where there had stood pagan temples before. He erected the church of St. Basil, in honor of the saint whose name Volodimir received in Baptism. In 989 he built a second church - the Most Holy Mother of god (called the "tithe" church because he donated a tenth of his wealth towards its erection), in which he installed the priest Anastasius, who had come from Corsunia with him.

He did not forget schools. He ordered his nobles to send their children to school to provide the church and nation with wise and enlightened leaders of their own kind. Not everyone understood this and for this reason mothers cried when the Prince commanded that children be sent to school.

For a nation which had so recently believed in wooden idols, all this was an unusual transformation. The whole system of relations changed, the nation entered into a wide field of cultural contact with other Chrisitian nations, and the kingdom put on a completely new face, while a new order prevailed, one founded on the truth of Christ's gospel.

Catholicism or Orthodoxy.

Volodimir recieved Christianity from the eastern center, from Byzantium, in the Eastern rite. Not seldom, the question of whether he was Orthodox or Catholic is raised. We cannot use today's standards to measure things at the time of the Christianization of the Ukraine. These two differentiating terms by which we understand Catholicism or Orthodoxy today were then nonexistent. There existed then a unity between the Eastern and Western Churches. Certainly, from time to time, misunderstandings flared up, even leading to estrangement and temporary disunity, but at the time when the Ukrainian ancestors received the Christian faith, there was unity and agreement between Rome and Constantinople. The Church was one, Christian, Apostolic and Universal, with the Pope as the visible head of the Church.

Good relations existed between the Ukrainian nation of Volodimir the Great and the Holy See. As early as two or three years after his baptism, Volodimir was sending messengers to the Pope (991). We do not know what the reason was for this legation, whether it was religious-ecclesiastic or political. But whatever the reason, it shows that Volodimir maintained relations with the Holy See. At the time of Popes John XV (985-996) and Sylvester II (999-1003), we see again living links between the Ukraine and Rome. Discussions, and an exchange of ideas and opinions took place.

We must remember that a very similar situation existed in Bulgaria after the reception of Christianity. The Bulgarian King, Boris, who also received Christianity from Byzanitum, turned at once to the Pope to ask that he send missionaries and bishops from Rome. Clearly he had important reasons for this.

Western Missionaries in the Ukraine.

There were also western missionaries in the Ukraine a few years after the official reception of Christianity. Thus, for example, the German chronicler Ditmar relates that the Magdeburgian archbishop ordained a Saxon missionary as an archbishop for Rus. At about the same time (c. 1002) another missionary, a bishop from Colberg, came to Kiev and brought the daughter of Boreslav the Brave, the Polish king, with him. She was the fiancée of Sviatopolk, Volodimir's son. This bishop preached for a time, but Western Christianity did not meet with much success. This is not because it was a western model, but primarily because it was preached in a language which was not understood; in this language the services took place and sacred actions were fulfilled. Such a rite could not compete with one which was understandable to the populace in its own (or a very similar Church Slavonic) language. But even though the nation did not favorably welcome the Western missionaries, the reason was not that it was a different faith, inferior to that which came from the East. The reasons for the lack of success of the Western, especially German, missionaries on Ukrainian lands should surprise no one.

When we accept that the western provinces of the Ukrainian land were Christianized earlier (than were the central ones), receiving Christianity by the missionary activity of the brother - Saints, Cyril and Methodius, then it becomes clear why the German missionaries were not liked and why their work was unsuccessful. Still in living memory were the persecutions of the first sowers of God's word among the Slavs by the German hierarchy, a persecution of the Cyril-Methodian pupils, and a slow setting aside of the services of Slavic character in those countries which had accepted eastern Christianity. Though the resources of information and communication were not so well developed as today, there is no doubt that news about different types of religious repression was passed on from community to community and was remembered for a long time.

8. The Organization and Extension of the Church.

At the end of the 10th century, that is, at the time when Rus-Ukraine received Christianity, Volodimir's kingdom embraced a huge area. In the north it reached the territory of today's Finland, in the south it was bounded by Greece, in the west it touched the Carpathians and in the east the Volga. To Christianize such a large territory, even with today's resources of communication, would be unusually difficult if there were not a large number of missionaries and well-organized administration which would direct the missionary work. Evidently there was neither an adequate number of missionaries nor an organized administration immediately after the Christianization of the Ukrainian people.

As the chronicle mentions, a certain number of priests came from Corsunia with Volodimir and perhaps some came from Greece as well, but this number was too small to serve the whole kingdom. It is also not known whether these newly-arrived missionaries knew the language of the Ukrainian ancestors. We may suppose that the Corsunian priests knew the Slavonic language since live commercial communication took place between Kiev and Corsunia; not improbably, some Slavs settled permanently in Corsunia as they did in Byzantium. But there were too few of these priests and because of this, Christianization spread first throughout the larger cities, the seats of princes, and only later in the more remote areas.

The spread of Christianity also depended on the level of civilization of the clans which were part of the fold of the kingdom of Kiev. In the south the new faith was accepted easily, without strife, but in the north, for example, in Novgorod, there was opposition. Here says the chronicler, Baptism was by "Putiata with a sword and by Dobrinya with fire". The populace here was more superstitious and believed in different magicians and fortune-tellers who persuaded the people not to accept the new faith. For a long time, these soothsayers were successful. In the northern provinces, paganism held out for at least a hundred years. But on the Ukrainian territory of today, Christianity spread very quickly, and by the end of Volodimir's life, there were not even traces of paganism left.

To Christianize a nation is not merely to baptize its people. Volodimir understood this very well and at once undertook the task of making his kingdom not only Christian in name, but in fact.

The building of Churches.

Immediately after the Baptism, he began the building of churches. The first churches which appeared in Kiev during Volodimir's reign were the "tithe" church and the church of St. Basil. Volodimir did not count the cost when erecting churches. As in other Christian countries of that time, so also in the Ukraine, the prince was the guardian and the protector of the Church. Volodimir the Great also sincerely occupied himself with the Church. He also taught each of his sons to do the same in the seat of his own territory. With the help and protection of the prince, the Church was able successfully to combat pagan influences wherever these influences occurred.

We have few facts pertaining to the preliminary organization of the church. We only know that, having built the "tithe" church, the prince set

Anastasius as a priest there. There must have been other priests and perhaps a bishop also in this church.

However, our chroniclers do not inform us of anything definite. Nor do they inform us how the functions of the religious were divided practically, what they concerned themselves with, or what were their laws. We have some information about this from the church statute and we can surmise the rest from the basic facts we have about the Greek or the Bulgarian church.

Historians believe that at the time of Volodimir there were five bishops' cathedrals, that is, five eparchies: Kiev, Chernihiv, Volodimir Volinks Rostov and Novgorod. But it is also possible that there were more eparchies though we do not have more exact information about this.

Along with the most important aspects of the organization of the Church, Volodimir also occupied himself with the building of schools. Mention has already been made of how mothers cried for their children when the prince ordered that they be sent to school. Schooling was of a high standard in Greece at that time, so the Prince decided to bring schools into his own kingdom as well. Above all else he needed many priests of his own who would know the customs and practices of the nation, its language, and its soul.

Education.

The first schools were taken care of by the Church and the first teachers were priests. It was the same in the west. It is a pity that we do not know more about how these schools were set up, how many of them there were, and how teaching took place. We may surmise that the basis of education consisted of the Holy Bible, the teachings of the Church Fathers, and some information about geography, astronomy and mathematics.

Astronomy was taught primarily so that one would be able to determine the feast days (the Easter cycle). But for those times this "booklearning" was a great advance. These schools gave us our first priests, bishops, and organizers of monastic life. Later, one of these was the metropolitan of Kiev, Ilarion, who was famous as a great preacher and theologian. The schools affiliated with the churches were organized by bishops' sees.

In the second half of the XIth century, with almost every bishop's cathedral there was an affiliated school which graduated new workers towards the enlightenment of the country. In this way the matter of Christianization of the country, organization of the church, and the strengthening of faith were put on the right track. The Apostle Paul had taught in the same way that the faith would be based on wisdom.

9. The first Metropolitans and Bishops and their Activity.

The lack of historic information.

In the ancient Ukrainian historical sources which refer to the beginning of the church, there are many unclear facts and omissions. Not much is known about the beginnings of her organization, about the form of her liturgical arrangement, about the origin of the first priests, or even exactly when and where Saint Volodimir the Great was baptized. One of the most unclear matters is where the first bishops or metropolitans came from. Such ambiguity tempts historians to all sorts of speculations backed by more or less - well grounded arguments.

The most widely-accepted view is that the first hierarchy consisting of a metropolitan and bishops, came to the Ukraine from Constantinople. Logic would indicate this as well: if Volodimir received the faith from the Greeks, why wouldn't he accept their bishops from them as well? But there is a different view, which sees the first bishops or metropolitans as not coming from Greece, but from Bulgaria. This view is held by some Russian and Ukrainian historians of the Church. They believe that had the first hierarchy been from the Greeks then factual sources would have preserved this - if not Ukrainian sources, then at least the Greek chronicles. Such sources do not exist. They do not exist because the Bulgarian Church did not have very friendly relations with the Greek Church in the time of the Christianizing of Rus-Ukraine. If our first bishops came from Bulgaria, then obviously there would be no mention of this in the Greek chronicles and as for the Ukrainian chronicles, perhaps such mention existed, even exactly, but was later edited out by rewriters as material which was displeasing to the Greeks.

What does the chronicle say.

It is difficult to say which of the above two views is the proper one. Nevertheless, on the basis of some secondary sources, we may suppose which of the possibilities is the more likely. We will examine the two views in order.

Ukrainian history tells us that Volodimir was baptized in Corsunia in the church of St. Basil, and that the Corsunian bishop christened him with the priests of Princess Anne. There is no reason to reject this assertion and we may accept it as true. Returning to the Ukraine, Volodimir took Anastasius and some Corsunian priests back with him, not mentioning any bishop. This means that Volodimir returned to the Ukraine without a bishop. This was not unusual; missionaries did the missionary work, not bishops, so there was no need for bishops to go to the Ukraine in 988. Only by 996, the chronicler tells us, bishops were reproaching Volodimir for not punishing murderers with death but by giving them a fine to pay. This is an interesting place in Ukrainian history.

Of what nations were the first bishops and metropolitans?

In keeping with an old tradition, there was no death penalty for murders and Volodimir kept to this tradition. In Byzantium it was different - there murderers were punished by death, so it would follow that the bishops who were demanding the death penalty for murderers were Greeks who saw nothing wrong in this penalty. This was the way things were in their nation. We may draw from this the conclusion that the bishops in the Ukraine were Greeks, but when they came, what their cathedrals were like, and what their names were is not mentioned at all.

31

There was a similar situation with the metropolitan. Monk Jakiw, who wrote "To the Memory and Praise of the Prince Volodimir" relates that there were bishops and a metropolitan at the time of Volodimir. A similar note is given in "The Regulations of Prince Volodimir" (a set of laws or a collection of rules given to clergy). Monk Nestor mentions first the metropolitan Theopemptes on the occasion of the dedication of the church to the Most Holy Mother of God (the tithe church which burned down and was restored by Prince Yaroslav). It is surprising that Ukrainian chroniclers have such little information about the first bishops or metropolitans. Nestor the Chronicler was himself a monk and spiritual matters weighed on him heavily; he mentions many trivial matters but has nothing to say about the archpastors of the church for fifty years after the reception of Christianity. Normally a young church surrounds its first bishops with great piety. They pass on into history as its founders, and the nation honors them, creates legends and oral traditions, and often gets them entered in the roster of saints - but here there is absolute silence. It is difficult to say what the reason for this was. It is probable that there was no metropolitan in the Ukraine immediately after the christening. But a church could not have existed for a longer period without a hierarch, and one or more must most certainly have existed. But bishops are only mentioned eight years after the christening and that very generally. Up until that time it is as if they had not existed.

The adherents to a second theory attempt to explain this historical gap. This theory is based on the premise that the first hierarchs came from Bulgaria - more specifically, from Ochrida. We have already mentioned Ochrida previously. It is a city in southern Yugoslavia, which in ancient times belonged to Bulgaria. The episcopal see, as has already been mentioned, existed already in the 6th century before the coming of the Bulgarians to the Balkans. Then this see belonged to the sphere of influence of the Roman Church. It was destroyed in the 7th century by the Avars and only in the 9th century, after the conversion of the Bulgarians, did this ancient Christian center gain a voice. During the Council of Constantinople in 869, Bulgaria was added to the Greek patriarchate and Greek metropolitans were in Ochrida until the 920's, when the Bulgarian Chruch was granted autocephaly.

Byzantine influences in Bulgaria.

Having occupied eastern Bulgaria, the Greeks did not disturb the Bulgarian Church but left it its autonomy for a time (until 1025). In 1019, the Byzantine emperor Basil took over the remaining lands of Bulgaria and put an end to the Bulgarian kingdom for almost two centuries. Such were the relations between Bulgaria and Byzantium during the Christianization of Rus. Until the end of the 880's the liturgical language in Bulgaria was Greek and only the students of Methodius (after his death in 885), who had been driven out of Moravia, succeeded in spreading the liturgical use of Bulgarian in Bulgaria.

Adherents to the Ochridian theory suggest that Volodimir knew about the

Greco-Bulgarian relations and what the Greek hegemony portended and so he was in no hurry to recruit Greek bishops. Instead of approaching Greece, he asked for bishops, and maybe even a metropolitan, from Ochrida. The reasons for this policy were that the Bulgarian bishops, first of all, spoke a language understood by the populace and secondly, being themselves set with hostility against Greece, gave the guarantee that they would guard the interests of the Kingdom of Kiev and not those of Byzantium. Such a state of affairs was not, understandably, to the liking of the patriarch. He was just waiting for the opportunity to push the Ochridian bishops out of Kiev. The chance came when after 1025, only Greeks were being ordained as Ochridian hierarchs. That is why the first mention of the name of a metropolitan from Kiev, Theopemptes, a Greek, comes so late in the history of the Ukrainian Church. If there had been bishops from Bulgaria earlier in the Ukraine, then either the chronicler had to keep silent about them or, even if he mentioned them, later rewriters of the chronicle omitted these notes.

This is an interesting theory and one cannot deny it has a certain logic. Nevertheless, in the absence of direct proofs, it remains for the time being just a theory.

Of course, with the divergence of views on the origin of first ecclesiastical hierarchy, it is very difficult to arrive at a list of the first bishops. Some historians maintain that the first hierarch was Michael, others claim it was Leon (or Leontius, who died in 1004). Still others give the following order: bishop Anastasius, archbishop Ivan, metropolitan Theopempt, metropolitan Kyrylo, and metropolitan Ilarion.

The Church Rule of Volodimir.

As for the activity of the first hierarchs, it is clear that their most important act and obligation was the consolidation of the new faith. Nevertheless, apart from purely ecclesiastic-religious functions, the religious occupied themselves with other matters as well. These matters were subject to the statutes or laws set for the Church. We have a copy of such a statute for the Ukrainian Church at the time of Volodimir, the so-called Church Rule. This statute primarily standardizes the matter of ecclesiastical courts. The extent of the jurisdiction of ecclesiastical law was very wide, both for the matter arbitrated by ecclesiastical courts and for those persons falling under its jurisdiction. The ecclesiastical courts judged not only priests but also their families, the church functionaries, outlaws, and administrators of hospitals, hotels and refuges. Under the jurisdiction of the law were marital matters, inheritances, transgressions against the faith, witchcraft, and similar offenses against faith or morals. In addition, the religious also had control over weights and measures. All this brought the Church, especially the hierarch, a large income. In the era of early Christianity, princes were extremely generous towards the Church and the religious, but with time these privileges became limited or abolished, and some functions, for example the control of weights and measures, passed under civil control.

The activity and Financial Position of the Church.
In brief, the activity of the first hierarchs was determined by the needs of the time, local conditions, and traditions. Above all, they directed missionary activity, supervised schools, trained young priests and along with this performed the functions of judges.

In its early stages, the Church did not have lands, but acquired them only towards the end of the 11th century. By then the Church had developed stable organizational forms, established the divisions of the eparchies, developed education and founded many monasteries. Because of this, the Church needed financial protection. The actual number of religious and clergy is not recorded, but since the forms of the ecclesiastical order and administration developed here in the manner of the Greek or other Eastern Christian traditions, then the number must have been very large because at the main churches and metropolitans' or bishops' cathedrals there were hundreds of religious. In Constantinople at St. Sophia in the middle of the 6th century (under the emperor Justinian) their number was 425, and somewhat later, under Heracles, at the beginning of the 7th century, there were still more. From this we can draw the conclusion that the bishop or metropolitan administered over a very large ecclesiastical organization. To this organization belonged priests, deacons, deaconesses, subdeacons, readers, cantors, torchbearers and other ecclesiastical functionaries.

10. Church and State.

The affairs of Church and state were tightly interwoven in ancient times. The Byzantine emperor, for example, had in the Church if not a controlling, then a very important vote. He had the last word in the appointment of a patriarch, in the convoking of synods, in the formulation of ecclesiastical laws, in the resolution of religious conflicts, and in many other matters of ecclesiastical and religious life. A similar situation existed in the West. Charles the Great, the Frankish king interfered even in matters of dogma, considered himself the sole protector of Christianity in Western Europe, determined church laws, formed eparchies, appointed bishops, and even directed the preaching of sermons. The German emperor Otto I became a similar defender and protector of the Church after the ancient Corolingian empire had been replaced by the Holy Roman Empire in the German Nation in 962. Otto even went so far as to demand the right to decide who should be Pope.

Volodimir's Relations with Church.
In the Ukraine of Volodimir's time, matters between Church and the state were settled amicably. We are unaware of any disputes or misunderstandings between the prince and the church hierarchy. Without a doubt, Volodimir, as the ruler of a large and newly Christianized kingdom, was not indifferent as to how and whom the new Church administrated. He must have known that the patriarchs, to whom the hierarchy was subordinate, were to a large measure dependent upon the emperors. The matter was

34

known about in the Ukraine. For this reason it is completely understandable that given the situation and in keeping with the common practices of that time, Volodimir did not let the Church or its hierarchy out of his view. As has been said above, the beginnings of the Church administration and hierarchy were so entangled that it is not exactly known where the principal church authority originated and to whom it was subject.

Volodimir's Ties with Rome.

The conjecture that Volodimir hesitated into which sphere to attach the Ukrainian Church, the Eastern or the Western has a completely serious foundation. His legations to the Pope and the Pope's legations to him were not mere courtesies but must have had some aspect of business. It is not necessary to seek a political side in the strict sense here because the political interests of the Kingdom of Kiev did not conflict with those of the Papacy, and so they did not require resolution. Complications could only arise with church matters and, more specifically, hierarchical matters. It would seem that Volodimir, as a good leader, was very concerned with safeguarding the best possible opportunites for growth for the Ukrainian Church and isolating her from such foreign influences as could negatively affect her development and place the kingdom in danger of foreign domination. This cannot however be regarded as interference in church affairs. The matter of church politics is one thing, while the matter of religion and theology is another one completely. Neither Volodimir nor other princes interfered in purely religious matters, leaving the decisions on these ecclesiastical matters to the Church.

One of the important issues in Church-state relations was that of church administration and tied into this, various privileges given to the Church by the leaders of state. These privileges were standardized by separate statutes or regulations; there has already been mention of such regulations of Volodimir. It was not a small matter to set aside for the Church such a large jurisdiction because in this way, fixed and strong norms of judgement became widespread and besides that, the kingdom lost its source of income. Yet our princes, in deference to the Church and its functionaries, gladly took such steps, understanding that it was not proper for the kingdom to judge offences which had elements of religion at their core, nor to judge those persons who had devoted themselves to the service of God and the Church. Such agreement between the worldly and spiritual rulers created an atmosphere of harmony, mutual trust and co-operation. The new law, the law of love of neighbor, had a favorable influence on the character of the nation which had, up until now, been used to brutal wars, to unscrupulous behaviour with the conquered, to debauched pagan traditions and to other vices. All this was not favorable to the development and cultural rebirth of the country and for this reason, the role of the Church was unusually important.

The influence of Christianity on Volodimir's Character.

We see a great influence of Christianization on the very character of Volodimir. Before, he had been a tough warrior, a cruel and unprincipled ruler who let no scruple stop him on the road to his goal. Now he became gentle to the point that even the bishops themselves believed it necessary to remind him of his obligations as a worldly ruler to punish wrongdoers with death. In the tradition of the nation he left behind him the memory of a great benefactor who protected the "loved ones" - that is, the poor, those without shelter, widows and the sick. This newly - baptized prince understood the idea of Christianity much better than many of today's Christians. This influence of the Church on a worldly ruler could not help but have an influence on the civilian populace. Volodimir, by his example of a religious and God-fearing life, was an apostle of Christ's teaching and an example fit for imitation. On the one hand, he tried to mark out for the Church the way to her best future development and on the other hand, he sincerely respected her as an institution of God's order and accepted without reservation truths proclaimed by her. We cannot say the same about today's rulers. Such a position as that of Volodimir and many of his successors creates an intelligent union of two authorities, the worldly and the spiritual, and had this position been understood in later Ukrainian history, then the fate of the Church and nation would perhaps have been very different.

11. Religious and Cultural Life

What is culture? Culture in general is a complicated notion. It is the sum of the spiritual wealth of many generations. Is it not formed in a year or two, by the power of any act or by the efforts of a group people. Culture is a long re-forming process of the way of life and thought of large masses of people within a nation. When we speak here of culture, we have in mind Christian culture, that is, wordly experience, thought, understanding of values, and a manifestation of all the convictions of a nation, a manifestation in line with the rules of Christian faith.

Christianity was quickly accepted in the Ukraine, but this does not mean that all of society at once concerned itself with the ideas of Christianity and threw out the old way of life. Such a phenomenon did not occur anywhere - nor did it occur in the Ukraine. The Christian culture spread for ages, recasting the remains of the old world view of the Ukrainian ancestors, their customs, practices, conceptions, and feelings to conform to the truths of Christian teaching. In other words, in history there are no known mass conversions of whole nations in the course of one or a few years to a different culture. In the Ukraine as well, the Christian rebirth developed organically out from the centers of greatest influence, from the main foci to the furthest ones of the great kingdom above all, by the pressign work of the Church and schools but also by the example of single worldly figures.

The role of the Leaders.
In the history of every nation, in the changing of the forms of its life, key

individuals play important roles. Usually they are leaders, ecclesiastical or secular, whose example influences society more extensively and more considerably than the words of a preacher. What, for example, would be the use of a sermon by a missionary if people knew that he himself did not live as he preached. Would the law of a ruler find understanding and obedience if his subordinates were to see that he himself did not respect this law, did not believe in it, and proceeded contrary to what he demanded of his citizens.

Ukrainian history is replete with examples of worldly figures at the beginning of Christianity. The Ukrainian Church has been commemorating Saint Olga for almost a thousand years and venerates her for her example which no doubt, had an influence on the Christianization of the country. The baptizer of the Ukraine himself, St. Volodimir, having accepted christianity, completely changed his life. Instead of waging wars and military marches, he concluded peace negotiations with the neighboring rulers - Boleslav the Pole, Stephan the Hungarian, and Andrew the Czech prince, - and generally lived in "the fear of the Lord". The large land needed calm, peaceful, and friendly coexistence with its neighbors, because only in peaceful times is cultural development possible, as is the growth of material wealth. With his care, Volodimir embraced the "lesser ones" those who most needed help - above all.

The exemplary Life of Volodimir.

The chronicler narrates that in his court, the prince ordered meals for the poor and the beggars and had food taken to the homes of invalids or the sick. We do not know any other example from history where a ruler would so zealously carry out the advice of the gospels. We can imagine how this influenced the nation, with what trust, respect and love the nation treated their ruler and how his example inspired generous ideals along with the new faith. This example had a greater influence than does force based on military or police power. This example did not simply call one to obedience or imitation; it renewed the person, obliged him to think and compare the new ideas with the old, and gave evidence of the nobility of the Christian religion.

As we already know, Volodimir cared about schools. He himself loved learning and, for his time, was a highly enlightened person. The chronicler says that Volodimir "loved booklearning". For a chronicler so stingy with words, this note about Volodimir loving learning means that the prince must have assigned much importance to education. It could not have been any other way. It is true that many goals may be reached by brute force, but it is not possible to rule a kingdom by force, nor to create spiritual values, nor to contend with nature. But God gave man not only strength but also and above all wisdom. The prince understood this and for this reason he took so much care to raise his nation to the heights of human dignity.

The Saintliness of Boris and Hlib.

We will mention other devotees of the beginning era who influenced the spread of Christianity by the saintliness of their lives. Such, for example, were Volodimir's two sons, Boris and Hlif, who died at the hand of their brother Sviatopolk, not long after the death of their father. They must have been very righteous princes, because the Church entered them in the roster of Saints only six years after their death (1021). An assassin's hand found St. Boris as he was at prayer, singing psalms. Such events did not happen without consequences. In some people, the example of the righteous prince strengthened their faith; in those who were inclined towards paganism, it brought out the question of whether a kingdom where a brother goes against his brother with force can survive.

The Ukrainian Church has examples not only among princes, but also among the champions of the monastic life. There will be more said later about monasteries and the monastic life; here we shall just mention these lights of Christian righteousness who laid the foundations for our Christian life. Here belong Saints Anthony and Theodosius of the monastery of the Caves (Pecherska Lawra), who were the originators of the monastic life in Ukraine; the pious Varlam, also a monk of the monastery of the Caves, who was perhaps the first Ukrainian to make a pilgrimage to the Lord's Grave in Jerusalem; the pious monk, Nestor, who wrote the oldest history of Ukraine; St. Policarp, the archimandrite (abbot) of the monastery of the Caves; the holy Ahapit, and many many more saintly men whom the Ukrainian Church honors.

St. Stephan the Bishop.

Of the first hierarchs one should mention St. Stephan, the bishop of Volodimir-Volinksy. He came from a distinguished noble family, but from youth he was drawn to the monastic life. So he left home and went to the monastery of the Caves, where the superior at the time was the holy Theodosius. The holy Stephen was so renowned for the saintliness of his life and his monastic deeds that the monks chose him to be superior after Theodosius' death. At the end of his life he was ordained bishop of the Volodimir-Volinsk eparchy and left behind him the memory of a great and saintly man and a sincere supporter of church unity.

From its inception the Church embodied in the Ukraine the focus not only of religious, but also of cultural-educational life. Thanks to the Church, already in the reign of Volodimir there began to appear works translated from Greek to the Ukrainian language of the time. First of all, of course, appeared the Holy Bible, the Gospels, the Epistles, and other books used in liturgical services. Books were very costly in ancient times. They had to be copied by hand and this took a long time. Even copiers were scarce in the first years of the existence of the Church.

More books appeared during the reign of Yaroslav the Wise. The chronicler says that Yaroslav loved books and read them "day and night". Many books were copied for the edification of the people during his time, because Yaroslav knew that "there is great benefit in learning from books". Books in the words of the chronicler, are rivers which irrigate the land; they are sources of wisdom and comforts in grief; whoever reads books speaks with

God or saintly men and because of this he gains great benefit for his soul. It seems that the first library appeared at the time of Yaroslav. The chronicle reads, "Yaroslav, as has been mentioned, loved books and wrote many of them and put them in the church of St. Sophia, which he built". Apparently he did not write the books himself but only procured the books and passed them on to the church of St. Sophia. Since there were "many" of them, this is a sign that not only the Gospels and liturgical books were there, but also a considerable number of translations of the Church Fathers, sermons, biographies of the saints, morally-instructive and perhaps also historical works. About Yaroslav there is also the note that in 1031, while staying in Novgorod, he gathered about 300 children together and sent them to school. For those times, this was a large number, so we may surmise that education was sufficiently well-developed.

Meanwhile, in neighboring Poland, when Boleslav the Courageous died (1030), a revolt against the Church took place. "In revolution the people beat their bishops and priests and warriors, and there was rebellion in them". It is interesting to compare how the Ukrainian rulers approached Christianization and what success they had with what successes the Polish kings had not considering the fact that the Christianization in Poland was under the care of numerous western missionaries. For this reason we must emphasize the great wisdom of the rulers, who wished to unite the general cultural-educational reshaping of society with Christianization. Such a policy proved advantageous and brought great benefit both to the Church and the nation.

Of the translated works, an extremely important chronicle of the Ukrainian past is "Sviatoslav's Anthology" (1073 and 1076). This is a copy of a Bulgarian anthology dedicated to king Boris, the enlightener of Bulgaria, who died in 907. This anthology was copied for Prince Sviatoslav of Chernihiv, son of Yaroslav and represented a kind of encyclopaedia of the whole body of Greek scholarship of that time. Included are philosophical, historical, and theological articles as well as many others; this shows that the Ukrainian princes were interested in all achievements of human culture.

A separate class of the Ukrainian scholarship is evidenced in the homiletic and pastoral-moral works, works of a certain type and authorship. Here we should mention the teachings of Theodosius to the brethern of the monastry Pecherska Lavra, where he shows different vices which undermine society, in particular the retention of certain pagan practices - gluttony, drunkenness and others. Interesting is his sermon to the lay people. He suggests they do not pray overlong during meals, but only before and after them. An existing practice was to sing the troparians during lunch, and against such a practice the venerable Theodosius said, "The practice of singing many troparians during a meal was not thought up by servants of God, but by servants of abomination, so that they could drink all the more after the troparians".

Sermons.

An outstanding leader preacher was Ilarion, the Kievan metropolitan. There is little information about him and it is obvious that he cared little for his own fame. It is only known that he was a "holy, literate and abstentious man". Thus he embodied all the finest Christian virtures. He was the Metropolitan of Kiev in the final years of Yaroslav, perhaps at the time when some dispute arose with the Greeks and the Greek Metropolitan had left Kiev. Than Yaroslav had Ilarion named Metropolitan (1051). From him we have the wonderful, "Word on the Law and on Grace", a sermon ina historical-dogmatic context on the theme of the redemption of the human race. The sermon ends by addressing itself to Prince Volodimir, asking that he arise from his grace and see the deeds which he initiated, the flowering churches, the multiplication of the faithful, and the fertile blooming of the Christian culture which he sowed.

Cyril, the bishop of Turiv (in Polysia) was also renowned for his leadership. He appears in the 12th century. In Turiv there was the monastery of the brother saints, Boris and Hlif, and probably Cyril was a monk there. He left behind a few sermons which show the high caliber of his homiletic artistry. Comparing him with other preachers of his time, we see at once in Cyril a great skill, an extensive knowledge, a beauty of form and a clarity of theme. The basis of his theme is the moral development of a human being. A similar splendid preacher-moralist was Luke Gydyata (11th century), a bishop of Novhorod, but betwen him and Cyril there is a great difference in form and expression.

To the moral-pedagogical class of ecclesiastical literature we may also add the "Teaching for Children" of Prince Volodimir Monomach. This is a very valuable example of ancient Ukrainian literature because it mirrors the understanding and the practical application of the truths of the Christian faith by princes. Monomach is a perfect example of a Christian prince. The basic theme of his "Teaching for Children" is "fear God above all things" for the fear of God is the beginning of wisdom.

As we can gather from this short overview, the princes and the Church in the Ukraine took diligent care that along with the spreading of God's word, there was a widespread enlightenment that fostered a love of learning, wisdom, reading and spiritual values, and not a love of the material order. They give us a good example to follow today, almost a thousand years later.

12. Monasteries and the Monastic Life

Monasteries appeared in the Ukraine very soon after the introduction of Christianity. Perhaps in the final years of the tenth century they did not exist, but they had already existed in the second quarter of the 11th century. The chronicle first mentions monasteries in 1037, at the same time that Yaroslav the Wise built the cathedral of St. Sophia - The Supreme Wisdom of God. In the same year he founded two monasteries, St. George's and St. Irene's, and to this work his wife contributed a great deal. The chronicler says that Yaroslav especially liked the "black-robed", that is, the monks, and he writes that these monks "began to multiply and other monasteries began to spring up". In the monasteries most books were copied, thus Yaroslav also had a practical goal in aiding the development of monasticism. The monks, along with the basic goal of a monastic life towards spiritual perfection, were bound to serve the wider goals of Christianization and the cultural development of the nation. They supplied needed groups of clergy; from monasteries came the bishops, metropolitans, theologians, writers and advisors of princes.

The Monastic Rule.
About the earliest monasteries, except for a short mention, we have no information. We do not know what sort of monasteries they were, under what rule they functioned, what was their number, and what sort of abbots they had. However there is more exact knowledge about the foundation of the Pecherska Lavra monastery in Kiev, which entered Ukrainian history as one of the most important cultural, religious and political centers. The chronicler relates that in 1051 "Yaroslav set up Ilarion as metropolitan in St. Sophia, the bishops' Cathedrale". This Ilarion was once one of the priests in the church of the holy Apostles in Brest near Kiev. He loved the monastic life so he dug himself a cave on the shore of the Dnipro river and he went there to pray. In 1051 Yaroslav made him a metropolitan and he was perhaps the first Ukrainian metropolitan, because the chronicler does not neglect to mention this in particular. Soon after the holy Anthony settled in Ilarion's cave. He was from Lubech in Chernihiv and had previously stayed on the Holy Mountain of Athos. The history of the Monastery of the Caves (Pecherska Lavra) begins with Anthony. About twenty monks gathered around him, among them the holy Theodosius, Varlaam as abbot and dug himself a new cave. In 1062 Varlaam accepted the abbotship of the monastery of St. Demetrius and in his place the monks of the caves chose the holy Theodosius as abbot.

The first Monasteries.
The nature of the earliest rule which the holy Anthony set up for the monks of the Monastery of the Caves is not known. Probably it did not suit a community life for soon the holy Theodosius changed it to the rule of St. Theodore the Studite, which was practiced by the monks of the monastery of St. Theodor the Studite in Constantinople. At that time, the Monastery of the caves already numbered over a hundred monks. In the preliminary stage of development of Ukrainian monasticism, life in monasteries was very severe. The monks spent long hours at prayers, in fasting, and in self-mortification. They concerned themselves with physical works and learning as well, especially the copying of books. The ambition of every prince or distinguished nobleman was to found a monastery. They bestowed on these monasteries special care, goods, and privileges. In time a wish for comfort, ease and a pursuit of honors stole into the monasteries; the earlier, stricter way of life disappeared and this, understandably, did not have a good influence on the improvement of monasticism. Princes also entered monasteries, for example, Mykola Sviatosha, the Prince of Chernihiv and Luts, who entered the Monastery of the caves; Sviatoslav, the son of Yaropolk, Ivanna, the daughter of prince Vsevolod, and many others.

41

Historical sources do not indicate the number of monasteries which existed in the Ukraine in the pre-Mongilian era, but there were tens, if not hundreds of them. Monasticism was very popular in the Eastern Church and monasteries were populous. This was probably the case in the Ukraine as well. The rules by which the monks lived were largely based on the Rule of the Monastery of the Caves, which immediately gained great respect for itself, but this Rule did not unify Ukrainian monasteries into one larger whole. Each monastery was self-sufficient, independent of everyone (except the Bishop or the metropolitan) and the monks elected their own abbot and other monastic leaders. These monasteries sprang up across all the Ukraine, in Kiev, Chernihiv, Volyn, Polysia, Halychyna (Halych, Synevidsko, Peremyshl, Plisnesko and others).

Types of Monastic Practices.

Monastic influences came to the Ukraine from the eastern Churches. In the East, two types of monastic life developed: desert-dwellers and monastic. The desert monks lived alone, and were also called hermits or poledwellers, depending on their way of life and ascetic practices. This type of monasticism was not popular among Ukrainians. The second type was called monastic, that is, those who lived together in monasteries. This type of monasticism was widespread in Egypt, Palestine, Syria, Mesopotamia, Greece and also in the Ukraine. One document from the beginning of the sixth century relates that there were 54 monasteries in Constantinople and a few years later (in 536) there were 68 men's monasteries. Eastern monasteries were populous. For example, the monastery of St. Sava in Jerusalem numbered 150 monks in the sixth century, the monastery of St. Theodosius had 400 monks, and the monastery of the Nev Lacra had 600 monks.

All monasteries, in the same way as those of Greece, were relieved from the different duties; monks were relieved of their responsibilities to society (for example, service in the military). Some monasteries were acquiring great earthly wealth, and this obviously, was not to the benefit of the nation. Thus on the one hand, monasteries brought with them a certain benefit but on the other hand, (especially in the later era), because of the lack of a strong central leadership and control, monasteries evidenced definite negative characteristics as well.

The greatest service was rendered by the Monastery of the Caves in Kiev. Out of it came many Ukrainian bishops, metropolitans, learned theologians, great preachers and ecclesiastical authors. The cultural-pedagogical role of the Monastery of the Caves in Ukrainian history is great. For many long years it was the center of the printed word and the nucleus of religious and national enlightenment. But there were also times when the monks concerned themselves with politics. Nevertheless the bright pages of the history of the Monastery of the Caves are unassailable; it played a very prominent role in the development of Christian culture in the Ukraine.

42

13. Churches and Church Arts

The Influence of the Religious Cult on Secular Life.
The history of every nation shows that religion has a great significance in all areas. It forms the nation's character, habits, way of life, legal system, and also its cultural insights and spiritual creativity. Christianity too, from the very beginning of its spread in the Ukraine, had a great influence.

At first Christianity spread through the preaching of the Holy Gospel. However, in every religion the external forms are important. This external display of worship is called a religious cult. If we accept as true Volodimir's mission to various countries and how he chose which religiion to embrace, we see what a great impact the service in the Church of St. Sophia in Constantinople had on the envoys. They didn't know, says the chronicler, where they were - on earth or in heaven. There is no exaggeration here. The greatness of the temple and the holiness of the external display of the worship, that is, the spirituality of the form and the content of the prayer, can move the most indifferent person to reflection, meditation, reappraisal of moral values and by God's grace, set him on the one true way to eternal life.

Temples of God.
In the Christian religion, as opposed to all others, the temple of God is a holy place where great mysteries, the Holy Sacraments set up by Jesus Christ, take place. For this reason, from the very beginning of the existence of Christianity, converted nations made the greatest effort to produce churches condusive to the cult of God's worship.

Church architecture began in the Ukraine even before the acceptance of Christianity. We know that in Kiev in the ninth century there was the Church of St. Nicholas on Askold's grave. Obviously, St. Nicholas was reverenced in the Ukraine even when there were relatively few Christians. In the times of the Princess Olga there is mention of the church of the prophet Elias. But the building of churches on a large scale began in the Ukraine only at the end of the tenth century, after the acceptance of Christianity and its spread to the masses. The chronicles relate that at the beginning of the eleventh century, there were 400 churches in Kiev alone though the great fire in 1071 destroyed about 700 churches. Even if these numbers are somewhat exaggerated, it is nevertheless apparent that there were many churches in the Ukraine and that the building of churches was a widespread practice.

Usually, wooden churches were built, because they were more easily and quickly erected. The first brick church in the Ukraine was the church of the Assumption of the Blessed Virgin Mary, also called the "Tithe" Church, built by Volodimir the Great and consecrated in 996. Greek craftsmen probably built it in the style of churches in Byzantium. The Prince ordered this church decorated and painted, for which he gave a tenth of his income. For this reason it was called the Tithe Church. This Church stood until the Mongolian invasion in 1240. It was seriously damaged then and was rebuilt by Metropolitan Petro Mohyla in the 17th century.

The Sobor of St.Sophia.

The most monumental church was St. Sophia's, that is, the church dedicated to the Supreme Wisdom of God, built in 1037, at the time of Yaroslav the Wise. This church was modelled on the St. Sophia in Constantinople and surpassed in beauty all churches which had been built at any time in the Ukraine.This church survived all disasters, Tartar invasions, invasions of northern princes, and all occupations. It was a testament to the glorious and hard moments in the life of the Ukraine and we believe that it will survive today's times as well.

At about the same time there was built in Kiev the church of the Annunciation of the Blessed Virgin and somewhat later (1073), the church of the Monastery of the Caves in Kiev in honor of the Assumption of the Blessed Virgin Mary. The church of the Assumption was destroyed during the last World War. It should be noted here that the bigger churches normally of brick, were built by princes with their own resources, while the smaller ones, usually wooden, were built by individual communities. Not only princes, but also distinguished and rich nobles built churches as well. The building of churches went hand-in-hand with the growth of Christianity, not only in Kiev, but also in the smaller cities, towns or villages. Not many early churches in the towns survived, for most were wooden. But there were also those made of brick, for example the cathedral in Halych (built at the time of Yaroslav Osmoysl), in Cholm, Peremyshl, Brest and in other centers.

Architecture.

The earliest architectural form of Ukrainian church buildings reminds one of the Greek, or Byzantine style. It is distinctive in that its base is a square divided into three naves and with domes on the roof. The influences of this style came to the Ukraine from Greece, Bulgaria, Macedonia, and other eastern countries to which the Byzantine archtectural style had spread. At the end of the 11th century, western architectural influences become apparent in the Ukraine as well, with St. Michael's monastery and the previously-mentioned church of the Blessed Virgin Mary built in that style.

These various influences do not signify that there is nothing original in Ukrainian Church architecture. Foreign architectural forms were not simply adopted by imitation. They were adopted only as an example which builders took as a basis, developing and evolving it in keeping with the regional understanding of architectural beauty and artistic tastes. There is nothing bad about borrowing good ideas or artistic forms from another, more cultured nation. In the west the same situation existed. The Gothic style, which originated in France, swept through all the countries of western and central Europe, but in every country it found a native restructuring, a definite, different national expression. A similar occurence took place in the Ukraine with the Byzantine influence.

As for the interior appearance of the churches, they looked somewhat the same as the present day churches of the "conservative" style, with an iconostasis which isolated the sanctuary and with the Royal Doors. There were no benches in the churches and the faithful prayed either standing or kneeling. The larger churches were much decorated with frescoes, mosaics, painting and carvings.

Internal Decorations.

As to the decoration of a church, first of all as to painting, there came to the Ukraine a Byzantine influence as well. At that time the Greeks were the best masters of the art of painting, and the Byzantine influence reached even western Europe. The bases of the painting were themes from Holy Scripture, especially from the life of Christ, from the life and Acts of the Apostles, Fathers of the Church, martyrs, great ascetics and those regional, pious individuals who are numbered by the Church in the roster of Saints.

Byzantine Church painting, or iconography as we call it, differed from other forms of visual representation of that time in that it tried to make bodily form reflect spirituality. The body has a secondary function here; it only serves as the background onto which the eternal and immortal soul is projected along with its contemplation of the eternal divine truths and its wish to serve the Lord.

Icons were either rendered in mosaic, that is, put together from little stones or pieces of glass, or were painted. Paintings were painted either on boards or on freshly-prepared masonry. The latest type of painting was called "fresco". This was a great skill which today, despite all the achievements of technology, painters cannot duplicate.

Church Singing.

The verbal form of prayer, that is, church singing, also belongs to ecclesiastical art. From the very beginnings of the Ukrainian Church, church singing was widely used and developed. In the earliest church books which have been passed down to us, the Oktoyich (of eight tones) is mentioned, and Prince Volodimir, in his Formulary, differentiates "among church people - those who sang in the krylos", meaning cantors. We know that Yaroslav brought in cantors and that holy Theodosius, according to the chronicler, copies the form of the "monastic way of singing" from Michael, a monk of a Studite monastery. From this it is clear that a great emphasis was placed on the liturgical form and the expression of worship, perhaps greater that that which we place today. Thus we may learn much from the early Ukrainians.

14. The Metropoly of Kiev and the Patriarch of Constantinople.

The Church Organization.

The organization of the Church as we see it at the end of the 10th century, that is, at the time of the acceptance of Christianity by the Ukraine, was already more or less definitely determined. Territorially it was divided into five great provinces, called patriarchates, which were headed by patriarchs: Rome, Constantinople, Alexandria, Antioch and Jerusalem. The Roman patriarch as the visible head of Christ's Church always had the first place. The First Ecumenical Council in 325 at Nicea first talked about patriarchs and their rights. The authority and honor of patriarchs is not an authority established by God but only the result of the development of the Church in the first three centuries in the direction favored by the church. Patriarchs were bishops of the most important centers of Christianity which were founded by the apostles and for this reason had acquired great authority and were recognized as the original, "first" Churches of those single large provinces.

In the Eastern Churches, the patriarchates were divided into metropolies, and metropolies into episcopacies or eparchies. To better understand the attitude of the Metropolitan of Kiev to the Patriarch of Constantinople, we must speak somewhat more about the organization of the Eastern Church in general.

In the eastern patriarchates, the greatest ecclesiastical office, both as to dignity and to authority, was that of the patriarch. The bishops of some ecclesiastical provinces (for example, Armenia, Georgia, Selevkia and others) had similar power, and were called "catholicos". They wielded the same power as the patriarchs and bishops to metropolitans. There were so-called elder metropolitans and autocephalous metropolitans. The elder metropolitans had approximately the same authority that the Latin archbishops had. They ruled the larger ecclesiastical province and had bishops who were subject to them as helpers. The autocephalous metropolitans did not have bishops who were subject to them, they ruled over only one eparchy and evidently were subject to the patriarch. There were few of these autocephalous bishops; for example in the sixth century in the patriarchate of Constantinople, there was but one such metropolita - the one from Chalcedon. There were also archbishops. We first see this title in the sixth century in reference to the Alexandrian archbishop. Later the title was bestowed on bishops of prominent towns; but the 6th Ecuminical Council (in 787) reserved this title for but ten bishops in the whole church. Nevertheless, church practice encouraged the bestowal of the title as well on those ecclesiastical hierarchs who were the heads of independent churches, that is, autocephalous churches; for example, the Bulgarian, or on those bishops whom the patriarch wished to remove from the dependence on their archbishops and whom he wished to subordinate directly to himself. In all, there were 51 such archbishops in the patriarchate of Constantinople in the 10th century and by the end of the 11th there were only 39.

The Authority of the Patriarch.

Further down in honor and authority came the bishops. The eastern bishops had less power than the western bishops and were, strictly speaking, helpers of the metropolitan. There were many such bishops in the eastern patriarchates. In the 6th century, the patriarchate fo Jerusalem had 3 metropolies with metropolitans and 56 bishops; in Antioch there were 12 metropolitans, 5 autocephalous metropolitans, 2 archbishops, and 125 bishops; in Constantinople thee were 32 metropolitans and 325 bishops, 1 autocephalous metropolitan and 34 autocephalous archbishops, all together 419 ecclesiastical administrative individuals. In the 10th century the patriarch of Constantinople already had 49 metropolies and 522 eparchias, and by the end of the 10th century there were over 60 metropolies.

A Synod of bishops elected the patriarchs, but in practice very often the Byzantine emperor had the deciding vote. A metropolitan was chosen by the bishops and he was approved and consecrated by the patriarch.

Nevertheless, if we speak of the non-Greek metropolies, the patriarch himself chose the metropolitan, not consulting the local bishops. This is what happened in the case of the metropoly of Kiev. Thus it is obvious that in their relations with the metropoly of Kiev the patriarchs did not hold to the Nomokanon Rule, that is, the operative church law, but decided according to the dictates of the patriarchal interests and the politics of the emperors. Because of this, as we shall see, many misunderstandings arose between the Ukrainian princes and the patriarch. It was important to the patriarchs not to grant too great an independence to the Churches of other nations because this interfered primarily with their ecclesiastical but also with their national policy. This is readily seen in the example of Bulgaria. We know that already by the end of the 7th century, (in 678) the Bulgarians were in very close contact with Greece, yet Christianity became widespread in their land only two centuries later. Some historians, Orthodox in faith, say that Christianity among the Slavs spread so late, that is, significantly later than among the Romance and the Anglo-Saxon nations, because the patriarchs were completely indifferent to converting the Slavs. When the Slavic nations took the initiative themselves and directed the Christianization, the patriarchs took care not to let the new Churches out of thier hands and tried to ensure that these churches measured up to the goals and interests of the Greeks.

The Metropolitans of Kiev in the first Era.

We will know chronologically go through the metropolitans of Kiev of the firts era and we will attempt to show what the real attitude of the patriarchs was to this metropoly. The beginnings of the Ukrainian hierarchy are very unclear and this has already been noted. To cast light on the question, very basic and patient study is required, free from all kinds of subjective orientation or prejudice. And perhaps, more will never be known about where the earliest Ukrainian metropolitans came from and who they were. For this reason there is no option left but to accept the view that the earliest metropolitans were naturalized from Greece. In chronicles and in other historical sources, there is no agreement as to who was first. Some submit that he was called Michael, others Leontius. Michael is supposed to have arrived with Volodimir when Volodimir was returning from Corsunia and baptized the populace of Kiev, but more sources mention Leontius. Therefore we will begin with him.

Leontius: The chronicle of Novgorod mentions him, there is allusion to him in Greek materials, and also tradition tells us that he was the first metropolitan of Kiev. Of course, he was a Greek and consecrated by the patriarch. Another question is whether these materials, which are from a significantly different time, reflect reality. Nothing is known about when this metropolitan arrived and how long he remained.

Ivan (1015 - 1037) He is mentioned by Jakiw Mnych and in the biography of Borys and Hlib as being the metropolitan of Kiev.

Theopempt (1037 - 1048) This would be the third metropolitan, appointed by the patriarch and sent from Greece. During his rule as metropolitan, war broke out between Yaroslav the Wise and the Greeks and he was forced to leave Kiev in 1048. Whether he left voluntarily or was exiled by Yaroslav is not known.

Ilarion (1051 - 1062) This was the first Ukrainian metropolitan. The chronicler Nestor says that, "God put it in the prince's heart . . ." Yaroslav set up Ilarion as the metropolitan of Rus in St. Sophia, chosen by the bishops. He was appointed without the participation of the patriarch but only chosen by the order of the prince and consecrated by the local bishops.

Gregory (1062 - 1072) - Greek.

Ivan II (1080 - 1084) A Greek, a "man clever with books and learning", he wrote "The Law of Jakiv Blackcassock", a polemic work against the Latins.

Ivan III (1089 - ?)

Ephrem (1089 - 1097) - A Ukrainian, earlier a bishp of Pereyaslav. There are conflicting opinions as to whether he was ordained by the patriarch in Constantinople or not. During his rule, the feast of the procession with the relics of St. Nicholas was instituted.

Nicholas (1097 - 1104) - A Greek.

Nikiphor (1104 - 1122) - A Greek.

Michael (1130 - 1147) - A Greek. He fell out with Izyaslav Mstyslavich, left his cathedral and went to Greece. Then the prince called a sobor (council) of bishops and told them to choose a new metropolitan - Clement Smolatych.

Clement Smolatych (1147 - ?) This is the third Ukrainian metropolitan. During his election a misunderstanding and division between the bishops of Greek extraction and the Ukrainian bishops came about. The Greeks asserted, contrary to the Nomokanon, that a metropolitan could not be set up without a patriarch. We see from this that the Greek bishops who were sent to episcopacies in the metropoly of Kiev must have been receiving separate orders and instructions. According to the Nomokanon, there was no obstacle to the election of a metropolitan by bishops. Notwithstanding, Clement was chosen and ordained metropolitan by the Ukrainian bishops, who used the relics of Pope St. Clement in the ordination. However the enemies of Izyaslav refused to acknowledge Metropolitan Clement and when they came to power they removed Clement and again put a Greek in the metropolitan's cathedral.

Constantine (1156 - 1158) A Greek. In 1158, Izyaslav again came to power and occupied Kiev. He removed Metropolitan Constantine who soon died in Chernihiv. For a few years, the cathedral was without a head - the reason is unknown. Perhaps there were discussions going on as to who was to lead the metropoly. In the end, in 1161, a Greek came in again.

Theodor (1161 - 1163) After his death, Prince Rostyslav wished to return the cathedral to Metropolitan Constantine, but the patriarch, not consulting with him, sent the Greek Ivan.

Ivan IV (1164 - 1167) - A Greek. On his account there arose a great conflict between Rostyalav and the patriarch and the prince was prepared to remove the Greek metropolitan. But Rostyslav's counselors advised him to accept the foreign metropolitan in the interests of peace in the Church. In the end the prince agreed, but stated that if the patriarch again sent a metropolitan without his consultation or agreement, he would decree that only Ukrainians could be elected and set up as metropolitans and that only at the command of the Great Prince.

Constantine II (1167 - 1182) - A Greek. During the rule of this metropolitan, Andrey Boholubsky first tried to obtain a separate metropolitan for the Suzdalian principality and to this end he sent his candidate Theodor to the patriarch. However the patriarch did not consent to this and only ordained him a bishop. Theodor came into conflict with the metropolitan who ordered Theodor imprisoned and later sent "mutilated", to a Persian island to be imprisoned for life.

Nykyphor II (1182 - 1201) - A Greek.

Matthew (1201 - 1224) - A Greek.

Cyril I (1224 - 1233) - A Greek from Nicea "a philosopher, a good academician and well-versed in the knowledge of divine literature".

Cyril II (1233 - 1236) - A Ukrainian, consecrated in the cathedral of St. Sophia. He was not confirmed by the patriarch and for this reason he is not mentioned in any list of metropolitans of Kiev except one.

Joseph (1237 - ?) A Greek. This was the last metropolitan of the pre-Mongolian era. He disappeared without trace during the Mongolian attack on Kiev.

The Policy of the Patriarchs.

With this roster of metropolitans of Kiev ends the first era of the history of the Ukrainian Church. Out of the 22 metropolitans there were only four Ukrainians; the rest were Greeks sent by the patriarch, for the most part without consultation with the prince and without ever comparing notes with the local bishops. It was not even necessary to consult the local bishops for the patriarch appointed metropolitans from among his own people, the Greeks, whom the Ukrainian bishops never saw beforehand and about whom they could not know anything. In such a manner the operative church law was applied only to metropolies in Greece. There the bishops of a metropoly elected a metropolitan and the patriarch just consecrated that metropolitan. The attitude to the metropoly of Kiev was different.

As to the rights of the metropolitan of Kiev, he led the Church with greater independence from the patriarch than did the Greek metropolitan. Though the Ukrainian Church did not regard herself autocephalous at that time, she really was and patriarchs did not interfere in the internal affairs of the Church. Territorially she was a huge unit larger than the whole patriarchate of Constantinople in which she ranked as the 60th metropoly. Obviously the patriarchs could not let such a metropoly out of their hands. The relations between Kiev and Constantinople were not always good, and for this reason the national interests of the emperors demanded that the Church in Kiev be very closely tied with the Greek Church and in this way influence the Ukrainian Princes to a favorable stand towards the emperors. This use of the Church for political ends was not confined to the Byzantines; a similar practice existed in the West beginning with Carl the Great, if not earlier.

The Greek Metropolitans of Kiev had different Ordens.

Besides this, the growing discord between Rome and Byzantium was felt more and more. Misunderstanding from the times of Patriarch Photius and the temporary break-up haphazardly taken care of made it clear to both sides that the situation and atmosphere which had existed from the break-up in the 10th and 11th centuries were far from amicable and harmonious. Thus is becomes clear why the Greeks made sure that our Church did not attain independence and did not eventually begin to think on her own in the categories of her own church policy. They had reason for this, for as we shall see later, the princes of Kiev were completely candid as to their feelings towards the west and towards a submissive attitude toward the western church. A heavy burden lay upon the Greek metropolitans who ruled the Ukrainian Church: to orient the thought, feelings and sympathies of the congregation subordinate to them to the Byzantine side. In terms of general respect toward ecclesiastical authority and the God fearing respect of the nation toward church law and the teaching authority of the church, the task was accomplished well and without much trouble. The Bulgarians defended their ecclesiastical independence somewhat more strongly and, though they ended up in the Byzantine sphere of influence, nevertheless they obtained a patriarchate for themselves along with the right to determine the fact of their church on their own. In the Ukraine there were also efforts to get out of patriarchal guardianship or at least to limit it. However, these efforts were somewhat sporadic stands, the effects of international friction rather than the results of a planned, unyielding and goal-oriented policy for the church for the distinction of her own self-development.

15. The Attitude of the Ukrainian Church toward Rome.

One can already get some idea of the attitude of the Ukrainian Church toward Rome and toward Latinism in general on the basis of that which has been said about her beginnings and her activity in the course of two and a half centuries. This attitude in her history is portrayed differently depending on the orientation of the historian himself. To write an objective history is not an easy matter and when one is dealing with a religious matter, it is doubly difficult. First of all, it is not easy because the historian will naturally defend that church to which he himself belongs; he will observe the facts and interpret the sources through the prism of the faith he professes. Secondly, it is not easy because the matter of religion is the matter of faith, where not everything can be proven with a mathematical formula. For this reason the interpretations of that source material which touches on the ties of the Ukrainian Church with Rome in the early era are sometimes incomplete opposition to one another.

As we already know, Christianity in the Ukraine may have begun its spread in the western provinces, filtering in from Moravia Major as early as the 9th century. We have no completely certain proofs of the extent of its spread, but such a distinguished researcher of the beginnings of Christianity in the Ukraine as A. Petrushevych cites much interesting material which really argues for the fact that the influences of Cyril-Methodian Christianity were strong in the Ukraine.

The brother-saints, notwithstanding the fact that they themselves came from the East and were spreading an eastern brand of Christianity, recognized the unity of Christ's Church, the Apostles' Capitol as her universal center, and the Pope as the highest teacher. The Holy See approved their work and often took their side in defending them against their oppressors. Logically speaking, the followers of Cyril and Methodius as well as the faithful may even then have drawn a distinction between Rome, the Apostolic Capital of St. Peter, and those Latin bishops who were attempting to capitalize on the Christianization for their own political ends. There is no doubt that after the death of St. Methodius in 885, after the banishment of his followers from Moravia and Panonia and the institution of the Latin rite and the Latin language, the attitude towards the Latins in these countries was not very positive. Religion and the visible form of its expression are very holy things to a person. When they are imposed upon someone or when a previously accepted form is forcibly changed, then enthusiasm cannot be expected as a result. In time such imposition may be forgotten; after a few generations a new tradition may be formed, but at the beginning there is much pain felt in a nation during an enforced reform. A person loves his individuality; every nation also has and loves its individuality, regardless of whether it is savage or cultured. Only those people - and there are generally few of these - who do not have any self-respect and have no feeling of individuality will be indifferent when some stranger imposes his own ideas on them and contradicts their own.

These first tensions in eastern Christianity brought about by the Latinizing process, or more exactly, by the hierarchy of one church, were not without effect on further mutual relations. Certainly they did not stop the cultural friction which was growing between the East and the West but, on the contrary, made it more complex. The Bulgarians, accepting Christianity in the 9th century, did not know themselves what road to take. They had bitter experience with the neighboring Byzantium; thus, though they had accepted Christianity from there, they reoriented themselves to Rome, only to return to the East again after a few years.

The differences between the Eastern and Western Churches.

In all likelihood there was a similar situation in the Ukraine. The undeniable fact is that the Ukrainian ancestors embraced Christianity of the eastern rite - a Christianity which did not fundamentaly differ from western Christianity. The only difference was that in the eastern Christianity, elements of culture of the East with its fondness for mysticism were reflected, and in the western Christianity, the fondness for strict juridicism and cold logic was reflected. But at that time no one spoke of these details nor took them into account; the effects of subordination to one or the other Christian center commanded the primary attention.

For this reason Olga, though she accepted Christianity from the East, made nothing of the "religious" difference between Byzantium and Rome and soon after her Baptism was trying to establish good relations with the western church. These relations of our Princes continued for at least two hundred years. Chronicles relate that after the conquering of Corsunia by Volodimir the Great, envoys from the Pope bearing Holy Relics came to him. The chronicler is stingy with his words, but nevertheless it is a very significant fact that on the eve of Ukrainian Christianization there was an amicable relationship with the Holy See. Similar papal delegations are mentioned twice more (in 991 and in 1000) and also one from Volodimir to the Pope. A tradition even sprang up in the Ukraine, which even Hrushevsky regards as

52

feasibly acceptable, that Volodimir accepted a crown from the Pope and was the first Ukrainian king. It is difficult to believe this tradition because kings were not made every day and there is preserved exact and undeniable evidence of two other kings of that time (St. Stephen of Hungary and the Polish Boleslav the Brave). There is not such evidence of the coronation of St. Volodimir. But this in no way weakens the assertion that friendly relations existed between the baptizer of the Ukraine and the Holy See.

A similar situation existed at the time of Jaroslav the Wise. He was married to a Swedish princess who was a member of the Latin church, and his children, with the exception of one daughter and Vsevolod, his son, both of whom were married into the Byzantine court, also married royally with persons who belonged to the Latin church. This is an indication that no difference was discerned between eastern and western Christianity at that time.

The Schism of Cerularius.

In the year of Yaroslav the Brave's death in 1054, a very sad event took place in the Universal Church; an event which is historically called "the schism of Cerularius".

The relations between Byzantium and Rome had been tense for a long time. The Byzantine emperors regarded themselves as the gretest single rulers in the world, heirs to the mighty Roman Empire. In 962 a similar empire, the Roman Empire of the German Nation was formed in the West, with the Pope crowning the German king Otto as emperor and thus putting him on the same level of honor as the Byzantine emperor. The tense relations between Rome and Byzantium did not diminish, but intensified. The Greeks made several complaints against the Latins as to rite and also as to faith; for this reason the Pope sent delegates to Constantinople in 1054 to look into the problem and settle the dispute. Not having reached an agreement, the papal delegates, under the direction of cardinal Humbert, excommunicated the patriarch and isolated him from the Church. For his part, the patriarch excommunicated the delegates, and the division in the holy Church was complete. The division has lasted to the present day, to the great sorrow of all Christians.

Western historians say that the papal delegation, returning from Constantinople, stopped in at Kiev and perhaps tried to inform the metropolitan of Kiev of the events which had taken place. The reason for this may have been to bring the metropolitan over to their side. Ilarion, the first Ukrainian metropolitan, was then in power; therefore the delegates could expect that there would be no difficulties in the matter. However, if the delegation was indeed in Kiev, it was not completely successful, for the Ukrainian church did not at once enter into the conflict. It is not difficult to guess why not. There were often conflicts, sometimes very sharp, between Rome and Byzantium, but with time all disputes were settled; hence the metropolitan did not think it advantageous to pull his church into the dispute. The Ukrainian church was young and needed as much peace as she could have.

53

Polemic Works.

The Ukrainian church maintained this roughly neutral stand until the end of the eleventh century, that is, about 150 years, despite the fact that the metropolitans after Ilarion, with the exception of Ephraim, were Greeks. It is true that in the 1080's there appeared a work, attributed to metropolitan Ivan, against the Latins; nevertheless, in comparison with the polemic works of the Greeks, this work was very restrained. Only during the rule of Metropolitan Nicephorus, a Greek, did the church take a clear stand on the side of the patriarch. The polemic works of this metropolitan bear clear signs of antagonism toward the Latins. Metropolitan Michael kept us this same animosity together with a few other Greek bishops; for example, the bishop of Nowhorod, Niphont, who wrote a pamphlet called "Voproshenie Kirikove" against the Latins.

However the Ukrainian princes did not allow themselves to be swayed by this influence and it is probable that the majority of clerics and faithful bore the Latins no personal animosity, simply because they had no reason nor need to do so.

We see that during his rule, in 1075, Izyaslav sent a delegation to Pope Gregory VII. Izyaslav sent his son Yaropolk to ask the Pope's help, for just at that time, his brothers had captured Kiev away from him. Yaropolk, at the command of his father, placed Rus under the care of the Holy See, and for this he received the title "apostolic prince". Orthodox historians call Izyaslav the "greatest Catholic prince", that is, or all the pre-Mongolian princes.

Even during Vsevolod's reign, though the prince was married to a Greek princess, good relations with the western, Catholic dynasties continued and Vsevolod'd daughter, Evpraxia, married Heinrich IV, the German emperor. Vsevolod kept in touch with Pope Clement III by correspondence, while Pope Innocent III sent two delegations to the Ukraine. Hence it is obvious that contact with the western world, and especially with Rome, was uninterrupted. Apparently these contacts occured either when the prince, for example, Rostyslav, had a say in the choice of a metropolitan or when the metropolitan was Ukrainian.

The Dominicans in Kiev.

At the beginning of the 13th century, during the rule of Pope Honorius III (1216-1227) there even appeared in Kiev Dominicans who founded a monastery and preached with complete freedom. They did not remain long, though, for by 1232 they had been banished from Kiev during the rule of Carl I, a Greek from Nicea. But the very fact that the prince did not forbid them to settle in Kiev, to found a monastery or to preach freely shows, if not a submissive, then at least tolerant attitude to the western church.

As can be seen from the presentation of dry facts above, there was not tolerance of nor animosity towards Christians of the Latin world in the Ukraine. On the contrary, Greek metropolitans had to work hard to succeed in building a mistrust of Latins. When one compares the works of the Greek metropolitans with the few works whose authors were Ukrainian metropolitans or bishops (for example, Luke Gydyata), one sees the fundamental difference right away. The letters or works of the Greeks almost always have the theme "the difference between faiths": while the Greek works were exposing the Latins, the works of Ukrainian bishops were almost exclusively concerned with matters of Christian morality, spiritual life and the perfecting of a person. This is very instructive and an alert leader cannot help but notice the difference.

16. The Organization of the Ukrainian Church in the First Era and Her General Characteristics.

The bases of the organization of the Ukrainian Church in the very beginning of her foundation become those sources of canon law and ecclesiastical practices which were in use at the time in the Western Church. Here belong the Rules of the Holy Apostles (or the canon of the Holy Apostles), the canons of the seven Ecumenical Councils, the Nomocaons, or collections of church law which also include the civil laws of the emperors regarding the church, and finally the practices of the Western Church, which developed in the course of many years. In the Ukraine this collection of ecclesiastical laws was called the "Managing Book", that is, a collection of canons and regulations by which the Church guided herself. In addition the Ukrainian princes issued their own laws which were called "Church regulations". There were six such regulations in the pre-Mongolian era. Two of these regulations, issued by Volodimir the Great and Yaroslav the Wise, referred to the whole Church and the others (two of Vsevolod's, one of Sviatoslav and one of Rostyslav) were of a local character - three referred to the eparchy of Novhorod and one to that of Smolensk.

The regulations more precisely defined the rights and privileges of the Church, of the clergy, and of the "church people", decided the matter of ecclesiastical courts, and so on.

The Rights of the Metropolitans of Kiev.

The metropolitan had the highest post in the metropoly of Kiev and within his juridiction he ruled in almost complete independence from the patriarch. Theoretically the patriarch was the highest court in the resolving of ecclesiastical squabbles, but we know of few referrals to the patriarch. The metropolitan consecrated bishops chosen by the sobor (council of bishops), but there were instances where the metropolitan himself set up bishops in cathedrals using his own judgement or in consultation with the prince. The metropolitan did not judge the bishops by himself - only a sobor had this right - but there were exceptions and abuses here as well (for example, Metropolitan Constantine judged bishop Theodor with all the severity of the justice of the times). The metropolitan also controlled canonization and the inclusion of the canonized to the roster of saints, the establishment of feast-days, the calling and leading of sobors, the supervision of bishops, and the everyday administration of the Church in general.

The bishops, who fulfilled their pastoral and sacred duties in the eparchies, were subject to the metropolitan. There were six eparchies at the death of Volodimir: Novhorod, Chernihiw, Rostov, Volodimir-Volynsk, Bilhorod and Kiev. In the mid-13th century, at the end of the first era, there were 15 eparchies: Chernihiw, Pereyaslav, Volodimir-Volynsk, Kiev, Polotsk, Novhorod, Smolensk, Ryazanks, Peremysl, Volodimir, Rostov, Bilhorod, Juriiv, Uhrovsk, Halych and perhaps' Zakarpathia (about this seat there is no exact evidence) and Tmutorokan. The last was perhaps under the direct control of the patriarch.

When one compares the 15-17 eparchies existing in that large empire with 419 episcopates existing in the 6th century in the patriarchate of Constantinople which was territorially but half the size, it becomes clear that the bishop's office was somewhat more important in Ukraine. The bishop's power was similar to the power of a minor prince, when at the same time in Greece each town had its own bishop or metropolitan (in the 10th century there were 60 metropolies and 51 archepiscopates) or archbishop. The eparchies in Ukraine were rich, and for this reason the Greeks came gladly to do Christianizing work in Ukraine.

Ecclesiastical Offices in the Sophia of Constantinople.

In Ukrainian eparchies, similar to those in Greece, the following clerical offices or ecclesiastical honors developed: the Protopresbyter, the first among priests, a bishop's helper; the Archdeacons, who served as bishop's helpers and in the administration of the eparchy (this title soon disappeared and in its place came another - protosyncel - which has remained to this day); the Aprocyzier, who represented the interets of the Church and the metropolitan at the prince's court; the steward, who administrated eparchial or metropolial property; the Skeophilacs (or kimeriarkos), who managed church finances and liturgical goods like cassocks, vessels and so on; the Chartophilacs, who managed church books and archives; the Chancellor, who ws the master of ceremonies, and other, lesser functionaries.

The clergy associated with the cathedrals were very numerous. While it is true that we have no exact index of what the clergy was like in Ukraine, we can nevertheless draw conclusion on the basis of the facts which are known about the Greek cathedrals. Thus, for example, during the reign of Heracles in the 7th century at the cathedral of St. Sophia in Constantinople there were:

Number of Clergy

80 priests	75 torchbearers
150 deacons	2 syncels (who fulfilled separate functions
40 deaconesses	determined by the bishop)
70 subdeacons	12 chancellors
160 readers	40 notaries
25 cantors	

In all, there were 525 persons. A relatively small church of Vlachern had 75 spiritual or "church people".

To this must be added a multitude of different types of beneficient or charitable organizations such as shelters for foreigners, old persons' homes, guardianship for beggars and the poor, orphanages, guardianship for the crippled, the sick, and so on and so forth. Usually these organizations were managed by monks under the supervision of a bishop. For the upkeep of the church, that is, the metropolitan, the bishops and their clergy, the government assigned a tenth part of its income.

What is a Desyatyna? A desyatyna (or a tenth part) first appears during Volodimir's reign. The matter of a desyatyna is also decided by Vsevolod's Regulations: a tenth part of the income from the prince's lands, from judicial matters, from trade incomes and from national goods. One can imagine that the incomes of bishops in the era of the princes were not small. In the 12th century the desyatyna slowly goes out of use and princes grant churches earthly produce or give them concessions for certain businesses (such as the sale of candles).

A large source of income was ecclesiastical courts. This was because the punishments were fines and since the circle of jurisdiction was very wide for the church courts, the church's treasury was by no means poor.

Achievements of the Christian Culture.

In characterizing this era of Ukrainian Church history, it must be mentioned that in two and a half centuries the Church conducted a complete Christianization of wide areas within the nation and successfully developed church administration in local areas. Thousands of churches were built in that time, hundres of monasteries were founded in which there were sometimes 300 or more monks, a certain number of schools were built, and a multitude of charitable organizations were set up. Christianity was accepted in Ukraine without the mass demonstrations, protests or dissent which occurred in northern lands or, for example, in Poland. From this can be drawn the conclusion that the preparation for Christianity proceeded through a long period of time - from the middle of the ninth century. One of the greatest gains for the Ukraine from Christianity was the institution of writing and of understandable language of worship. Cyril's script became the basis of the development of the language of Ukrainian literature.

The Orientation of the Ukrainian Church in the First Era.

In that time the Ukrainian Church went through, it may be said, three epochs. The first, initial one was the decision which way to go, to the East or to the West. This unclear period in the initial history of the Church lasted about 30 or more years. In the end, the former route was chosen. Nevertheless we see all the pains taken by the Ukrainian princes, and in some cases the bishops as well, to keep a wise balance between East and West. This second period lasted until the end of the 11th century. In spite of the ecclesiastical dependence on the patriarchs of Constantinople, the princes of Kiev kept their family ties with the western world, and maintained relations with Rome and the Latin Church, without prejudice - on the contrary, often with trust and friendship. In the third period, starting approximately at the beginning of the 12th century, an orientation towards the West took the upper hand in the Ukraine and slowly the Ukrainian Church began to give herself over to the antangonism which sprang up between the Roman and the Byzantine Churches in the middle of the 11th century.

The Second Era

From the Fall of Kiev (1240) to the Sobor of Brest.

1. The Fall of Kiev and its Effects on the Church.

During the reign of the Great Prince Yaroslav the Wise, the strength of the Empire of Kiev reached its peak. After a few years of fighting over the succession, "Yaroslav took the throne of Kiev" (1016). During his reign he built up the nation and fortified it. One of his greatest achievements was the collection of laws, "Ruska Pravda", which served as the basis of right living for the nation and for society. It appeared that this mighty princely empire had stood solidly on its feet and before it stretched years of magnificent growth. Yet not two hundred years passed after the death of this great prince when Kiev fell into ruin.

What were the reasons for the decline of this strong, modern-for-its-times nation? There were two reasons. The first was internal strife, misunderstandings between the prince-successors of Yaroslav's great inheritance. The second reason was the unceasing raids of nomadic hordes from the east against which the nation weakened by internal strife had no strength to defend itself.

In keeping with the practice of the times, the Great Prince of Kiev divided his lands among his sons, leaving the eldest the first throne in the city of Kiev, and dividing the primacy among the other, younger princes. But misunderstandings, disagreements, and wars broke out between the princes; one constantly attacked the other to sieze his lands and enlarge his own share. Such a nation, where brother fights brother, cannot stand. Its strength is used up in its own destruction.

The Destruction of Kiev in 1168.

The first intolerable blow to the State of Kiev was dealt in the middle of the 12th century and that at the very hands of the heirs of the great prince. In 1169, Andriy Boholubsky, son of the Suzdalian prince Juriy Dovhoruky and grandson of Volodimir Monomach, attacked Kiev and completely destroyed it. The chronicler relates that the Suzdalians looted and killed people for two days. They did not spare one church, not one monastery and removed all the icons, all the vestments, the church books, and even the bells. Having looted everything, they burned the churches. The chronicler ends his passage by saying that there was weeping and moaning in Kiev, "and sorrow and unconsolable grief and unceasing tears". This attack of northern princes signaled the decay of the state of Kiev. Between its center, Kiev, and the divided principates of the north there appeared an impassable boundary of hostility and animosity. A new national organization began to appear in the north which, mixed with different Finnish clans, became more and more removed from its maternal roots.

It was a mistake on the part of the builders of the Ukrainian primate state that they, having adopted much of what was good from their neighbors, the Byzantines, or other nations, did not want to adopt that which forms the basis of the existence, safety and development of a nation - a strong central authority. They knew from their own experience that the system of separate principates undermined a nation in its very foundations. It is lamentable that because of their obedience to the ancient tradition of dividing property among sons, they unintentionally set up the tragic end for their nation.

After the looting of Kiev by Andrij Boholubsky, whom the Russian Orthodox Church entered into the roster of saints, the princes of Kiev were nevertheless able to rebuild Kiev and more or less remove the traces of the barbarianism. But after seventy years a second misfortune came - the Tartars. The Tartars, Polovtsians and other nomadic tribes continuously raided Ukrainian lands from the east and the south. The compaign (in 1185) of Ihor Sviatoslavich, allied with other prince against the Polovtsians, ended with a grave defeat for the Ukrainian princes at the river Kayala. The strength of Kiev had been cut back. What weakened the strength of the state the most was the disharmony between the princes. And when it came time to repulse the attacks of the Tartars in the 1230's, the State of Kiev, not long before so mighty, had no strength left to do this.

Destruction of Kiev by the Tartars.

In 1240 the khan of the Tartars, Baty, conquered Kiev and completely destroyed it. The western missionary Plano de Carpini, who was travelling through Kiev a few years later, found about 200 homes left in all. The rest was all in ruins - about 600 churches, over 20 monasteries and all other costly tokens of the Ukrainian culture had been ground into dust. During this destruction of Kiev, Metropolitan Joseph was also lost without trace.

The fall of Kiev reflected itself very painfully in the Ukrainian church life. When the next metropolitan, Cyril, came, he found a wasteland. Chernihiw was similarly destroyed. For a time, the metropolitan resided in Halych, and later went on to Volodimir the Suzdalian in the north and remained there almost until the end of his life. Only for a few years before his death did he return to Kiev.

This metropolitan was a bishop in Cholm earlier. He was noticed by the patriarch and instated as patriarch only in 1250. He was a tool of king Danylo, but it is obvious that Danylo mistook him, for he was the first to bring the capitol of the metropoly of Kiev to the north. His name is tied with one of the first general sobors of the Ukrainian Church, called the sobor of Volodimir, in 1274, which decided on the "12 Laws about ecclesiastical matters and the activity of priests". He left other writings as well, among them, a "Teaching for Priests", which probably created the custom in the Ukrainian Church of passing on this "Teaching" to priests at ordination.

2. The Transfer of the Capitol of the Metropolia to the North.

Although Kiev, even before 1240, was not playing the same role that it had formerly, it was always to a certain extent at least a symbol of the great principate. The process of separation of the divided principates, which had already begun at the end of the 11th century, was reinforced now, after the destruction of Kiev. At the end of the 11th century, the western Ukrainian lands separated first, and at the beginning of the 12th century the north-western lands followed. This is the area where the center of Ukrainian statehood was slowly transferred. But these lands and princes who ruled here felt their organic and cultural unity with Kiev, and Kiev always belonged in their sphere of influence. On the other hand, the princes who ruled in the north did not feel such a tie with Kiev and always wished for a complete separation. The best evidence of this feeling of separateness was the destruction of Kiev by Boholubsky, which a prince with even a bit of feeling of cultural or clannish oneness with the ancient center of the great principate would not have been able to bring himself to do.

Before the destruction of Kiev 1167, the Suzdalian prince, Andriy Boholubsky sent the patriarch a delegation asking for the consecration of his candidate Fedor, as a separate metropolitan for his principate. But the patriarch would not agree to divide the metropoly of Kiev and to form another center at that time. After the destruction of Kiev, a new opportunity for this arose. As has been mentioned, during the attack of Baty on Kiev, Metropolitan Joseph disappeared without a trace and it was not known whether he had died together with his faithful or whether he had fled to Greece and was not letting anyone know his whereabouts. For a few years after this, the metropoly of Kiev was without a head. Only in 1243 is there mention made of metropolitan Cyril in the Volynian chronicle. Cyril did not have the blessing of the patriarch from the start but perhaps he obtained this blessing in 1250 in Nicea, where the patriarch of Constantinople had his residence then.

Although Cyril spent most of his years as a metropolitan in the north, he did not perhaps consider returning to Kiev to renew church life there. He negotiated some concessions for the clergy with the Tartars, particularly a release from tributes and a guarantee of Church freedom to exist and work. He came to Kiev in his later years, about 1276, and remained there for four years, as at the end of his life he wished to reaffirm his relationship with the capitol of all the metropolitans up to that time. He was buried in the cathedral of St. Sophia.

The successor to Cyril on the metropolitan's throne was the Greek Maxim, who ruled the Ukrainian Church between 1283 and 1305. In his relationship with the Tartars, he held to the same policy as did his predecessor, but being a foreigner, he always preferred to stay away from them. Nothing tied him to Kiev. Up until this time, he had resided in some Greek locale; therefore he was indifferent to the traditions of Kiev. At the beginning he resided in Kiev for a time, later moving from one town to another, until he settled in Volodimir on the Klyasma, in Suzdal, in the same Volodimir where his predecessor had resided before him. But where as his predecessor, Cyril, had only lived there without changing the capitol of the metropoly from Kiev, Maxim definitely relocated the capitol of the metropoly there in 1299. This was a heavy blow to the metropoly of Kiev.

The Authority of the Metropolitan of Kiev.

A metropolitan had a great authority in the era of princes, notwithstanding the fact that he was almost always a foreigner, a Greek. During the time of the mighty principate, he was regarded as the second unifying power of the great reaches of the nation. When the authority of the prince of Kiev diminished and principates with a separatist tendency began to grow, the metropolitan became the one power and authority which could have any influence on his eparchies in the divided principates. He remained the one symbol of the reality of the recent great nation. For Kiev he was the hope that hard times would pass and that Kiev, as the center of Christianity in all Eastern Europe, would rise again and heal its grave wounds. But Metropolitan Maxim did not perhaps wish to take upon himself the task of rebuilding the ruined capitol and, as the chronicle of Lavrenty relates, "not bearing the constraints of the Tartars, left the metropoly and fled from Kiev and all Kiev became desolate". In Kiev, which had been the center of the metropoly for almost 300 years, not even a bishop remained. The highest ecclesiastical authority left was an archpriest, as the local representative of the metropolitan.

Thus because of internal strife, there remained no strength to defend Ukraine against the barbaric nomads who dealt Kiev the final blow. The personal interests of individual princes took precedence over wisdom and a feeling of responsibility for the future fate of the State of Kiev and for the greatness and wealth which had been left them as a heritage by their forefathers. This lack of wisdom had its revenge on them as well, for not one hundred years passed before their inheritance became easy prey for their neighbors. In this way the greatness of the mighty Kiev, the "mother of the cities of Rus," began to diminish. With the reestablishment of the capitol to the north, a new center slowly grew there; different from Kiev in all its appearance, its understanding of Christianity and its contrasting culture.

3. The Halych-Volynian State
- the second Center of Church Life.

An Overview of the History of Halychyna.

The land of Halychyna belonged to the State of Kiev from ancient times, that is, from the 9th century. In the 10th century, the western borderlands had fallen into the hands of Poland, but Volodimir the Great took them back from Poland in 981 and joined them once again to the principate. Later, after the death of Volodimir, the Poles had again occupied the so-called cities of Chervenia for a short time (in 1017), but not for long, for in 1030 Yaroslav the Wise beat the Poles back and took back the lands. At the division of Yaroslav's principate, his grandson Rostyslav Volodimirovich (who died in 1065) received Halychyna, and after his death the district was divided among his three sons: Ruryk received Peremyshl, Volodar Zvenyhorod and Vasilko Terebovla. Volodimir's son Volodimirko relocated his capitol to Halych (in 1411), deprived the other princes of their shares, and took Halychyna under his own control. His son, Yaroslav Osmomysl (1153-1187), enlarged his nation to the Danube river, came to a comfortable agreement with Byzantium, strengthened the State internaly, established contacts with other foreign rulers and in this way brought the State of Halychyna to great power and wealth. This is the famous prince who is being praised by the author of "Slovo o Polku Ihorevi", who barred the way for the king, who closed the gates of the Danube.

His son Volodimir (1187-1199) was banished by the nobles and the Rostyslav dynasty died with him. For a time Hungarians occupied Halychyna, but the Volynian Prince Roman, drove the Hungarians out and joined Halychyna to his State of Volynia into one whole. In such a manner, at the end of the 12th century, just when the State of Kiev was leaning towards its fall, a new center of Ukrainian statehood, culture and church life developed. The Halych-Volynian State played a very large role in the life of the Ukrainian nation. Just at that menacing time when Kiev was destroyed, it assumed the yoke of defence of the Ukrainian lands against the greedy, neighboring Poles and Hungarians and against the danger of the nomadic hordes of the East. The Romanovich descendants fused together most of the Ukrainian lands, including Kiev, and were able to successfully guard Ukraine against assimilation and mastery by Poland and Suzdalia. This was already a completely Ukrainian nation, free from foreign and northern lands. The mightiest of the rulers of Halych was Roman, whom the chronicle calls "the despot of all Rus". In the West this state reached up to Ryashiw (today in Poland), in the south to the Danube and the Black Sea, in the east to the Dniepr and in the north it neighbored with Lithuania.

The Influences of the Western Church on Halychyna.

Western Ukraine, although under the influence of the Kievan Empire until the end of the 11th century and under the direct authority of the Kievan princes, leaned somewhat more towards western cultural influences, neighboring as it did more on Poland and Hungary than did Central Ukraine. The Church in the west, by will or by force, met with the Latin Church in various missions, was tolerated by Halychian rulers and by the same token was more familiar with the Latin influence that were eparchies further removed from the West and also under the influence of Greek propaganda.

As we have already seen, in all probability Christianity came to Western Ukraine in the 9th century during the time of the missionary activity of Cyril and Methodius, and because the brother-Saints were in union with the Holy See, the influence of the Christianity they proclaimed, even after the

Schism, was doubtless quite strongly felt. This is borne out above all by the tolerance of the Halychian princes to the Latins, in their marital ties with Catholic royal homes and their ties with Rome which they maintained themselves. The chronicles make note of two diplomatic misssions from Pope Innocent III (1198-1216) to Rus on Church matters and perhaps on the matter of the participation of the Ukrainian princes in the Crusades. Even in Novhorod, Catholic missionaries were seen and in Western Ukraine, Catholic chaplaincies were formed for the spiritual service of German and Hungarian colonists. The Galico-Volynian prince himself, Roman, was educated in the court at Cracow, married with a kinswoman of the Polish king, Leshko Bilyy, and was also related to the Hungarian prince Andrew. German sources recorded him as a benefactor of the Catholic monastery in Erfurt. Thus it may be assumed that the attitude of Roman Mstyslavich to the Latin Church was not inimical. It is true that one chronicler Voskresensky, relates that the pope sent Roman a crown which Roman refused, but this episode seems hardly authentic as other sources say nothing of it. It may have sprung up appreciably later under the influence of the anti-Latin propaganda in the 13th century, when the relations between the Greeks and the Latins were very hostile, and this prince was to serve as anti-Latin argument.

Not only were the Latins tolerated in Halychyna at that time, toleration was to a certain extent reciprocal. In the Hungarian kingdom, for example, there were no Latin monasteries until the 12th century, but there were monasteries of the Greek-Slavic rite. In Czechia, such monasteries survived until the first half of the 13th century. The saints of the Western Church often refer to the early literature of the Ukrainian Church, and no distinction is drawn between them and the saints of the Ukrainian Church.

Foundation of Eparchies in Western Ukraine.

The earliest Halychian episcopate is, without a doubt, that of Peremyshl, which was set up at some time in the first half of the 9th century, if not earlier. As for the episcopate of Halych, it was of later origin, perhaps at the end of the 11th century or the beginning of the 12th. Certainly it existed in the mid-12th century, for we have dating from that time a medal with an inscription by bishop Kosma of Halych minted on the occasion of the institution in the whole Ukrainian Church of the feast of St. Mary the Protectress.

The third ancient eparchy in the western Ukrainian lands, that of Kholm, was founded somewhat later, by King Danylo in 1235, although the colonization here had come earlier and there even existed a cathedral, built by Volodimir the Great, which indicates that church life thrived here.

Besides the administrative units in the form of eparchies, from the earliest times of Christianity in the Ukraine there sprang up monasteries, as in Plisnesk, Halych, Peremyshl, and other centers, which also contributed much to the buildup of church life in western Ukraine. All this - the princes' toleration of the Latin rite, and the ordering of ecclesiastical relations when removed from the unceasing wars between individual princes, helped create a calmer atmosphere which allowed ties with the western world to develop.

And when dark clouds gathered over Kiev, the Halychian lands were ready to continue the tradition which had been interrupted by the destruction of the capitol. It is true that there was no lack of war here either but these wars did not spread so much devastation as did the wars against the princes' throne.

After Roman's death in 1205, the nobles once again made themselves known - they banished the young successors of the dead prince and gave the Halych-Volynian State to the Ihoreviches of Chernihiv. Among the Ihoreviches there sprang up a dispute which ended poorly both for them and for Halychyna, for in 1209 the Hungarians took over Halych. I 1207 Pope Innocent III tried to bring the rulers of Halychyna to ecclesiastical unity and perhaps sent a delegation in regards to this matter. There is mention made of this in a letter to the Hungarian prince, Andrew, but whether or not there was a delegation is not known. In any event, the time was not opportune for this and the intermediary, the Hungarian king who had siezed Halych, was not suited to the task. In 1211, the Ihoreviches routed the Hungarians, began to rule in Halych and were beaten down to 500 strong by the noblemen with whom Roman had had trouble before. In 1214 the Hungarians again occupied Halych, set up a party of noblemen who were subordinate to them and began talks with Rome in the matter of the union of Halych with the Catholic Church. But nothing came of this, for the Hungarians at once began to bring in the Latin rite, thus alienating the people from them. A rebellion sprang up against them and they were driven out in 1219, while the throne of Halych was occupied by Mstyslav of Novhorod.

The Latinization of the Ukrainian Church.

After the death of Pope Innocent III (in 1216), there came a change in the Catholic action towards the union of the eastern Christians. Instead of delegations and persuasion, there was an enforced propaganda of Roman Catholicism. More and more often there appear in the Ukraine Dominican and Franciscan monks involved in their work. As has already been mentioned, they had founded their monastery (Dominican) at about that time in Kiev and had not called suspicion to themselves at first.

Nevertheless, at the beginning of the 1230's, there is observed a dispute against their action, against Latinization, and they are driven out of Kiev and other eparchies. This strained relations and brought about the distrust of the local populace. Such an action of forced Latinization only served to hinder the union of the Churches and to spread anti-Catholic propaganda still further. The relations between Rome and the Greeks were inimical even without this, for just at that time, the Crusaders had occupied Constantinople, driven out the patriarch to Nicea, and set up a Latin patriarch in his place. This action of the Latins could not but have an influence even on the Ukraine.

After a few years, the Tartars invaded the Ukraine and not coming across any adequate opposition, swept through all of Central Europe up to Silezia. Only there were they stopped and from there they returned to central Europe and there set up their state.

At this dreadful and restless time, King Danylo was in power and he finally won back his inherited throne and again united the Halych-Volynian lands in 1240.

4. King Danylo and his Church Policy

The Invasion of the Tartars.
The dreadful power of the Tartars which, having devastated the lands of Ukraine, pushed on into central Europe, wreaked great havoc in the western world. The Tartars destroyed Poland as well (at the battle of Lignitz in 1241), occupied Hungary and the northern Balkans, and, having suborned (meands "bribed") the Ukrainian and Moskovian princes, occupied areas around the Volga. Such a power could not be taken lightly and for this reason the Pope, in agreement with the emperor Friedrich II, called an Ecumenical Council at Lyons, to decide what action could be taken against this power dangerous to Christianity. One of the leaders of this coalition against the Tartars was Pope Innocent IV himself, who took pains to join to this action those rulers whose countries were in immediate danger from the Tartars. Danylo belonged to this group as well. The Ecumenical Council was called in Lyons (France) in 1245.

At this Council, a representative of the Ukrainian Church appears for the first time - Archbishop Peter, who, historians speculate, had been sent there by Danylo or one of the other Ukrainian princes. Mention is made of Archbishop Peter's participation in this Council in some western sources and these sources have stirred much debate on the questions: who he was, what kind of archbishop, where he was from, who sent him and what finally happened to him. From the sources it is evident that Archbishop Peter did not know the biblical languages, Greek or Hebrew; nor also Latin, thus he had to make himself understood through a translator. He was knowledgeable about the Tartars, their faith, customs, traditions, method of waging war, and relations with conquered countries. As a spiritual person, he showed a good knowledge of theology and did not raise any doubts among the priests at the council about the reality of his faith. It is obvious that he took advantage of the full trust in his personage, for he took part in a common service with the other priests of the council, as the afore-mentioned foreign chronicles relate.

On the theme of Archbishop Peter's involvement in the Council there has sprung up a great body of literature. Nevertheless this question remains incompletely illuminated. The difficulty lies in the fact that the rosters of Ukrainian metropolitans make no mention of Archbishop Peter thus there arises a suspicion that later rewriters of the rosters left him out or that he was at his cathedral for such a short time that he didn't make the rosters. As for the term "archbishop", this title was given only to the metropolitan of Kiev or the bishop of Novhorod, who was also called an archbishop after 1156. But the bishop of Novhorod of that time is well known, thus Peter was not he. He may have been the metropolitan of Kiev after the metropolitan of that time, Joseph, had disappeared without a trace, but there is no proof of this either.

A hypothesis was put forward by Tomashevsky who very carefully analyzed all the sources. Peter, according to Tomashevsky, may have been a metropolitan of Kiev who had been elected by the bishops but, not having patriarchal confirmation, ruled the metropoly of Kiev temporarily. This may be why he didn't carry the title of metropolitan, since he didn't have the patriarch's blessing. However nothing definite can be said in this matter. Yet neither can his participation in the council be doubted, for there are detailed records of this.

Having accepted as certain and proven the participation of a hierarch of the Ukrainian Church in an Ecumenical Council, we may conclude that behind such an important matter must have been a national authority, probably one of the princes. This may have been the Halych-Volynian ruler, Danylo, who had united his lands and worked out his policies not long before, or the prince of Chernihiw, Michael (as Tomashevsky postulated), who had good ties with the Catholic world and was related to the Polish Hungarian royal courts. But whoever he was, Danylo or Michael, the participation of the Ukrainian Church at the Council of Lyons portended new, widespread plans in the formation of Ukrainian national and ecclesiastical policies.

Papal Delegates in Ukraine.

The matter of the Ukrainian Church was treated with great interest at the council and already in that same year of 1245, the pope sent a delegation under the direction of the Italian Franciscan, Plano di Carpini, to the Ukraine and to the Tartars with the task of investigating the matter in detail firsthand and of gathering exact information about the Tartars, about the general state of mind and relations in the Ukrainian Church, that is, information which could serve as basis for further policy making.

The delegates arrived together with Danylo's brother Vasilko, who had met them in Silesia, to Volodimir of Volynia and here they had their first conference with the Ukrainian bishops. Discussion centred on the topic of the union of the Ukrainian Church with the Holy See, but the bishops did not wish to decide such an important matter themselves in the absence of Danylo. Danylo had at that time gone to the Tartars to reach a peace agreement with them, to recognize their supremacy, and in this way to safeguard the nation fron this dangerous neighbor.

Returning from the horde, Danylo met the delegation which was continuing on its way to the Tartars at the Dnipro, and here they acquainted him with the policies with which they had come. At home, Danylo found letters from the pope on the matter of Church unity. From the letters it is obvious that this time the matter must have been discussed quite often, because the letters also mentioned that the Holy See was ready to take charge of Danylo's nation, that the pope was sending a new delegation to Danylo and also that the matter of definitely holding the discussions and union itself was charged to the Prussion bishop, Eldelbert, who was a good friend of Danylo.

In 1247, the delegation of Plano di Carpini returned through Kiev to

Cholm. Here their second council with the Ukrainian bishops took place, this time in the presence of Danylo and his noblemen. Obviously the most important issue of the discussions was the church question. It seems that the Ukrainian hierarchy did not see any difficulty in the action and only bothered to ensure the inviolability of its eastern church rite and its own hierarchy, that is, in the same status as the Ukrainian Church had heretofore enjoyed, or an even higher status.

The Church Union of Danylo.

Immediately after this council,Danylo sent a delegation to the pope, to Lyons (in June, 1247), and by the end of August the delegation had returned with letters from the pope with the terms of the union of the Ukrainian Church with Rome. The pope, according to the terms of the agreement, took Danylo's nation "under the protection of St. Peter", which had certain political advantages. Under such protection, a given nation gained the benefit that meant no other Catholic nation could wage war on it. The pope left Danylo a free hand to conquer the neighboring lands to the north of the Prypiat river which had not yet been Christianized and Danylo soon took advantage of this. As for the church matters, the pope agreed to the aforementioned points, that is, the inviolability of the eastern rite and its hierarchy. It is obvious that Danylo's negotiations with Rome had a dual purpose: first of all, to obtain support from the western, Catholic world in the event of a raid by the Tartars, and secondly to safeguard the independent development of the Ukrainian Church, preserving the ancient traditions of the Christian East and strengthening her with the cultural achievements of the West.

The chronicles relate that in that same year of 1247, after the agreement was completed, the pope sent Danylo a king's crown, which Danylo did not accept at that time, however. He didn't accept it because, in accepting the crown from the pope, he would be exposing himself to danger from the Tartars, under whose supremacy he had been until that time. To accept the crown meant to break the tie of loyalty with them and this Danylo, without definite protection and help in case of need, could not do. For this reason he replied to the pope, as the Halych-Volynian chronicler relates, "I cannot accept your crown without your help." It is true that the pope had that year announced a Crusade against the Tartars, but these Crusades, which had lasted since the end of the 11th century (since 1096, in all, there were seven of them), were not met with enthusiasm any more and this time the pope's appeal was unsuccessful. Danylo knew of this and for this reason did not hurry to accept the crown. The crown itself, without tangible assistance, could not save his besieged nation, but on the contrary, in the given circumstances, could only do him harm.These discussions occurred in the years 1245-1247, and Danylo,fearful lest the Tartars find out about them, cut them short.

Danylo's return to the East.

In 1248 or 1249, Danylo renewed his contract with the patriarch of Constantinople, who then resided in Nicea, in Asia Minor, and sent Cyril to be ordained the metropolitan of Kiev. The patriarch agreed to this and Cyril was ordained to the metropoly of Kiev perhaps in 1250. After his ordination he returned to Halych, but did not remain there long. From there he went to Kiev and later further north and remained in Volodimir on the Clasma. It was doubtless important to Danylo to have a trusted person as metropolitan. When he saw that he could not depend on Cyril and that the metropolitan had, perhaps, received some instructions from the patriarch as to his See, he began seeking new ties with Rome. The political situation was also turning in this direction.

In 1253, the Lithuanian Prince Mendovg accepted Christianity in the Latin rite. The pope brought him under his protection and by the same token, Danylo may have had yet another unfriendly neighbor in the north.

In 1253, Danylo's ties with Rome were renewed. In that year, the pope again tried to organize a crusade against the Tartars and this obviously greatly pleased Danylo. If such a campaign were successful, the Halych-Volynian State would be rid of a continual danger from the Tartars and, having established amicable relations with the western world, would have a great opportunity to become one of the greatest powers of Europe.

The Coronation of Danylo.

Representing Rome, the papal legate, Opizo, conducted matters. The Poles did not favor Danylo's ties with Rome and when the papal delegates arrived and stopped in Cracow, the Poles tried to persuade them not to enter into discussion with Danylo, because Daylo could not be depended on. The delegates did not take the advice and their mission was successfully completed. It is true that Danylo did not show great enthusiasm in entering into an agreement with Rome at this time, not believing in their promises (of help against the Tartars); nevertheless the papal legate was able to convince him that the Polish king (Conrad Mazovetski) as well as the crusaders would come to his aid in the event of his need. Danylo finally agreed and accepted the papal crown. His coronation took place in the town of Dorohychyn in Pidliasha, in August or September of 1253. Danylo, and with him the bishops, made a vow on the entry into union with the Western Church, recognizing the pope's supremacy. Here once again, the inviolability of the rite and priviliges of the Ukrainian Church was confirmed.

The Breaking of Relations with Rome.

Danylo's fears were justified. Soon after, when he had accepted the crown, disagreements with the Tartars started. The Tartars began to advance on the State of Halych but Danylo's appeal for help fell on deaf ears. No one came to help and he had to bear the burden of the war himself. This time the outcome of the battle with the Tartars was not as bad. The Halych-Volynian powers repelled the Tartars and in the end, an agreement was reached between Danylo and the voyevoda of the Tartars, Kuremsa. Historians speculate that one article of the agreement was the demand of the Tartars that Danylo sever his ties with Rome. This indeed happend in 1256, three years after the Halych/Rome union. It occurred not through the fault of Danylo, but because Danylo saw no other choice. The West had been deaf when there was grave danger hanging over the Halych-Volynian State. It goes without saying that the pope was very dissatisfied with this.

In 1257, pope Alexander II, the successor of Innocent IV, issued a bull to Danylo, reminding him of his duty, calling him to return, and warning him of church punishments in the event of disobedience. But Danyulo, taught by bitter experience, did not support ties with Rome anymore. The break with Rome did not save his State. The Tartars, breaking their agreement, again attacked his state, destroying some cities and finally demanding that all fortifications be destroyed. Danylo himself fled to Hungary and his brother Vasilko, a good diplomat, made peace with the Tartars, acceded to their demands, and destroyed those fortifications which annoyed the Tartars. Danylo, who had been an unusually talented ruler, died in 1264. His attempts to unite the Ukrainian Church with the western world were sincere and thoughtful. The reasons for their lack of success must be sought elsewhere.

Some historians, especially foreign ones, accuse Danylo of insincerity in his talks with Rome and pose as the reason for the failure of the church union the fact that Daniel operated with primarily political aims.

As for the first accusation, Danylo's insincerity, he cannot be under suspicion. He himself was educated in the Polish and Hungarian courts and his mother was a Pole, thus a Catholic. With the western rulers he always maintained good neighborly relations; therefore, Danylo's negative attitude towards Catholicism cannot be confirmed. As for the second accusation, his political motives, this does not need to be defended. Danylo was not a theologian and theological or ritual differences between the eastern and the western churches interested him little. That he was motivated by political goals in his relations with Rome was normal, for he was a secular ruler, and besides that, Rome at that time was not an exclusively religious head, but was also a political power. In his place, probably any other Christian ruler would have proceeded in the same way.

For example, the Lithuanian Prince Mendovg, was converted by the Crusaders and, having been baptized, accepted a crown from the pope. Later, he completely fell away from Christianity, persecuted Christians and more than one hundred years passed before Rome was able to reunite Lithuania and bring in Christianity there. This happened only at the end of the 14th century, during Yagello's reign.

Danylo died, as has been mentioned, in 1264 and was buried in Cholm, in the church of the Assumption of the Blessed Virgin Mary, a church which he himself had built.

5. The Establishment of the Metropoly of Halych

The Endeavours of Danylo's Son Leo

After Danylo's death, his son Leo immediately took power in the state as the prince of Peremyshl (by 1268) and united the districts of Peremyshl and Halych into one whole. In 1272 he transferred his capitol from Halych to Lviv and from that time, Lviv began to grow as a new center in the western Ukrainian lands.

Although the years of his reign are filled with wars against Poland, Lithuania and the Tartars, he was perhaps the first to take serious pains to ensure that a new metropoly for the Ukrainian lands be formed. For though the metropoly of Kiev still existed, the metropolitan always resided in the north, was little interested in the Ukrainian eparchies and was really the metropolitan of the Suzdal-Volodimiran State. However, Leo was not able to have a new metropoly created during his lifetime. Only after his death, during the reign of his son George I, did the Halych-Volynian State receive a new metropolitan see.

These insistent attempts of the Halych-Volynian princes to have a separate metropolitan for their lands were understandable. They were natural heirs to the tradition of Kiev and preservers of the State of Kiev of Volodimir and Yaroslav and therefore interested in preserving the metropoly, which had been bound for three centuries with Kiev and which would properly be kept in the centers of the Ukrainian lands as well. But to force the metropolitan of Kiev, who preferred to reside in Volodimir in the north instead of in Kiev, was not feasible and for this reason they sought the formation of a new metropoly.

In 1303, a decree of Emperor Andronicus and Patriarch Anastasius appeared by which they raised the episcopate of Halych to the level of a metropoly. Halych, the capitol of the princes of Halych numbered 81st on the list of metropolies of the patriarchate. It embraced the eparchies of Halych, Peremyshl, Volodimir, Cholm, Lutsk and Turiw.

As it was with the metropolitans of Kiev, the first metropolitan here was the Greek Nifont. Who he was, where he came from and what he did is not known. He was not in power as metropolitan for long, for he died two years later, in 1305.

After his death, the monk Peter, a man of local origin, was elected metropolitan and sent to Constantinople so that he could obtain there the patriarch's ordination and blessing. But unexpectedly a situation arose in which the metropolitan of Kiev, Maxim, died in the same year as well. Therefore a candidate from the north came to Constantinople as well - Heronty, an abbott, nominated by Prince George.

The Protests of The Princes of Suzdalia

The matter took several years to settle, for the Suzdalian princes used all means to have the separate metropoly of Halych nullified. Even earlier, in 1303, when the patriarch was establishing the metropoly of Halych, the metropolitan of Kiev and the Volodimir-Suzdalian had raised a protest against the division of the metropoly. These protests had not died down and now the patriarch, who had not been happy to oblige the Halych-Volynian princes by establishing a metropoly, decided to take advantage of the opportunity that

71

both metropolies were without leadership by reuniting them. He was easily successful. He rejected Heronty and ordained Peter as the one metropolitan for the cathedral of Kiev and by the same token, abolished the metropoly of Halych which had been established a few years previous to this. Possibly the patriarch thought to appease both parties in this way, having ordained the candidate of Halych and sent him to serve the princes of Suzdalia. A situation existed in which the metropolitan of Kiev, who had for ten years resided in the new center of the metropoly (actually since Cyril's time, about 1250) and had no intention of returning to Kiev, carried the title of metropolitan of Kiev when Kiev belonged to another state, that of Halych-Volynia. To correct this anomaly, the patriarch gave Peter the title of "Metropolitan of Kiev and of all Rus." Understandably neither the princes of Halych nor the Ukrainian bishops were satisfied with this Solomon's wisdom. But there was nothing they could do.

Metropolitan Peter played an important part in the deliberations between the northern princes. There, a battle was going on between the Moscovian and the Tverian princes for primacy. Peter took the side of Moscovy, that is, he sided with Ivan Kalyta and by his influence shifted the balance of victory to his side. This is the glory he prophesied for Ivan Kalyta: "When you build a Church to the Blessed Virgin in your city, you will become more famous than other princes, your sons and grandsons will be honored, this city will be famed in all the cities of the land of Rus, saints will live in it and my bones will be buried in it". He kept his word and transferred the capitol of his metropoly to Moscow. Russian historians say that Peter's assistance to the prince of Moscow strengthened his political and moral position among all the northern princes and pushed the Moscovian state into primacy. In this way, a native of Ukraine helped the growth and strengthening of a foreign state.

Doubtless this was a strong blow to the ambitions of the Halych-Volynian princes. What measures they took immediately after this for the renewal of the metropoly of Halych is not known. In 1329 the primacy over the eparchies of the metropoly of Halych was already held by the metropolitan of Moscow (that is of Kiev and of all Rus), the Greek Theognostus.

The Fate of the Metropoly of Halych
As the second metropolitan, Theodore, the sources are in disagreement as to the time of his appointment as well as about its manner. According to the Russian sources, this Theodore "bought" himself the metropolitan see in 1345 from the patriarch, but he did not benefit by the see for long, for two years later he died. These sources add that the patriarch agreed to grant the wishes of Halych, so it seems that Theodore was a candidate, sent with "a request and a supply of money" for any need which should arise.

Ukrainian sources indicate that Theodore was a bishop in Halych earlier and became metropolitan in 1331; however he began to rule as metropolitan only in 1341. After his death in 1347, the metropoly of Halych was definitely abolished.

When the Romanovich dynasty died out in 1340, the Halych-Volynian State became the prey of its neighbors. There did not remain any source of strength in the ideals of tradition and culture, there were no more princes who were symbols of the independence of the Halych-Volynian State. With their death, their great history broke off. There began the history of slow decline. The first evidence of this was the abolishment of the metropoly itself. There was no one to stand up for the interests of the Ukrainian Church. Some sources mention yet another investing metropolitan, not one of Halych but of Kiev, nevertheless not the one who resided in Moscow but the one who resided in Kiev. Thus in 1352, Metropolitan Theodorus, who had been ordained by the Bulgarian patriarch, appeared in Kiev. It is not known who he was, whether Ukrainian or Bulgarian, but that he existed there is no doubt. It seems that these were the final attempts to save the independence of the Ukrainian Church, through the help fo the Bulgarian patriarch. But this metropolitan did not survive for long. In the same year, he was ejected and forbidden to practice as a priest by a patriarchal (Greek) synod.

The Abolition of the Metropoly of Halych

It was all the same to the Greek patriarchs whether or not the metropoly of Halych existed. The metropolitan of Moscow, Theodorus, together with Prince Symeon the Proud (son of Ivan Kalyta), sent a delegation during the life of Metropolitan Theodore (in 1245) with a significant sum of money to the patriarch asking him to abolish the metropoly of Halych because on account of the division there was a danger of loss of the true faith in the eparchies over which the metropolitan of Moscow did not have jurisdiction. The patriarch waited until the death of Theodore and just as he closed his eyes, the metropoly was abolished. From that time all the Ukrainian bishops were to yield to the metropolitan who resided in Moscow.

After the death of the last of the Romanoviches, the nobles of Halych called the Lithuanian Prince Demetrius Liubart to the throne. Here began the history of the Lithuanian-Rus State. By an agreement with Poland in 1366, the Lithuanian prince Olgerd passed Halychyna into the hands of the Polish King Casimir. It was all the same to Casimir to whom the Ukrainian eparchies which found themselves in his state were loyal. He did not want the jurisdiction of the metropolitan of Moscow to extend into his lands. Understandably he would rather Latinize them all, but the organization of the rather strong Church stood in his way along with the nobility which was firmly tied to its Church.

From the Ukrainian nobility came a new initiative, pressure on the king that he ask the patriarch for a separate metropolitan for Halych, because, as the nobles said, "a land cannot be lawless" that is, it could not exist without a leader, who in the Ukraine, had always been the metropolitan.

The Renewal of the Metropoly of Halych

In 1371, Casimir wrote to the patriarch, reminding him of the old metropolitan rights of the district of Halych and notified him that either he renew the metropoly of Halych, or Casimir would begin Latinization of the occupied territories. As could be expected, such an argument was successful, and the patriarch, disregarding the contrary opinion of the metropolitan of Moscow, appointed to the metropoly of Halych the candidate Anthony, sent from Greece, in 1371.

Territorially the metropoly of Halych embraced the same eparchies as before: Halych, Peremyshl, Cholm, Volodimir-Volynsk and Turiv. Having separated the metropoly of Halych, the patriarch sent the metropolitan in Moscow a letter, in which he put the full blame for the separation on him. The patriarch accused him, the metropolitan, of not caring about the other eparchies, of staying in one place and leaving without "pastoral leadership, teaching and spiritual care" other eparchies further away from Moscow and for this reason the blame for the separation should fall on him. The metropolitan of Kiev in Moscow was Alexei then, of noble birth of the Pleshcheyevs, the first native Moscovite at the metropolitan's cathedral.

The metropoly of Halych did not have the luck of long lived metropolitans. Anthony died in the following year, 1371. After Anthony's death the Polish King Yagello, sent John, the bishop of Lutsk, to Constantinople to be ordained. But John was not ordained and returned empty handed. Not discouraged by the rejection, he ruled the metropoly until 1401 by the consent of the bishops. The patriarch, meanwhile, did not bother him. When the possibility came that John could unite with Rome, the patriarch became agitated and sent Michael, the bishop of Bethlehem, to deprive John of the rule of the metropoly. After a while, Michael was successful. John lost not only the power to rule the metropoly, but even his own eparchy in Lutsk. In 1401 this lengthy battle for an independent metropoly by the Ukrainian bishops ended. An important role was played here by another foreigner, a Serb (according to some sources, a Bulgarian) who at first ruled the metropoly of Lithuania and after Alexei's death (in 1379), took control of the whole metropoly of Kiev.

6. The Metropoly of Lithuanian-Rus

When the Romanovich dynasty ended, the Ukrainian lands fell into dependence on their northern neighbour - Lithuania. The Lithuanians, who were still pagans at that time had, during the time of the last Ramanoviches often attached the northern and eastern Ukrainian lands and by the time of the last Ukrainian princes, they ruled the districts of Turovo-Pinsk and Brest and in 1341 they occupied Kiev. Somewhat later, other Ukrainian land fell under the influence of Lithuania, with the exception of Halychyna and Cholmshchyna, which went to Poland.

The Lithuanian princes, although pagan, dealt tolerantly with the Ukrainian populace and left the church in peace. The Ukrainian culture of that time was significantly higher than that of Lithuania. For this reason the Lithuanians easily fell under the Ukrainian influence, accepted as official the Ukrainian language and slowly, Christianity began to spread among them.

The attitude of the Lithuanian princes to their eastern neighbors, the princes of Moscow, was inimical and for this reason, as a logical outcome, there arose the question of the church allegiance of those eparchies which found themselves under Lithuanian rule. It is hard to determine when this question first came up but already in the 1320's, perhaps the metropoly of Lithuanian-Rus existed. In the roster of metropolies subordinate to the patriarch of Constantinople there is mention made that during patriarch John Hlyka's rule (1282-1320), the Ukrainian lands under Lithuanian rule were formed into a separate metropoly. When exactly this happened and who the first metropolitan was is not known. Nevertheless, in the first half of the 14th century, when there was a dispute raging over the existence of the metropoly of Halych, there is no mention made anywhere of the metropoly of Lithuania; therefore, it may not have existed at that time. Only during the reign of Olgerd did the matter become actualized.

As has already been mentioned, at the beginning of the 1350's, there appeared a metropolitan in Kiev, Theodoret, who had been ordained into the metropolitan's cathedral by the patriarch of Bulgaria. By whose initiative metropolitan Theodoret appeared in Kiev is not known, but it is possible that he arrived there thanks to the Prince of Lithuania, Olgerd, under whose power Kiev found itself. As has been said, Metropolitan Theodoret was removed by the patriarchal synod (in 1354) and he had to leave. The eparchies which came under the influence of the State of Lithuania again returned to their dependence on the metropolitan who resided in Moscow.

The Metropolitans of Lithuania and of Moscow

But Olgerd knew the importance of a metropolitan for a nation. For this reason, after the death of Theognostus, the metropolitan of Moscow, he sent to the patriarch, Roman, his own candidate, with the stipulation that he be ordained for the cathedral of Kiev. The prince of Moscow also sent a candidate, Alexei Pleshcheyew. The patriarch, not wishing to make any enemies for himself, ordained them both metropolitans of Kiev and all Rus with the proviso that Roman would direct the eparchies under Lithuanian rule and Alexei the northern eparchies. In this way, a second metropoly, that of Lithuania was created. There was no harmony between Roman and Alexei, and when the latter arrived in Kiev, Olgerd ordered him imprisoned and took away his vestments, with Alexei saving himself only by fleeing. Roman was the metropolitan of Kiev until 1362. After Roman's death, the metropoly of Lithuania was without a leader for a long time. The patriarch, heeding the protests of the metropolitan of Moscow (who was still titled ". . . of Kiev"), was in no hurry to give Lithuania a hierarch, but to reconcile Olgerd with Alexei, he sent his delegate, Cyprian, to Lithuania. Olgerd was so impressed with Cyprian that he sent Cyprian back with a document addressed to the patriarch, in which he asked that Cyprian himself be made metropolitan. Just as Casimir did, Olgerd warned that, in the event of refusal, he would turn the eparchies of Lithuania into Latin ones. Like it or not, the patriarch was forced to agree. He ordained Cyprian to the metropoly of

Lithuania with the clause that after Alexei's death, he would take the whole metropoly under his direction.

The Battle for one Metropoly

After Alexei's death (1378), Cyprian had to wage a hard battle to take power in the whole metropoly because the princes of Moscow were again attempting to gain a metropolitan for themselves. In the cathedral of the metropoly of Moscow, Pimen and Dionysius appeared one after the other; however neither of them had either the patriarch's ordination or his blessing. Only in 1386 did Cyprian take power in the whole metropoly, with the exception of the eparchies which belonged to the metropoly of Halych, and by 1401, he had power over them all.

With the fall of the metropoly of Halych, in which Cyprian was instrumental to a significant degree, the episcopacy of Halych fell as well. From 1414 on, it was without a leader, and the bishop's position was taken by a "vicar" of the metropolitan of Kiev.

Having been made metropolitan of all Rus, Cyprian showed great initiative in the goal of having closer ties with Rome. He didn't stay in Moscow as did his predecessors, but resided in Lithuania. In Halych, he had discussions with Yagello who tried to convince him to join with Rome. Furthermore, he tried to understand the local situation well, trying to determine whether the terms of union with Rome were acceptable. Nevertheless, having a great insight in church matters and in Byzantine diplomacy, he did not wish to conduct the talks towards union himself, on his own, but only with the agreement and sanction of the patriarch. He was reaching an agreement with the patriarch in this matter, but the situation was not amenable to this for the Turks, having taken the Balkans in 1386, were a continuous threat to Greece from the north. Thus all attention was centered on the defense of the country.

Cyprian was one of the few instruments of the Greek patriarch who took church union and understanding seriously. Not having reached anything concrete with the patriarch, he nevertheless did not give up the idea of church union even until his death. In 1405 he even called a conference of bishops in Lithuania and there, once more with Yagello's agreement, the matter of church union was discussed. The princes of Moscow took an antagonistic stand towards the deliberations, but this did not stop Cyprian in the action he had already begun. His plans were frustrated by his death. He died in 1406, leaving behind him the memory of a godly, sincere, and talented pastor.

After his death, the Greek Photius (1406-1431) took control over the whole metropoly of Kiev on the plea of the bishops and the prince of Moscow, who, ignoring Vitovt, the prince of Lithuania, prevented him from having Gregory Tsamvlak ordained. For a few years it was peaceful. When Photius, immigrating from Moscow, set heavy taxes on the churches, he was arrested in 1414 in Lithuania, imprisoned, and later banished.

The new Separation of the Metropoly of Lithuania

The Ukrainian Bishops now elected Tsamvlak and Vitovt referred him to the patriarch so that he be confirmed. But the patriarch would not hear of it. Then the sobor of bishops once again confirmed the election and, referring to precedents in the earlier history of the metropoly of Kiev (for example, Klym Smoliatych), made him the Lithuanian-Rus metropolitan without the patriarch's blessing. In this way, the metropoly of Kiev, momentarily united (during Cyprian's rule), was again divided. Photius, angered at such a reversal, anathematized Tsamvlak and all the bishops who took part in his election and confirmation. But the anathema did not help matters any; no one feared it, and Tsamvlak was recognized by all the Ukrainian eparchies, both those which were in the the Lithuanian Rus State and those which were under Polish rule. Tsamvlak died in 1419 and again the metropoly united. Photius made peace with Vitovt, made a statement of his loyalty, and ruled the metropoly until 1431.

After Photius' death, a sobor of the bishops of Moscow elected as his successor Jonah, the Ryazansky bishop in 1433 and in Lithuania, bishop Herasym of Smolensk was elected. Herasym did not remain long on the metropoly. He became involved in politics and called upon himself the suspicion of Svedrigallo, the Prince of Lithuania, who ordered him imprisoned and then burned alive at the stake in 1435.

Jonah, the elected metropolitan of Moscow, did not remain long in the metropoly either. When, after his election, he arrived in Constantinople to be ordained, it came out that Isidore had already been ordained as the metropolitan of Kiev. Jonah finally received his post in 1448, when Isidore condemned the sobor of Moscow for its participation in the Florentine Ecumenical Council and then himself left the metropoly (1441). Finally and definitively, the old metropoly of Kiev was divided in 1458 into that of Moscow and that of the Ukraine-White Rus, that is of Kiev.

7. The Unions of the Lyons and Florence (1274 and 1438-39)

The history of the Ukrainian Church is part of the history of the Ukrainian Church, it is necessary to examine the relations in the Christian Church of that time, especially the relations between Rome and Constantinople.

East and West. The Estrangement Deepens

The estrangement between the two centers of Christian culture of the first millenium grew for many years and in the end led to a complete division between the Eastern and the Western Churches. The center of the former became Constantinople, the center of the latter Rome.

Up until the mid-11th century (1054), misunderstanding existed between Rome and Constantinople but in general, relations were peaceful and unity was maintained. By the end of the 11th century, when Islam occupied the lands sacred to every Christian this brought great discouragement in the West and soon initiated a movement for the freeing of holy places from Muslim rule. Thus the Crusades started and lasted from 1096 to 1270. During the 6th Crusade the Latins occupied Constantinople and established the "Latin Empire" there. The patriarch and the emperor fled to Nicea in Asia Minor and remained there until the fall of the Latin Empire in 1261. Of course the occupation of the capitol of the Greek Empire and the establishment of a new patriarchate and emperorship and the bringing in of a patriarch of the Latin rite angered the Greeks very much. The rift between the Churches, which had occurred in 1054, deepened, and the hatred of the Latin by the Greeks became even greater.

The Byzantine Emperor and the Roman Pope

In 1261 the Latin Empire fell. The emperor of Nicea, Michael Paleologus VIII (1259-1282), with the help of the Genovans, recaptured Constantinople and returned the Byzantine Empire. But his position was very difficult. Baldwin II, who was the Latin Emperor, began to organize another campaign against Constantinople from the other side of Byzantium. The Bulgarians were a threat from the north and the Latin princes who still ruled Polyponesia threatened from the south. The internal situation in the nation was also difficult. The emperor Michael Paleologus himself had taken the throne illegally, having blinded the young successor to the throne who was John, son of Theodore II Laskariz. Patriarch Arseny sided with the nation against Michael. The emperor set up a new patriarch-Herman-and banished Arseny. But Herman, under the pressure of public anger, had to leave the cathedral and Joseph, the spiritual advisor to the emperor, was made patriarch. But even this did not satisfy the roused nation and soon it was besieged by dangerous internal movements. Understanding the situation very well, the emperor entered into discussions with Pope Urban IV and later with his successor, Clement IV, with the goal of reconciliation and church unity. The discussions went on for almost ten years and only during the rule of Pope Gregory X, who personally and diligently applied himself to the matter, did they reach a successful conclusion.

In 1274 an Ecumenical Council was held in Lyons at which the union of the Eastern and Western Churches occurred. But this union was not easily achieved. Almost exclusively, the discussions were led by representatives of the emperor who had his national and political interests at heart and they did not refer much to the interests of the masses and of the clergy. When the Greek delegation was preparing for the Sobor, it was obvious that there were two parties, one amenable and one antagonistic to church union. To the antagonists also belonged the patriarch, though he owed his rule to the emperor. The patriarch even sent a circular to the other neighboring patriarchs preaching harmony with the Latins. The matter ended when the emperor sent the patriarch to a monastery, persuaded a learned theologian, John Vekk, who had formerly been opposed to union, to join his side, and immediately drafted a document with his supporters in the name of the Greek clergy for the delegation at the Sobor. In this delegation, the former patriarch Herman participated, as well as the great logofet, Gregory, Acropolites. At the fourth meeting of the Sobor, the writings of Michael Paleologus and his son Andronik were read in which they, in the name of the Greek clergy, recognized the supremacy of the pope and accepted the terms of union given them, with the exception of the "Filioque". The Great Logofet Gregory made a vow in the name of the emperor in which he rejected church division and promised to uphold the collective faith. The spiritual participants and delegates to the Sobor made a similar vow in the name of the Greek nation.

The emperor was very happy with such an outcome at the Sobor. The pope immediately appeased his enemies and peace was made between Carl Angou and the emperor. Patriarch Joseph, who did not favor the union, was forced to resign and his position was filled by John Vekk.

Another Church Rift

But the nation and the lower clergy were not satisfied. Disagreements and complaints were followed by propaganda against the established union. The patriarch earnestly tried to calm the nation with his emissaries, but did not have much success. In some churches the pope was recognized, in others he was not. Possibly the nation would have become calmer after a time, but when Martin IV took power as pope, knowing that the completed union did not really exist, he excommunicated the emperor and refused to see his emissaries (1281). This was the fateful end of the Union of Lyons. In his turn Michael Paleologus did not stay unavenged - he forbade the mention of the pope in church services.

With the death of the emperor (1282), the union ended as well. His son Andronik II was on the side of the orthodox. Patriarch Vekk was forced to leave the post of patriarch and was sent off to exile. The churches which had formerly recognized the pope had to be reconsecrated. For ten years, some churches held to the union, but after that, no trace of the union remained.

At the beginning of the 15th century, the Greek Empire, pressured by the Turks, found itself in mortal danger. The emperors did what they could, travelling to the West themselves, asking for help, indicating the common danger to Christianity and to political order in Europe, but their persuasions were without success. Then John VI Paleologus decided to try his last resort. He entered into negotiations with pope Eugene IV and suggested a union of Churches in the hope of obtaining help from the western Catholic world. The pope agreed to the proposition. It was decided to call an Ecumenical Council which would concern itself with rectifying the church division as soon as possible. At the end of 1436, the emperor and Patriarch Joseph went for a Sobor to Ferrara in northern Italy, with representatives of other eastern patriarchs and Greek bishops. The representative of the metropoly of Kiev, Metropolitan Isidore came to the council as well.

The Council of Ferrara - Florence

At the turning point of the 14th and 15th centuries, the Ukrainian Church was very interested in church union. It has been shown how sincerely Metropolitan Cyprian strove for this. It is certain that he found many supporters among Ukrainian bishops who were already tired of the unceasing dissensions between the candidates for the metropolitate and realized that the weakened authority of the patriarch could not serve as a support for the Ukrainian Church. Cyprian's successor from 1414 was his relative, Gregory Tsamvlak. Tsamvlak took part in the Council of Constantinople between 1414 and 1418, which had been called to settle the internal matters of the Catholic church, to settle the so-called papal schism, and to reform church discipline. At the council, Tsamvlak spoke, underlining the importance of Church unity and asking the pope to call a separate council for this purpose. But the times were not favorable to church union. At that time in the Catholic church there were currents which were inimical to the pope and his supporters and for this reason the question of church unity was put off to a later time. In any case there were already talks going on between the pope and the emperor to this end.

The Role of the Ukrainian Church

Isidore, of Greek origin, came to the metropoly of Kiev in 1437 and in the following year had already taken part in the Ferraro-Florentine Council. About 200 persons of his retinue came with Isidore, among them Abraham, the Suzdalian bishop, who was so important to the success of Isidore's endeavors. There was a very inimical attitude towards the idea of church union in Moscow, but Isidore was nevertheless able to persuade Basil, the prince of Moscow, who agreed to send a delegation from the metropoly of Kiev to the council.

From Greece came the emperor, Patriarch Joseph II, many Greek bishops, and representatives of the eastern patriarchs. On the Greek side the most active were the metropolitan of Ephesus, who represented the patriarch of Jerusalem, and Vissarion, the metropolitan of Nicea, the former an unreconcilable enemy of the Latins, the latter a sincere supporter of union.

The matters which the sobor considered revolved chiefly around these questions: the statement of faith "and son", the primacy of the pope, the sanctuary, and certain differences of the Latin rite such as unleavened bread, and so on. The discussions were spirited and lengthy. Finally, for the Creed, a formula which appears in St. John Chrysostom, who was greatly respected by both eastern and western theologians, was decided upon. As for the unleavened bread, the council agreed that the Holy Eucharist was just as valid with leavened as with unleavened bread, without further debate, for there was strong support for this even in the works of eastern theologians. As for the primacy of the pope, the following order was decided upon: The Roman pope, the patriarch of Constantinople, the patriarch of Alexandria, the patriarch of Antioch and the patriarch of Jerusalem.

The Ukrainian metropolitan also played a significant role in the council and, like a good theologian, did not yield anything in the discussions to Mark, the metropolitan of Ephesus.

Patriarch Joseph became seriously ill a month before the closing of the council and died on the 17th of June, 1439. Before his death he wrote "The Final Profession of Faith" in which he accepted all the decisions of the council.

The solemn act of the council on the union of the Church was signed on the 5th of July, 1439. All the bishops or metropolitans signed for the Eastern Church except Mark, the metropolitan of Ephesus, and the emperor. One hundred fifteen bishops signed for the Latin Church. Metropolitan Isidore signed the act of union for the Ukrainian Church, being the representative of the patriarch of Alexandria as well. In this way a great deed was accomplished - union of the hitherto divided Church into one mystical body of Christ.

It can be believed that this time the wish for unity was sincere on both sides. It is true that the motives for the union, especially at the beginning, were less of a church-related than of a worldly nature, but nevertheless the discussions held during the council indicate that the Fathers participating in the council treated the points of conflict with great attention and no one yielded easily. But this is important. If the Greeks had wanted union "at all cost", it could have been achieved without any further endeavors.

The Union of Florence was not accepted in Greece. It was also not accepted in other Churches of the Christian East. The reason was that the estrangement was too great, its roots reaching deep into the soul of the masses of the nation. The act of union itself was not enough; for this was needed a long period of preparation, mutual understanding, and peaceful times. Precisely this was what was lacking.

The Reaction of the Greek Populace

The lower Greek clergy and people, hearing of the completed act of union, called their delegates heretics. All the antagonists to the union rallied around Mark the Ephesian and were joined by the patriarchs of three other Eastern Churches as well. They called a council in Jerusalem in 1443 at which they excommunicated from the Church all the supporters of the completed union.

The emperor used any means at his disposal to bring peace and order to the Church and appointed only supporters of the union to the patriarchate (Patriarch Mytrophan, Gregory Mammas), but the situation did not improve and on the contrary relations became more strove. Shortly before the fall of Constantinople, the eastern patriarchs gathered for a council once again (in Constantinople,) and again condemned the participants in the Council of Florence and removed Gregory Mammas from his patriarchate (1450). His place was taken by the orthodox Patriarch Athanasius. Three years later, Constantinople fell, and with it collapsed the Florentine Union.

This was the final attempt to reconcile the divided Church. After the fall of the Greek Empire, the patriarchate fell into almost total dependence on the rule of the Sultan. It is true that the Turks left the organization of the Church intact and guaranteed freedom of belief, but in effect the patriarchs became puppets in the hands of the Muslim rulers. The first loss was that of the largest church of the East, that of St. Sophia. The Turks transformed it into a mosque. This was an intolerable blow not only for the Greeks, but for all believing Christianity. It is a pity that to this day the Christian world, after more than five centuries, has not gained enough power or influence to return this great temple to those to whom it rightfully belongs.

8. The Division of the Metropoly of Kiev

After the close of the Council of Florence, Metropolitan Isidore returned to his metropoly. Even before his departure, the pope nominated him as his legate with powers of jurisdiction over all the Latin eparchies in the metropoly of Kiev. By this the pope wished to underline that they saw no difference between the Latin and the Byzantine-Ukrainian rites. In addition, the pope made him a cardinal together with Vissarion, the metropolitan of Nicea. But difficult tasks awaited the metropolitan at home. He knew this possibly, because he knew of the prejudice of the princes and hierarchy of Moscow against the west. His fellow-traveller, bishop Abraham, became separated from the metropolitan along the way and succeeded in reaching home sooner. Here he did not neglect the situation but before the metropolitan arrived, inimical feelings were already well-prepared.

From the road, Isidore sent a delegation to the hierarchy and the faithful of his metropoly, in which he expressed his joy and called all others to rejoice for the completed act of the Union of Churches.

"Rejoice", wrote the metropolitan, "for now those of the Latin and those of the Greek rite are all equal. Accept this union, so that there will be no division between us. And you, Latins, recognize all the Greek temples as true sanctuaries of God, come to them for the Holy Mass and behold Christ's Body with repentance as in your own, for Christ's Body is identical in levened as in unleavened bread. This was decided upon by the council of Florence in 1439".

Isidore, without doubt, was a great church figure, highly educated, a brilliant theologian, and well acquainted with the relations in the Greek Church. The one thing which he underestimated perhaps was the negative effect of the militant Latins within the boundaries of Poland and Lithuania-Rus. The Latins here had been able to create such disharmony that the decision of the council could not erase it easily or without trace. Relying on the power of of the nation, it always scornfully viewed Christians of the Eastern rite and thereby called hatred upon itself. This was a great fault of the Latins and for this reason they can share a definite part of the blame for the following events.

Returning home, the metropolitan stopped by New Sanch as well, territories populated mostly by Ukrainians but already with a strong inflow of foreign, Latin-Polish elements. Instead of going to his own church, Isidore decided (to manifest the equality of the rites) to celebrate Mass in a Latin Church. He did not accomplish anything by this, but lost much. The Council had performed no miracles and had not removed the inimical feelings of the faithful of the Eastern Church to the Latins, feelings which had been so long ignored. Isidore, being a Greek and moreover new in the metropoly, did not understand this. This was his first misstep. It must also be kept in mind that the Polish Catholics of that time were not as orthodox and as tied to Rome and the pope as they were later.

The Matter of the Pre-eminence of the Pope over the Council

Already at the Council of Constantinople there appeared a diversity of views about the primacy of the pope in the Catholic west itself. Under the leadership of Parisian theologians, a teaching about the pre-eminence of a council over the pope was promulgated. This discussion continued at another council, at Bazel (Switzerland) in 1434. The primate of Poland, the archbishop of Gnezno, Nicholas Tromba, as well as most Polish bishops, belonged to this anti-papist group. Isidore must have known of this and must not have been very inspired by the Polish Latins. That this movement was very strong in Poland is borne out by the fact that in 1449, Poland officially took the side of the Council of Bazel against Pope Eugene. Similarly, Bishop Matthew of Vilen took an antagonistic stand towards the union at Florence and considered that council non-canonical. Thus the Ukrainian metropolitan was needlessly tarrying among the Polish Latins and in this way provoking his clergy and the faithful.

Having been in Lviv and in Cholm, Isidore went on to the Lithuanian-Ukrainian eparchies. He found his greatest support and understanding in purely Ukrainian lands. In the Lithuanian eparchies, the afore-mentioned Bishop Matthew had great influence and set the populace and the clergy against Isidore. The Ukraine, on the other lands, Isidore met with good will from Olelko, the Prince of Kiev, who was a great supporter of church union, as well as from Svedrygallo. Olelko warmly welcomed the metropolitan and in his document returned all the wealth which had once belonged to St. Sophia. In his document he writes that the "master and father of Kiev gives all this wealth to Father Isidore and all which belonged to St. Sophia."

He was also welcomed warmly and amicably in the White Russian eparchies, where Matthew's whispering campaign was not heeded.

In the end, Isidore reached Moscow. Here there was already a group prepared against him. Matthew, the Latin bishop of Vilen, had sent a report on Isidore ahead, stirring up those who were already against the Catholicism of the princes of Moscow. The rest was completed by Abraham and some other members of Isidore's delegation to the council. At first the Muscovites treated him cooly, but with restraint. The metropolitan celebrated Mass, in the vestments of a cardinal and no one interfered with him. After the Mass, he ordered the reading of the decree of the Council of Florence about union of the Churches. Some historians say that immediately in the Church, the Prince of Moscow became angry and had Isidore imprisoned.

Moscow condemns the Metropolitan of Kiev.

Nevertheless, the sources do not mention such a spectacle. They say that only after the service were the bishops then present in Moscow assembled and at that assemblage Isidore was cond mned as a heretic and imprisoned in a monastery. Prince Basil wanted t' know what the patriarch would say about the union of Florence. When ne found out that the patriarch of Constantinople had signed the act of union as well, he nevertheless did not change his position, proving that in its hatred towards the Latin Church, the Church of Moscow surpassed all others.

Isidore was able to flee from prison and reach Italy where he met with the pope in Siena in 1443. The metropoly of Kiev remained in fact without a metropolitan. It is true that there is mention made that Isidore was fulfilling the duties of the metropolitan of Kiev from beyond the borders of the Ukraine and that all the bishops of the metropoly recognized him, with the exception of those of Moscow. However the metropolitan see was in Moscow and there "their" metropolitan was called a heretic. There was trouble with the foundation of a new metropolitan in Moscow.

The Greek patriarch had signed the Florentine union and would not agree to ordain a new metropolitan of Kiev during Isidore's lifetime. Moscow meanwhile, did not wish to separate with Constantinople. The matter dragged on until 1448 in this way. In that year, by the "will of the state" a council gathered in Moscow and Metropolitan Jonah was elected and established without the patriarch's blessing. This Jonah was the same one who had been a candidate before Isidore. By this action the metropolitan of Moscow fell into schism with the patriarchate, because he accepted ordination during the life of Isidore who had been properly established.

Poland contributed to this schism, especially through Casimir Yagellovich. In an agreement with the relentless enemy of the eastern Church and Ukrainianism, the Vilenian Bishop Matthew, the king ceased recognizing Isidore as the metropolitan of Kiev and assigned the Latin-Ukrainian and Halych eparchies to the Muscovite Jonah. Here the motives were not religious. Poland had given herself over faithfully at that time to the pope. The motives here were exclusively political calculations. The Poles did not want a union in which the Ukrainian Church could grow and develop. They preferred either a complete Latinization or a blunting under the protection of the metropolitan of Moscow, because the then stupefied unorganized nation could easily become an object of exploitation and subjugation. The Poles thought in terms of the future. Thus they had to destroy the union and uphold the Orthodoxy of Moscow. In 1449-1450 Casimir ordered a council of bishops and removed the metropolitan from his see. The Catholic king sent the following document to Jonah of Moscow: "We are pleased with Father Jonah and have given him the metropoly of Kiev for this reason; our princes and bishops, priests and all the nation of Christians of Rus are to obey him."

The only resistance to this action was offered by the Ukrainian bishops and the Prince of Kiev, Olelko.For example, only after four years did the bishop of Volodimir-Volynsk recognize the metropolitan of Moscow and submit to him.

Isidore, who remained in Rome for the most part (he also took frequent trips to Constantinople), was the metropolitan of Kiev until 1458. In this year, he resigned and the patriarch put Gregory in his place.

The Separation of the Metropoly of Moscow.

Gregory took over the metropoly of Kiev in 1458 and ruled it until 1473. It was clear that Moscow would not recognize such a metropolitan and for this reason it was decided, with the agreement of the patriarch, to reorganize the metropoly of Kiev as an ecclesiastical unit. The eparchies of Moscow were separated from it. The metropoly of Kiev received a new canonical statute in 1458. This cleared the air. Gregory took charge of all the eparchies of the Latvian-Ukrainian State and the Ukrainian eparchies under Polish rule. The following eparchies were in his jurisdiction: Kiev, Smolensk, Polotsk, Jurivsk, Lutsk, Volodimir-Volynsky,Berestia, Peremyshl, Halych and Cholm, eleven all told. This division remained until the appropriation of the Ukrainian Church by the patriarch of Moscow at the end of the 17th century.

Both the Prince of Moscow and Jonah protested against the division of the metropoly. They sent delegates to the bishops with pleas and threats, but neither their pleas nor their threats had any effect. In 1461, Jonah died. In his place, the council of bishops of Moscow elected Theodosius as metropolitan and the tsar established him, without asking or pleading for a blessing from the patriarch. The new metropolitan accepted the title: metropolitan of Moscow, without even putting forward protestations to the blessed metropoly of Kiev.

9. The Post-Florentine Period in the Ukrainian Church

The early years after the Council of Florence, were distinguished in the history of the Ukrainian Church by the battle for and against the union completed by the council. Until the division of the metropoly, the Ukrainian eparchies fell under one or the other jurisdiction. For a long time, they recognized Isidore as metropolitan; later, under pressure from the Polish king, they fell under the rule of the metropolitan of Moscow. The division, or the separation of the northern eparchies which found themselves under the influence of the princes of Moscow and Teveria from the metropoly of Kiev put an end to this situation.

Kiev again the Seat of the Metropolitan

With the taking of power by Metropolitan Gregory (in 1458), Kiev again became the center of all the Ukrainian lands. The ancient tradition was renewed and, having rid herself of the protection of the declining patriarchate and especially the unrestrained pretensions of the metropolitan who resided in Moscow, the Ukrainian Church revived. The tasks of the new metropolitan were not easy. He realized that the completed union in Florence was not yet everything. Old traditions tied with Constantinople still lived in the

Ukrainian Church. Constantinople, understandably, did not have the same attraction nor brilliance after its occupation by the Turks that it had before.

Nevertheless, Gregory did not wish to enter into conflict with the patriarchs. There are even indications that he maintained some contacts with Constantinople, but it is hard to determine whether these contacts were of a church-leadership nature or an exchange of thoughts on account of the recent events. Gregory is considered a complete metropolitan and there are no signs that he was subordinate to the jurisdiction of the Orthodox patriarch of Constantinople. Metropolitan Gregory died in 1473.

After Gregory's death, a council of Ukrainian bishops elected the Missael Pstruch as metropolitan; he ruled the metropoly between 1474 and 1480. Even before Missael's election, the Ukrainian bishops referred to the pope by mail, complaining of the unbearable attitudes on the part of the Poles and asking him to defend the Ukrainian Church. It was to be expected that after the church reconciliation, the Ukrainian Church would be free to develop. But the events that followed were to prove otherwise. The Polish national ambitions took precedence over wisdom and over Polish Catholicism. After the union of Florence a forced Polish Latinization began in the Ukrainian lands. After his election, Missael, together with the bishops, again turned to the pope in the memorable letter of the 14th of March, 1476. Besides the metropolitan, Prince Michael (son of Olelko), Prince Dmytro Bilsky, Prince Vyazemsky, Joseph Soltan and some other prominent persons signed this letter. In the letter they submitted that they had found out about the Polish slanders of the Ukrainian Church in Rome and wished by this to assert that the Ukrainian Church stood by the union of Florence and recognized it. They recognized the truths of faith as they had been formulated by the council. They regretted the abasement of the Ukrainian rite by the Polish Latins, the rebaptizing of children baptized in the Ukrainian Church, and other persecutions which the Ukrainian clergy suffered at the hands of the Polish nobility and bishops.

The relations of the Metropolitan of Kiev with the Patriarch

The pope replied to metropolitan Missael's letter with a bull in which he recognized the eastern rite as equal to the Latin. Missael probably had no ties with the patriarch. Two years after his election, the patriarch sent his candidate to the metropoly of Kiev,but he was not recognized. Here he was imprisoned and accused of serving the interests of the Turks, and when he was set free, having also had a taste of the prison of Moscow, he returned home.

Between the 15th and 16th centuries, the emphasis on union slowly diminished in the Ukrainian Church and from time to time the Ukrainian metropolitans looked in the direction of Constantinople. Between Rome and the Ukrainian lands there stood a barrier — Poland, which neglected nothing in order to damage the Ukrainian Church. There is mention of the ties with the patriarch from 1497. The metropolitan-elect, Joseph Bulgarinovich, then referred to Patriarch Niphont, asking that he give his opinion of the union of Florence. Surprisingly, the patriarch praised the Council of Florence, recognized its decision as binding and advised Joseph to respect the decision of the council. He also sent him his blessing and ratified the election of the metropolitan. This metropolitan died in 1501.

After his death, the Ukrainian Church leaned unceasingly towards decline. This may be termed the dark age in the history of the Ukrainian Church. Moscow came to power and in its dissent with Poland, it entertained overly great aspirations to rule in Eastern Europe. The Latvian royalty, having intermarried with that of Moscow, created a favorable environment for this.

The Latvian prince Alexander, wishing to improve relations with Moscow, married Princess Olena of Moscow, the daughter of Prince Basil. Alexander thought that he would convert her to Catholicism. However, not only did he not convert her to Catholicism, but he also fell under her influence. At the establishment of a new metroplitan, Olena made the condition that a candidate who was favorable to the Orthodoxy of Moscow be set up. Jonah was made metropolitan (1501-1507) and he broke the ties with Rome and rejected the act of the union of Florence between the Ukrainian Church and the Catholic. Beginning with his rule, there began a complete collapse of the Ukrainian Church. At the end of the century this situation forced several Ukrainian hierarchs to give a new direction to the Church.

10. The Metropolitans of Kiev in the 16th and 17th centuries.

Mention has already been made of the metropolitans of Kiev in the post-Mongolian era in the discussion of events tied to the life of the Ukrainian Church. Here, for a better overview, each will be studied in turn and the most important facts of their lives and actions will be concisely noted. The first metropolitan of Kiev who opens the roster was Cyril III.

Cyril III (1238-1280). At the beginning, he was a bishop of Cholm, possibly a candidate of Danylo. After the seat of the metropoly of Kiev became vacant, Danylo sent him (to the patriarch), to be ordained, not immediately but only in 1248 or 1249. He received the patriarch's blessing in 1250. He resided almost all the time in Volodimir on the Klasma and in this way set a precedent for the new center of the metropolitans of Kiev. In1274, he called a council in Volodimir to organize matters of the Ukrainian Church. There, the "Twelve Laws on Church Matters" were accepted. He is also credited with the "Teaching for Priests" and other writings. He died in1280 and was buried in St. Sophia in Kiev.

Maxim (1283-1305) A Greek by origin. During his rule as metropolitan, he also changed his center a few times, finally taking up permanent residence, thus taking the capitol of the metropoly to the north to the Suzdalian Volodimir on the Klasma. He had good rapport with the Tartars and arranged certain privileges for the clergy.

Peter (1308-1326) from Halych, who was sent by the grandson of King Danylo to the patriarch with the plea that he be ordained for the metropoly of

Halych. The patriarch did not agree to this but ordained him metropolitan of Kiev with his seat in Volodimir. Although Volodimir was the capitol of the metropoly (the canonical capitol was Kiev), nevertheless Peter lived continuously in Moscow, supported Ivan Kalyta against the Teverian princes and contributed much to the growth of the State of Moscow. He died in 1326 and was canonized a saint by the Orthodox Church.

Theognost (1328-1353), a Greek. He transferred the seat of the metropolitans from Volodimir to Moscow. He took an active part in the political life of Moscow and also supported Kalyta against his enemies, whom he anathematized.

Alexei (1354-1379), the first metropolitan from Moscow, of the noted family of Pleshcheyev. The patriarch ordained him as an exception and decreed then that, in the future, the metropolitans of Kiev should only be of Greek origin. During his rule, the Latvian-Ukrainian metropoly was created; its metropolitan became Roman, a candidate of the Great Prince Olgerd. There were continuous disagreements between Alexei and Roman about the boundaries of the eparchy. Sometimes certain eparchies belonged to one metropoly, sometimes to the other. Alexei did not want to return Kiev to Roman and, on the other hand, Roman ruled the eparchy of Teveria, which really belonged to the metropolitan of Moscow. Also, during Alexei's reign, the metropoly of Halych was renewed in 1371 and the Western-Ukrainian eparchies were severed from the metropoly of Kiev and suborned to the metropolitan of Halych. Then Athony became the metropolitan of Halych.

Cyprian (1386-1406), A Bulgarian or Serb by origin. He was ordained the metropolitan of the Latvian-Ukrainian metropoly in 1376. After Alexei's death, there was a long battle for the metropoly of Kiev between the candidates of the prince of Moscow and Cyprian, who was supported by the patriarch. In 1836, Cyprian took control of the whole metropoly, including the eparchies of Halych. He strived for church unity, tried to convince the patriarch in this direction, and called a council of bishops in Myrolub (in White Rus) to discuss and prepare for church union. In this he recieved help and understanding from Yagello, the Polish king and Vitovt, the Great Prince of Latvia.

Photius (1409-1433) a Greek, sent by the patriarch. He lived about a half a year in Kiev and then moved to permanent residence in Moscow, against the wishes of Vitovt, who had agreed to his candidacy only under the stipulation that he would remain in Kiev. Then the bishops of the Latvian-Ukrainian lands elected a separate metropolitan of Kiev, a relative of Cyprian, Gregory Tsamvlak.

Gregory (1414-1419), a Serb or a Bulgarian. He continued Cyprian's actions. He took part in the Council of Constantinople, calling for agreement toward church union. He was elected and set up without the patriarch's blessing and for this reason, the patriarch took an inimical stance towards him. He died unexpectedly during an epidemic. After his death, Photius again took control of the whole metropoly and ruled it until the end of his life.

Isidore (1433-1458) a Greek. After Photius' death, the prince of Moscow sent his candidate, Jonah, to be ordained, but the patriarch had already ordained Isidore as the metropolitan of Kiev. This created great enmity between Jonah and Isidore. In Latvia, Harasym (1432-1435) ruled that Latvian-Ukrainian eparchies for a few years, being a supporter of Tsamvlak even so far as initiating communication with the pope. He let himself be drawn into the political strife against Prince Svedregallo and when the matter came to light, died by fire at the stake. During Isidore's rule the Council in Florence took place, at which the agreement for union between the Eastern and the Western Churches was completed. Isidore deserves much credit for this action, because, with his influence, knowledge and authority, he convinced many Greek bishops and urged the signing of the act of union in Florence. He was welcomed gladly in the Ukraine and inimically in Moscow. Imprisoned upon his arrival, he was able to flee to the west, where he took permanent residence in Rome. In 1458 he resigned from the cathedral of Kiev and in this year, the eparchies of Moscow were separated from the metropoly of Kiev. This was the most active metropolitan of the metropoly of Kiev in the second, post-Mongolian era.

Gregory II (1458-1473) "The Metropolitan of Kiev, Halych and All Rus" — this was a new title of the metropolitans of Kiev, beginning with Gregory. He remained faithful to the union of Florence. He lived on good terms with the Ukrainian and the White Rus bishops. Even the hierarch of Novhorod recognized him as his superior.Gregory resided in Novhorodok, in Latvia, where the capitol of the metropoly of Latvia-Ukraine was at the time, or in Vilna.

Missael Pstruch (1474-1480), earlier a bishop of Smolensk. He was a sincere defender of the Ukrainian Church against the Poles. He is known for his letter to Pope Sixtus IV, in which he defended the Ukrainian Church against the slanders of the Poles and stated that the Ukrainian Church accepted and upheld the decision of the Florentine Council. During his rule, the Latin propaganda increased greatly and the enmity of the Polish clerics against eastern Christianity grew. His relations with the patriarch were not good, for in 1476, the patriarch had sent his candidate Spiridon Tverych, to be metropolitan of Kiev, but he was not accepted in the Ukraine.

Simeon (1481-1488). There is little information about him. Whether he had the patriarch's blessing or not is not known. He is mentioned in the polemic work of Kopistensky "Palinodia".

Jonah (1488-1494), earlier a Polish archbishop. There is no information about him either. Probably he had some ties with the patriarch, but he is considered a supporter of the Florentine union.

Makary (1495-1497). Until his establishment as metropolitan, he was an archimandrite of a Trinitarian monastery (of the Holy Trinity) in Vilna. The bishops themselves ordained him, and after his ordination and establishment as metropolitan, sent a document to the patriarch asking that he approve this. The patriarch gave his approval but stipulated against such a practice in the future. He was killed by Tartars on his way to Kiev in 1497.

Joseph Bulgarinovich (1498-1501), earlier a bishop of Smolensk. He came from a distinguished noble family and was a relative of the Latvian Chancellor Sapiha. He supported the union of Florence, but was also on good terms with patriarch Niphont of Constantinople. He approached the patriarch to ask about the Council of Florence and the patriarch, obviously sympathetic to church unity, replied, "Maintain the Florentine union, brother, in the rite of your forefathers". He was in contact with Pope Alexander VI and asked the pope to approve his metropolitanship. The pope approved his metropolitanship. This was the last metropolitan who supported the Florentine union.

Jonah (1501-1507). He was set up under pressure from the Moscow court. A strong antagonist to unity, from him began a line of metropolitans who returned to orthodoxy.

Joseph II Soltan (1507-1520) of the Boyar class. He received approval from the patriarch of Constantinople. He attended a Council in Vilna in 1509 which brought in many profitable reforms to the church. Simony was condemned, priests were forbidden to transfer from one eparchy to another, higher qualifications were placed for candidates to the priesthood (for example, a widower priest could not perform priestly functions but had to enter a monastery), the stubbornness of the Polish nobility was bounded, the assignment of parishes was organized, and solidarity was assured between all the bishops against secular rule in the case of overstepping of the canons of the church. Through his participation in the council, Joseph accomplished much good for the Ukrainian Church.

Joseph III (1522-1534) There is no information about him besides the fact that during his lifetime he set aside or sold the metropolitanate to the bishop of Lutsk, Makary.

Makary (1534-1555), formerly a bishop of Lutsk. On his establishment there remains a note by the Polish King Zigmund (Gilmont), "N.N. asked me if we would give him the spiritual bread; speaking for him were Queen Bona and the princes and we gave him the metropoly because even Joseph II had yielded it to him." This clearly shows the relations in the Ukrainian Church of that time. During his metropolitanate, the episcopate of Halych was renewed and transferred to Lviv (in 1539). The first bishop of Lviv was Makary Tuchapsky.

Sylvester (1555-1568). From 1551 he was the archimandrite of the monastery of the Holy Trinity in Vilna, although he was a civilian. Only after Makary's death did he accept priestly ordination and later that of bishop.

Jonah (1568-1576) according to the information, he sold the metropoly before his death to Illya Kucha.

Illya Kucha (1576-1579). During his rule, the Church reached its greatest decline. Spiritual offices were bought and sold. The same held true for monasteries and archimandrites. Protestantism began to spread among the Ukrainian nobility. This is not surprising, considering the decadence which they saw in the Church.

Onysyphor Divochka (1579-1589). During his metropolitanship, the

Ukrainian nobility, observing the decline of church life, wrote to the metropolitan, asking him to save it.Divochka was removed by Patriarch Jeremiah of Antioch, who was then visiting the metropoly on the request of the patriarch of Constantinople. He removed him because he had illegally taken control of the metropolitanate, having been, up until that time, twice married. With this metropolitan, the roster of leaders of the second era ends.

As can be seen from these short notes, a wide horizon opened up before the Ukrainian Church after the Florentine union. The early post-Florentine leaders showed great Christian zeal, care and pastoral wisdom.The onslaught of Polish Latinism set them immediately against the West and later completely repelled them. For this reason, the chief blame for the failure of the Florentine union in the Ukrainian Church must rest primarily with the Catholic Poles.

11. The Church-Religious and Monastic Life

Religious and monastic life can grow and develop when the relations in the Church are peaceful, the forms of leadership are stable, and the Church itself is free from interior or even exterior political influences. Order and peace in a nation are important prerequisites of the development of Church culture and spiritual life. These conditions did not always exist in the Ukrainian state, even during the times of the princes. Frequent internal strife between the princes, brother-killing (fratricidal) wars for divisions of or over the first throne of the state of Kiev, attacks by the nomads – all this retarded the growth of religious life. Nevertheless while the state remained independent, the Church found protection – that is, the protection of princes, patrons and defenders. The situation worsened when no princes remained.

After the destruction of Kiev, as has been mentioned, the center of church life was transferred to the north, far from Ukrainian lands. The invasion of the Tartars destroyed hundreds of churches, monasteries, schools, killed many priests, and greatly weakened the life of the Church. Episcopal cathedrals were ruled mainly by local people, Ukrainians who were organically bound with the nation. The influence of Western culture and western literature also contributed to the general education of large masses of people. Unfortunately, more detailed information about the spiritual, educational and monastic life of the Ukrainian Church of that time has not been recorded historically. However, one can assume with certainty that the Church was very active and that the attachment of the faithful to the Church was great and sincere, for in any other case the Church would not have withstood foreign invasions that threatened her very existence. The Ukrainian language was in general use and held out very successfully in competition with the Latin which was the main language in the higher echelons of society of that time. This was primarily the influence of the schools run by the Ukrainian Church.

Between Byzantium and Rome
The general decline of the Orthodox Church also contributed to a certain

weakening of religious life. The Byzantine patriarchate, besieged by the Turks, could not offer much to the Ukrainian Church and the continuous changes in the Byzantine church policies – once with Rome, then against Rome – contributed to a state of uncertainty, indecision, and, not infrequently, confusion in the Ukrainian Church. The actual and later canonical division of the metropoly into that of Kiev and that of Halych, and later into the Latvian-Ukrainian as well, (a movement conditioned by state-political motives), also did not prove beneficial to the development of church life. The metropolitans instead of giving their attention to the spread and building up of the Church and church institutions, often fought among themselves for the right to have eparchies and for church property. This is never favorable for the growth of spiritual life.

One of the most interesting documents of the spiritual life of the Ukrainian Church in the early part of this era is the Council of Ukrainian bishops at Volodimir in 1274, which concerned itself with the internal matters of the Ukrainian Church, set higher requirements for candidates to the priesthood, condemned simony, taught how the Mass should be celebrated, and introduced other valuable reforms.

At the end of this era, the religious and cultural life of the Ukrainian Church declined sharply. Ukrainian lands under foreign rule lost their ancient rights and the state rule aided the Latin Church, which began an unceremonious attack on the Ukrainian rite in the 14th century and tried to enforce Latinization. This also hurt spiritual life, because the Ukrainian Church was spending all her energies in the defense of her existence. A great blow to the development of the Church was the so-called right of patronage, or the giving of "spiritual bread", which made the Ukrainian churches dependent upon patrons, these being mostly foreigners. Undesirable elements of society came to power, persons who bought "spiritual offices" for money from patrons or kings; for such "church officers", it was not the spiritual life of the Church but only the church properties that were of interest.

Many of the Ukrainian nobility went over to the other camp, either to the Latins or to Portestantism and this also considerably weakened the Ukrainian Church and her religious life. With the coming of the Jesuits to Poland, the situation in Ukraine slowly began to change. The Jesuits began to develop schooling on a grand scale. This encouraged the more active circles of Ukrainian society who also began to organize themselves better and develop similar schools in their lands. The greatest service in the development of church schools in the Ukrainian lands was rendered by the Church brotherhoods.

Monasteries and Monastic Life

There is not much to say about monasteries in that era. During the Tartar invasions, almost all of the monasteries had been destroyed. The only ones which remained were in the areas where the Tartars seldom came – that is, in the province of the Carpathians. In time, the monastic life was renewed in

Volodimir-Volynsk, Cholm, and other northern eparchies, but the monasteries played almost no church-religious role. As it is with Churches, spiritual life in monasteries can only develop when the church authority is so strong, and ordered that it can maintain control over monastic life, support it, and correct its faults. These conditions did not exist; thus the Ukrainian monasteries in the 16th century declined and also became "spiritual bread". There were far fewer monks there than there had been in the first pre-Mongolian era.

The situation within the monasteries in the province of the Carpathians was somewhat better. Here the relations were peaceful, the Tartar invasions did not often penetrate, and quarrels for eparchies or spiritual breads did not reach this area. Some of the ancient monasteries remained in this area, and besides that, new seats of monastic life sprang up in the Carpathian Ukraine, such as the ancient monasteries in Drahow, in Ulia, in Zarichya, in Imstichev, in Mukachev, in Bila Tcerkva and in other areas. These monasteries had a better opportunity for development because the life here was more peaceful and there was better supervision, especially after an episcopate was established in Mukachev (in 1440).

These developments indicate the great vitality of the Ukrainian Church and if it weren't for the heavily-strained political relations and misunderstandings between the Byzantine and the Roman Churches, the life of the Ukrainian Church would have developed very intensively. In the Carpathian province and in some other eparchies of the Halych-Volynian State, a number of monasteries prevailed. One was St. John the Baptist, near Halych, founded perhaps in the early 12th century; this was the burial place of Prince Rostyslav, killed by the Hungarians in 1189 and his grandfather Rostyslav Volodarevich, who died in 1126. There was a monastery in Synevidsk and another in Lelesov (in 1213). During king Danylo's rule, there were two monasteries in Lviv, St. George's and St. Onufriy's, a monastery in Danylov, in Plisnesk, in Gydych, in Bashevsk (in 1244), Polonynsk in the Carpathians, St. Onufriy's in Lavrov (in 1270), the Blessed Virgin's in Volodimir-Volynsk, Michael's, the Holy Apostles', the Verchratsky monastery (on the Belzchyna) and others. In the mid 16th century, under the influence of Church brotherhoods and the remaining Ukrainian nobility, new monasteries were founded to combat different heresies, chiefly that of Protestantism. To these belong the monasteries of Dorohochynsk (1563), Berestia, Rogansk, Spask, (near Cholm), Zabludivsk (1565), Dermansk (beginning of the 17th century) and others which sprang up at the beginning of the 17th century, such as the Eveysk, Bytensk, Hustinsk,Girovits, Lutsk, Stavropilsk, Pinsk, the Holy Epiphany, and others.

All the Ukrainian monasteries of that time based themselves on the same rule, that which was practiced in the Monastery of the Caves, with insignificant changes. Many monasteries maintained contact with the monas-. teries maintained contact with the monasteries on the holy Mount of Athos and many Ukrainian monks journeyed there, fleeing the world. One of these was the well-known Ivan Vishensky, a great and zealous defender of Orthodoxy, who with his letters, inspired the society in Halych to fight the Latins, especially those in Lviv.

12. Church Fraternities

The Oppression of the Ukrainian Church

It is said that ill-fortune teaches wisdom. Whether this is true or not is another matter, but this wisdom was confirmed in the Ukrainian Church in the 17th century. Having again turned to the East, to the patriarch of Constantinople (the Catholics themselves not blameless for this), the Ukrainian Church began to feel herself ruled by the hand of an inimical state. During Yagello's reign, in the so-called decrees of Horodelsk (in 1413), the rights of the Ukrainian Church were severely curtailed and Orthodox Ukrainians, according to those decrees could not be allowed to hold higher state positions.

After the Florentine union, these decress with regard to the Ukrainian Church were seemingly cancelled, but, as has been seen, in practice the Latin Church of Poland did not change its attitude, but on the contrary used any means to destroy the ties between the Ukrainian Church and Rome so as to give herself a free hand to stamp out Orthodoxy and bring in Latinization. To this end, the Polish hierarchy worked hand-in-hand with the Polish national officials. The success of such a policy increased while the Ukrainian Church weakened. Ukrainian nobles began going over to the Latin Church, community life was disorganized, education was poor, schooling was very poorly organized, and church leadership was very often in inappropriate hands. The culminating point of this weakening of the Ukrainian Church was the mid-16th century.

As has been said, people who had little connection with Ukrainian Church interests often held the office of bishop, sometimes even buying these "spiritual favors", so it was a waste of time to accept any help for the Church and the nation from that quarter. At that time, a class of organized citizens came to power.

Church fraternities existed in the Ukraine long before the 16th century. Researchers say that they sprang up together with church communities. At the same time that the church was being organized in a given area, a fraternity also was springing up. Obviously this was not the same kind of fraternity which we see in the 16th century. These primary fraternities were spontaneous organizations of the faithful which cared for the church, guarded it, held feasts with common meals,helped the poor, took care of funerals, and did other similar good Christian works.

The Ukrainian citizenry, closely linked with its Church, decided to take advantage of the structure of such a fraternal organization for the furthering of the wider goals of the church and nation.

When the Ukrainian Church, under the continual pressure and oppression of foreign rule, began to lose ground, to its rescue came the citizenry which played an important role in her defense and the enlivening of the Ukrainian national culture.

The Programme of Activity

This process began somewhere in the 1520's. The chief task the brethren set for themselves was the raising of the Church from her decline, reviving her and, in general, reviving the oppressed nation. There were two such task centers in the Ukrainian Church of that time: the one in Lviv which organized the Ukrainian forces and the second in Vilna, which took charge of the White Russian eparchies.

In the beginning of the 1530's the fraternity in Lviv was quite strong and well-oprganized and played an important role in the renewal of the episcopate of Halych and its transfer to Lviv (in 1539). Its work gathered strong impetus in the mid-16th century and earned it a widespread fame and respect even in the courts of foreign (Moldavian) Princes. With its work and dedication to the Church, the fraternity ensured itself the unconditional authority of a representative of the whole society of Halych. In 1583, the brethren, together with the bishop of Lviv, Balaban, bought a printing press and began publishing. At the same time they organized, or reorganized the school existing there, in order to "teach the Holy Scripture, Greek, and Slavonic languages, so that there would not be anyone who did not know them."

This was a very important step. Without education, knowledge, and enlightenment, neither the Ukrainian Church nor the nation could live, grow, and develop.

In 1586, the patriarch of Antioch, Joachim, who had been granted full authority over the Ukrainian Church from the patriarch of Constantinople, travelled to Lviv and stayed there. The brethren turned to him with their complaints and their plans. They complained about the decline of church morals and discipline, the ignorance of the clergy, and similar submissions which were undermining the Church. Perhaps the patriarch had not met such people elsewhere, because he was very much uplifted by this meeting. He ratified the fraternity's statute and appointed the fraternity the chief one among all the others which already existed or which were to be formed in the future in other cities and towns of Halych.

The primary task which the fraternity set for itself was the moral, spiritual, and educational uplifting of the Church and society. The fraternity brought in a strict supervision of the behaviour and way of life of its members, applying heavy punishments for transgressions or for behaviour against a brother. The fraternity also received from the patriarch the special privilege of overseeing the life and activity of the clergy and even of the bishop.

The Schools of the Fraternity

The fraternity achieved a great deal of good. After reorganizing a school, it brought in the best teachers, making this school famous across all the Ukraine. In 1592, the fraternity received a document from the king in which he ratified the foundation of the Fraternity of the Assumption and allowed it to found schools and spread its program of education. Many Ukrainian activists, bishops, and priests came from this fraternity and it became the central force of enlightenment for all of the Ukraine and gave back the nation a faith in its own powers.

Under the influence of this Fraternity of the Assumption, which was also called the Holy Cross Society, similar fraternities sprang up across all of the Ukraine, in bigger and smaller centers of Ukrainian community and church life. We know of such fraternities in Rohatyn, Ternopil, Tysmenytsia, Lutsk, Volodimir-Volynsk, Berestya, Bilsk, Peremyshl, Komarno and in many other areas. An uncommonly important and active fraternity was founded also in Kiev. This was the Brotherhood of the Epiphany (1616) whose member-founders were the most notable representatives of Ukrainian society, such as Hetman Sahaydachny, the later Metropolitan Job Boretsky, and others.

Although the fraternities were affiliated with churches and took as their main tasks church-religious goals, nevertheless their activity did not stop at this. In the organizations of the fraternities were centered all the creative forces of the nation and because they founded their activities on the ideals of Christian morality, service to the Church, and education, the fraternities became the cornerstones of the Ukrainian national awakening.

13. The Organization of the Latin Church in the Ukraine

Latin Monastic Orders in the Ukraine

Small colonies of the faithful of the Latin rite appeared inthe Ukraine in the pre-Mongolian era. In Kiev, for example, in the 12th century, there was already a Benedictine (Scottish) monastery. In other, larger cities like Halych, Volodimir-Volynsk, Novhorod, and other trade centers, there were also German, Hungarian and Czech colonies which apparently had their own spiritual leaders. In the beginning of the 13th century in Kiev there appeared Polish Benedictines and Dominicans. The Dominicans were not accepted in Kiev and after a few years they were told to leave (in 1233 or 1234), but the Benedictines, who were perhaps less aggressive, remained in Kiev until the Tartar invasion.

Generally speaking, there was no plan to organize the Latin Church in the Ukraine on a larger scale in the first era. Nor was there any opportunity for this. At that time, the Ukrainian Church was in quite a strong position and besides that, it had support from the princes; thus the attempts to bring the local populace over to the Latin rite would not have been successful anyway. The Ukrainian Church was in quite a strong position and besides that, it had support from the princes; thus the attempts to bring the local populace over to the Latin rite would not have been successful anyway. The Ukrainian Church, although under the rule of the Byzantine Patriarch, had a somewhat more tolerant attitude to Rome and the Latin Church than did the Greeks.

Rome was continuously interested in the Ukrainian Church and the Ukrainian princes had good relations with the western Catholic royal families; therefore Rome hoped that sooner or later a union could be effected. The Lateran Council of 1215 issued a resolution which placed the Latins in non-Latin eparchies under the jurisdiction of the local bishop. When Danylo's union failed, there came a significant change in the policy of the Latin Church, a change towards the spread of the power of Latin bishops to territories populated by the Orthodox, that is, jurisdiction over the Latins in non-Latin eparchies.

The Attempt to Latinize the Ukrainian Church

With the fall of the Halych-Volynian State, this movement spread still further, especially in Halych which, along with Cholm, found itself under Polish rule. Casimir, the Polish king, had already tried to bring the western Ukrainian populace over to the Latins, but he was not successful in this because the church traditions in the Ukraine were always strong and he feared internal disturbances.

After Casimir's death, a Latin metropoly sprang up in Halych, to which the eparchies of Peremyshl, Volodimir-Volynsk and Cholm were to owe allegiance. According to the plan, the Orthodox bishops of those eparchies were to be removed. In the Latin metropoly of Halych there appeared the Hungarian Matthew. Nevertheless, to remove the Ukrainian bishops from the eparchy was not a simple matter. The Latvian who took this task upon himself was Yagello, who became the Polish king in 1386. In 1412 he took the cathedral of Peremyshl by force and gave it to the Latins; thus the Ukrainian bishop in Peremyshl had to reside in Sambor or Syanock. From the begining of the 15th century, Yagello also stopped the assignment of anyone to the eparchy of Halych, turning it over instead to the Latin metropolitan who appointed a "Representative" of the metropolitan of Kiev. These representatives were very often lay people who did not belong to the Church. In 1417, a new Latin episcopate was formed in Cholm which somewhat later was joined to the episcopate of Lutsk. At approximately that same time, the episcopate in Kamyanets Podilsky was founded through Vitovt's endeavors.

It is not hard to guess where Poland's policy was headed. Thus when the Union of Florence came, it spoiled all the plans of the Poles and the Polish Latin hierarchy. According to the resolutions of the council, foreign minorities (Latins) were to fall under the jurisdiction of the local hierarch. This meant that in the Ukraine, the Poles and other Latins were to be subject to the Ukrainian bishops, because after the acceptance of the union, there was no longer any difference in faith. However, the Poles did not think in this manner. Catholicism did not matter as much to them as did the spreading of the boundaries of their own nation. From this quarter came hatred, instigation, and propaganda against the union. In the 15th century, the Latin metropoly was transferred from Halych to Lviv and the Latin propaganda started coming out from there.

A key enemy of the Ukrainian union with the Catholic Church was the aforementioned Vilenian Bishop Matthew, who preferred to co-operate even with clerics of Moscow inimical to Rome and to the Council of Florence, rather than with the papal legate and cardinal of the Roman Church, Isidore. The union of Florence slowed down the crafty plans of the Polish hierarchy for some time. Another impediment was Protestantism, which made great strides in Poland in the mid-16th century. For this reason, the Polish hierarchy had to use all its strength to paralyze the danger of Protestantism in its lands, and this saved the Ukrainian Church to some extent from complete destruction and Latinization in an era when her defensive power was minimal, that is, beginning with the second quarter of the 16th century.

Generally speaking, the plans of the Ukraine's western Latin neighbor to undermine the Ukrainian Church fell apart at the end of the 13th century. For 300 years, until the Union of Berestya, in spite of all the perturbations and weakness within the Ukrainian Church, the success of the Latins, even with help from the state, was very poor. The Ukrainian Church did not learn anything good from the Latins, except perhaps caution and mistrust of the Latins in general.

14. A View of the Second Era

The Metropoly of Kiev between East and West

The Reasons for the Fall of the State of Kiev

The misfortune which met the Ukrainian principate in the first half of the 13th century may be explained in different ways. Historians explain that because of internal squabbles, quarrels, and battles between the princes for a better share, the state squandered its powers to such an extent that it was not able to repel the Tartar horde moving in from the east. This doubtless was the chief reason for the defeat of the Ukraine. Political thinkers believe that poor state organization of the Ukraine was the main factor behind the crippling and that had the Ukraine had a strong central system of rule, the Ukrainian state of that time would not have collapsed. A Ukrainian preacher of the mid-13th century explained this tragedy which had fallen on the Ukraine as a punishment for her sins, for her dual faith – this being an allusion to the fact that in some places in the Ukraine, paganism had remained.

Perhaps all of these must be taken together as important reasons for the fact that the great inheritance from Yaroslav collapsed from one strong blow. As for the Church, without doubt one can imagine a somewhat better organization, a somewhat greater influential power, allying and unifying. But the Ukrainian Church of that time was relatively young and also under foreign rule. It was in the first historical stage of its organic development and, like it or not, was dependent upon state – political factors, especially the system of share – dividing among the princes, every one of whom primarily guarded his own interests. For this reason the Church could not avoid the fate which awaited and pressed down on both her and the state.

After the fall of Kiev, the see of the metropoly during two and a half centuries suddenly became barren. The new metropolitan, Cyril, having wandered here and there, took everything that was left in Kiev, including Serapion, the abbot of the Monastery of the Caves, and went to the north to Volodimir on the Klasma. By this action, he set the initiative for the liquidation of Kiev as the Christian center of the European East. It is true that he was involved in the Church in many ways. He held the first council of the metropoly of Kiev in history, a council which concerned itself with the internal matters of the Church. It was Cyril who wrote "Teaching for Priests", which showed the great worthiness and great responsibility of a priest. However, his accomplishments did not rectify his failure to maintain the capitol at Kiev. The transfer of the capitol to the north and its dependance upon the despotic rule of the leaders of Moscow of that time and later times, did great harm to the Church. If the center of the metropoly of Kiev and eastern European Christianity had remained longer under the system of rule which proceeded from the north, the history and development of the Ukrainian Church would have gone a totally different route.

An Overview of the Metropoly of Halych

After the fall of the State of Kiev, a new Ukrainian center arose in Halych, and the Halych-Volynian State grew in the western Ukrainian lands. The church felt the lack of a pastoral superior and in time, through the efforts of Yuriy I of Lviv, Halych received a separate metropolitan (in 1303). This did not last for a long time, for after a few years there was again but one metropolitan whose seat was in Volodimir or in Moscow. Part of the Ukrainian lands, as early as the beginning of the 14th century, found themselves under Latvian rule. The Latvian princes also did not want the eparchies in their state under the rule of the metropolitan of Moscow, with which neighborly relations were poor. The patriarch was forced in 1362 to ordain a separate metropolitan, Roman, for Latvia as well. The next metropolitan in Latvia, Cyprian, again united all three metropolies, those of Halych, Latvia-Ukraine and Kiev. However, after his death (in 1406), they would again divide.

Cyprian brought in new ideas to the Ukrainian Church and first began the attempt to unite the Churches of the East and of the West. This action was furthered by his successor at the Latvian-Ukrainian metropoly, Gregory (Tsamvlak). The atmosphere of the church union grew in proportion to the growth of the danger to the Greek Empire from the Turks. It would have been better had the motives for resolution of the church disputes been less worldly and more religious; then the Florentine Council, which was to have mended the wounds in Christ's Church would have had better and longer lasting effects.

Metropolitan Isidore

Nevertheless, the Council of Florence constitutes the most important event in the history of the Ukrainian Church of that era. She was represented by Metropolitan Isidore, a distinguished church leader, a brilliant theologian, and a great authority on the whole Christian Orient. The fact that the Florence union was accepted neither in Greece nor in many eparchies of the metropoly of Kiev does not diminish this role. The history of the Ukrainian Church will always consider him a great figure and a true Apostle of Christ's teaching that all are of one Body.

In the Florentine times, the soul of the Ukrainian Church became apparent. For at least 60 years the Ukrainian metropolitans remained faithful to the Florentine agreement. After the division of the metropoly of Kiev (in 1458), the northern eparchies, inimical to Christian unity, fell away from it and this eased the freedom of the Ukrainian metropolitans to choose their own orientation. The beginning of the 16th century brought a change in this orientation, but this was not the fault of the Ukrainian Church; here the causes were external foreign factors which were inimical to the universal Church.

The Ukrainian Church of that time fell under the influence of the ununited Byzantine patriarch. This change stimulated the Polish Latin clergy of the Polish state in their attempts to undermine the Ukrainian Church to the point where she would easily yield her spoils. That the Florentine union was not to the liking of the Poles there is more proof available than necessary. The growth of the nationalistic ambitions of Poland was innate to the Polish nobility as it was to the church dignitaries. Contrary to papal bulls, in which the eastern rite was equated with the western, the Polish Latins did not regard the eastern rite as Catholic enough. They did not regard it as such because it constituted an obstacle to the assimilation and de-nationalization of Ukrainian society under Polish rule. For this reason it had to be replaced with the uniform, the Latin. Help could not be expected from the patriarchs of Constantinople, for the patriarchate, having fallen under the yoke of the Turks, needed help himself. Thus the Ukrainian Church was left at the mercy of fate.

The Alarming State of the Ukrainian Church Fraternities

In proportion to the growth of Polish power and the spread of Latin influence on Ukrainian noblemen, the impoverished and persecuted Ukrainian Church was slowly but inexorable declining.

In the mid-16th century, the Church's position was so alarming that her complete collapse seemed imminent. But God is merciful. At this grave moment he sent her help in the form of that vital Ukrainian experience which still remained with the nation. Church fraternities sprang up, becoming the activating force behind the Ukrainian Church's motivation. This was the first push to action, to some sort of work, to enlightenment, to battle.

The fact that the Ukrainian Church did not die away in its darkest hour shows that there was much dormant power in the nation which had to be tapped. At the end of the era there came new people, people who graduated from the schools of the fraternity, people who were active and not afraid to take the responsibility for important decisions.

Generally speaking, the Ukrainian Church in this era slowly tore itself away from the tight embrace of the Byzantine patriarchate and tried to create her own independent orientation. Reserving the rite and other cultural gains of previous centuries, she showed a sincere wish to belong to the one and only Church of Christ. And although she was not successful in this and she remained within the jurisdiction of the patriarch for some time, nevertheless this first step was significant. This first step brought her to the second, more decisive one – the Council of Berestya.

The Third Era

From Berestya to the so-called Council of Lviv 1596-1946

1. The State of the Ukrainian Church at the End of the 16th Century

The Influence of Protestantism on the Ukrainian Church

In the 16th century two important events took place which influenced the fate of the Ukrainian Church to a great extent. The first event was that of the so-called Reformation or the Protestant movement in western Europe against Catholicism, which in turn brought a reaction from the Catholic Church, known as the anti-reformation. A key role in the anti-reformation action was played by the monastic orders, chiefly the Jesuits. Because Protestantism had spread strongly in the Polish-Latvian-Ukrainian State of that time and had embraced great circles of the Polish and Latvian intelligentsia, the Polish cardinal Stanislav Hozy brought the Jesuits into Poland in 1564 and assigned them the task of fighting Protestantism. The Jesuits manifested themselves as a great and very active power. This was a young order but very well organized, disciplined, and conscientious in the fulfilment of its duties. The Jesuits organized a wide network of high theological schools in which more than a few Ukrainians studied as well. Having been successful with the Protestants in Poland, the Jesuits turned their attention to the Ukrainian Church as the next task to be taken care of.

The Protestant movement in western Europe and the countermeasures of the Catholic Church significantly reflected themselves in the life and history of the Ukrainian Orthodox Church of that time. On the one hand, the Orthodox Ukrainians sought allies among the Protestant to be able to repel the inroads of the Catholic Poland and on the other hand, studying in Jesuits colleges, themselves fell under Catholic influences to a greater or lesser degree. More than a few of these students, having completed their studies, changed to the Latin rite and became lost to Ukrainianism. And since these were usually the sons of the Ukrainian nobility, such a change to the foreigner's campaign represented a severe blow and a great loss to the Ukrainian nation and the Ukrainian Church. How could the weak organization of the Ukrainian Church stand up against this.

The Union of Lublyn

The second major event was the union of Lublyn in 1569. Up until this time, Poland had been connected to the Latvian-Ukrainian state since 1385 in a so-called personal union, that is, each of the two states was separate but had a common king. In 1569 these two states were joined in so-called real union, that is, one state was indeed rightfully created in which the power was obviously held by the Poles. The Ukrainian lands, which had up until this time belonged to the Latvian-Ukrainian State, changed hands to complete dependence upon Poland. Understandably, in such a situation, the life of the Ukrainian Church became more complex.

As has been mentioned before the Jesuits, having uprooted Protestantism, if not completely, then at least strongly dampening its power, threw themselves with zeal at Orthodoxy. The Ukrainian Church, collapsed and impoverished, seemed to them an easy mark. She did not have state support, her clergy obtained its education from the Catholic clergy, and monasteries and monastic life could not compare at all with the activeness of the western orders. When the continual fleeing of powerful young hopefuls to the foreigner's camp is added to this, an approximate picture of the position of this Church at the end of the 16th century can be seen.

The Fraternities

It is true that in the second half of this century the activity of the Ukrainian Church fraternities sprang up and education was rejuvenated. The fraternities took upon themselves the main role in the defense of the church as an organization, as a cultural inheritance from the Ukrainian ancestors and as the Church-teacher of high moral ideals. For this reason the members paid diligent heed not only to the material safeguarding of the Church and the clergy but also to enlightenment and a moral life.

The fraternal schools, which up until this time had shown a weaker involvement, gained new life, gathered around themselves talented Ukrainian and foreign teachers, and tried to fill the need which was so gravely reflected in the life of the Ukrainian Church: to train an enlightened clergy.

One of the most important achievements in the field of Ukrainian education at that time was, without a doubt, the Ostroh Academy founded by Constantine Ostroh in 1580. Here we gathered the finest educational figures and here sprang up an exemplary press which published the first Bible printed in the Old Church Slavonic (in 1581), as well as many other works of theological and polemic literature.

The achievements of Prince Ostroh for Ukrainian culture were great. Were it not for him, the Ukrainian Church would hardly have withstood the overwhelming power of Polish Latinism. And although he did not support the action of the Ukrainian bishops at the end of the 16th century, nevertheless, with his uncompromising stand, he helped in many ways to further the action which he opposed. He helped because he inspired such a strong opposition that the proponents of a complete Latinization of the Ukrainian Church had to take it into account. Obviously it would have been somewhat more beneficial if this nobleman had given his talents, his strength and influences to the matter of church union, and if he had led this action and had tried to extract from it the maximum benefit for the Ukrainian Church and nation. Regrettably this did not happen. If it had, then the path of the Ukrainian Church's rebirth and perhaps even the national rebirths would have been other than the path which the Ukrainian nation has been forced to tread to this day. Nevertheless, his activity awoke the dormant sources of energy and moved the masses to action, to organization, and to thought.

The Right Patronage
One of the greatest evils in the organization of the Ukrainian Church of that time was the so-called right of patronage. Polish kings understood this right in their own terms. When the right of patronage gave the king the right to approve persons chosen by the hierarchy to higher church offices, they understood this privilege to mean that they themselves were to assign metropolitans, bishops or archimandrites. For this reason, people were appointed to the higher church offices who were completely inadequate, without spiritual enlightenment, without a consuming interest in the fate of the Ukrainian Church, and infrequently, even Latins as well. It was pointless to expect any good from such pastors. The battle for influence, for riches, for wages and honors spread – and such goals are completely different from those goals which Christ set for the Church.

The right of patronage for lower church offices was also held by local noblemen, towns and church fraternities. This, on one hand, had its advantages because, for example, the fraternities carefully watched the behaviour of the priest and allowed those whom they considered the best to hold church offices. But, on the other hand, the continual interference of the fraternity in the affairs of the leadership of the Church often led to misunderstandings between the members and the bishop, weakened the authority of the bishop and reduced him to the role of the doer of the will of the fraternities. The bishops did not want to give in to this and they protested against opposing fraternities. This of course, was not to the Church's benefit, and when such misunderstandings multiplied, they resulted in making the bishops search for solutions and help.

Traces in the Literature of that time
It can be seen that the disorders and lack of agreement between pastors and pastorages in the Ukrainian Church of that time was a phenomenon so widespread that this was reflected even in literature. In one ancient anthology the author gives a solution to the improvement of relations in the Church. He says "The Ukrainian Church will grow and spread and metropolitans and bishops will not be lacking (that is, the bishops' cathedrals will not be left vacant) only when they will properly witness about God and when they preach about wealth before God as before man, when they uproot sins and sow good deeds, when they obey God's commandments. Then they will live in God and God in them . . . "

2. The Orientation to Rome

The Visits of the Patriarch and the Holy Cross Society
At the end of the 16th century, two eastern patriarchs visited the Ukrainian Church. First in 1586, the patriarch of Antioch Joachim came to the Ukraine

and later, in 1589, travelling through to Moscow, the patriarch of Constantinople, Jeremiah, visited the Ukrainian metropoly. Both of these patriarchs turned their attention to a new and hopeful factor in the Church – the church fraternities. They praised the zeal of the members, their moral life, and their care for Church matters. Joachim gave the members in Lviv the rights of a Society, that is, he made them independent of the bishop and made the fraternity dependent on the patriarch. In this way, the authority of the fraternity grew greater while the authority of Hedeon, the bishop of Lviv, weakened. The patriarch of Constantinople, Jeremiah, affirmed these rights and made them greater still, thereby creating an even greater enmity between the bishop and the members.

The patriarch ruled perhaps with good intentions, safeguarding the exceptional rights of the fraternity; nevertheless, not being familiar with the situation, he did not repair relations but on the contrary, he sharpened the dispute between the bishop and the faithful. The patriarch also removed the metropolitan of Kiev, Onysyfor. He removed him because the metropolitan, before his ordination, had already been twice married. Church law of the eastern Church did not permit those twice married to receive ordination as bishops. In the future the patriarch ordered that the cathedrals of the bishops should be occupied only by monks. In accord with this, the removed Metropolitan Onysyfor was replaced by the archimandrite of the monastery at Minsk, Michael Rohoza, who was ordained by the patriarch himself.

The Exarch with Control over the Metropolitan

However, the patriarch did not trust Rohoza either and for this reason, appointed the bishop of Lutsk, Cyril Terlecky, as his (that is, the patriarch's) representative – exarch. Metropolitan Rohoza was unpleasantly stung by this and openly showed his depleasure. This diminished his authority at a time when authority was precisely what the Ukrainian Church sadly lacked. How could the metropolitan bring order and discipline to the clergy when he, the metropolitan, remained under the watch of his own bishop. With this thoughtless action, the patriarch merely quickened the process of fermentation in which the Ukrainian church found herself at the end of the 16th century.

Right after the departure of the patriarch, Bishop Hedeon of Lviw began talks with the Polish bishop of Lviw, Solikovsky, on the matter of union. To this end he also allied other bishops who were unhappy with the rulings of the patriarch, that is, the bishop of Cholm, Dionysius Zbirusky, and the bishop of Pinsk, Leontius Pelchynsky. But the oddest part is that the patriarch representative – exarch, the bishop of Lutsk, Cyril Terlecky, also joined this group. Prince Ostrosky also considered union, though later he became its avowed enemy. He considered it because, as Orthodox historians themselves say – he had lost all hope of any kind of help for the Ukrainian Church from the East.

The Idea of Union among the Orthodox Bishops

Having reached an agreement the bishops began to convince the metropolitan to call a council at Belz to discuss the unbearable attitudes which had arisen in the Ukrainian Church. Nevertheless, the metropolitan did not agree to a council in Belz and called it in the following year, in 1590, in Berestya. All the same, the bishops gathered somewhat earlier in Belz and unanimously decided to urge the metropolitan to make all efforts to unite the Ukrainian Church with Rome. The matter of church union was not decided upon at the Council in Berestya in 1590; only a letter was sent to the king complaining of the pressure on the part of the Poles against the Orthodox faith. Possibly there was no consensus of opinion among the bishops and also perhaps there was opposition from the bishop of Volodimir, Meletius Chrebtovich, whom Patriarch Jeremiah had raised to the position of "prototronius", that is, the eldest bishop after the metropolitan. In 1593, Meletius died and was replaced by Ipathy Poti, a highly-enlightened person who was respected in the home of Prince Ostrosky. From that time, the efforts towards church union were redoubled. In two years, 1593-1595, the bishops held four or five councils: in Sokal, Krasnostav, Kobryn, Berestya and perhpas in Lutsk (in August 1595) for discussion and a decision on the matter of union.

At that time Prince Ostrosky was interested in this matter. He had even outlined a plan for and conditions of a church union on his own. These conditions, known by the name "The Sokalian Articles", required that the Catholics leave the Ukrainian rite intact, that the transfer of faithful of the eastern rite to the Latin rite be disallowed, that the Ukrainian Churches' church properties and institutions be safeguarded, that the rights of the Ukrainian clergy be equalized with those of the Polish Latin clergy, that relations within the Ukrainian Church be repaired, and that education and spiritual enlightenment be developed.

The prince also believed that other eastern Churches, that is other eastern patriarchs, should be united in the cause of union so as to end the division which had arisen in the 11th century. All these prerequisites which Prince Ostrosky set down, with the exception of the participation of other eastern churches, were realized at the union of Berestya. If the matter of union in the understanding of the Ukrainian bishops and Prince Ostrosky was a holy action and good in its foundation, then the lack of participation by other eastern churches does not diminish its holiness and does not cancel its intention of sanctity. Certainly neither the Ukrainian bishops nor the prince, who was a deeply religious person, could see any theological or canonical obstacles that should prevent the Ukrainian Church from entering into prayerful union with the Catholic Church.

The Ukrainian and other Eastern Churches

The wish that other eastern churches take part in the union, no matter how holy it was, was nevertheless not a serious prerequisite, because it would be pointless to make the future of the Ukrainian Church dependent upon the other eastern churches; upon those under whose influence the Ukrainian

Church had been for long years and had not come out the better for it. Almost all of the eastern churches, with the exception of the newly-formed patriarchate of Moscow (in 1589), found themselves in the sphere of influence of the foreign and anti-christian Muslims, to whom it was crucial that church peace among the Christians not be allowed to be reached. The patriarchs of Constantinople, to whom the Ukrainian Church was subject enjoyed some religious freedom but were nevertheless completely dependent on the rule of the Sultan, who appointed them or removed them according to his wishes. Understandably, in such a situation, the Ukrainian bishops, who felt themselves directly responsible for the fate of the Ukrainian Church, preferred to decide by their own wisdom and according to their own conscience, regardless of the fact that by tradition the Ukrainian Church had remained under the authority of the patriarch of Constantinople for a long time. It must be added here that at precisely this time, the patriarch of Moscow was formed. The Byzantine patriarch gave his agreement and blessing to this and in this way, made the metropoly of Moscow, according the will of the people and the will of the patriarch, could become independent and decide its own matters according to its own wishes. If Moscow could do this, then why did the Ukrainian metropoly, much older and richer in terms of church culture than that of Moscow, have to remain any longer under foreign rule, the rule of the Greek patriarchs who moreover did not help her in any way because they themselves needed help. The Ukrainian bishops saw all this and understood it perhaps better than it is understood today.

The withdrawal of Bishop Balaban

Although the bishops' efforts towards union were not a complete secret, nevertheless the bishops did not hurry with a public proclamation of their efforts. Only in December 1594 did bishop Terlecky, in the name of the Ukrainian episcopacy, announce that the Ukrainian Church intended to join the Catholic Church, retaining the eastern rite and ancient rights. In January 1595, Bishop Balaban participated in a council at Lviw with the clergy and some foreign bishops who were visiting him at the time and this council also approved the union of the Ukrainian Church with the Catholic. But not a half-year passed before Balaban rejected his efforts towards union, made peace with the fraternity with which he had continually fought, denied his participation in the preparation to union and became its firm antagonist.

In June 1595, the matter was finally clarified. The conditions of union were signed by Metropoplitan Rohoza and all the bishops except Hedeon Balaban of Lviw and Michael Kopystensky of Peremyshl and the furthering of the matter was entrusted to Bishops Terlecky and Poty.

The opposition of Prince Ostrosky

But now, against the efforts of the Ukrainian bishops, with all his power and decisiveness, came its recent supporter, Prince Ostrosky. He heavily accused and condemned the Ukrainian hierarchy for abandoning the patriarchs and seemingly giving in to Latinization. He issued an appeal to the populace

107

in which he called on it not to obey its bishops and to oppose their plans. This behaviour of the prince frightened the bishops of Lviw and Peremyshl and they separated themselves from the movement for union.

Why exactly Ostrosky came out so strongly against union, in which he himself had recently taken part, remains a mystery. Historians say that it was as if this mighty magnate (he ruled over 700 villages and 30-odd cities) was strongly insulted because the bishops decided matters of union themselves and did not ask for his approval. If this guess is correct, then this was indeed their fault. For although the matters of the Church, according to Scriptural teaching, were to be decided only by bishops,all the same they should have taken into account the whole of this important act and the exceptional position of Prince Ostrosky in the nation. But whether or not this guess is true is difficult to say. In his message Ostrosky seems an ardent defender of Orthodoxy, the ancient rights, the rite and the everlasting traditions of the Ukrainian Church. But he was unable to hold even his children to this Orthodoxy and during his lifetime, they became not Uniates but complete Latins and Polish patriots.

This was not his fault directly and it is pointless to blame him for it for who knows whether or not they would have remained faithful sons of their nation if they had converted to that Church which their father so zealously defended.

Ostrosky also tried to convince King Gihmont to call a council of the Orthodox Church to revise the decisions for union, but he was unsuccessful in this. In September 1595, the king announced in a proclamation that the hierarchy of the Ukrainian Church had decided to unite with Rome. In the fall of that same year, Bishops Cyril Terlecky and Ipathy Potiy left for Rome for the definitive and formal signing of the agreement for union.

3. The Council of Berestya of 1596

The Conditions of the Union of the Orthodox Church with Rome

In Rome in December 1595, representatives of the Ukrainian Church signed the conditions for the union of the Ukrainian Church with the Catholic Church. The Ukrainian Church, according to these conditions, unyieldingly affirmed her eastern rite, her ancient rights as to the rule of the metropolies and episcopates, the old calendar, and the right of the lower clergy to marry if they chose. In a word, the conditions of union did not bring any radical changes to the life of the Ukrainian Church. Of course the Ukrainian Church recognized the pope, bishop of Rome, as the primate-hierarch of the whole Church of Christ. Pope Clement VIII accepted these conditions, equalized the rights of Ukrainian clergy with those of the Latin clergy, and in a separate letter to King Zigmont, asked that he care for the Ukrainian Church at this important moment.

The Participants in the Council and their Division

For the celebrated announcement of the act of union, Metropolitan

Rohoza called a council on the 6th of October, 1596. All the Ukrainian bishops čame to the council, as well as many archimandrites, abbots, priests and lay people. Supporters of and antagonists to the union came. Those present at the council became divided at the very beginning of the Council into those who wished to bring the Ukrainian Church to new ways, to bring it closer to the western world and those who believed that it would be best for the Ukrianian Church if she remained under the rule of the patriarch of Constantinople. The bishops of Lviw and Peremyshl joined those against union, and under the direction of the representative of the patriarch and with the participation of several foreign bishops, held their own discussions separately. This Orthodox Council condemned Metropolitan Rohoza and the bishops who had accepted the union and sent delegates to the king asking that he approve this condemnation. These discussions were led, as has been mentioned, by the protosynkel of the patriarch, Nikiphor, who did not know Ukrainian and used a translator at the council. He also did not know of the relations which existed within the Ukrainian Church, for the patriarch was not very interested in that church. However, this did not stop him from denying the Ukrainian metropolitan and bishops their right to decide the fate of their own Church and faithful according to their own consciences. Obviously, no one would have paid any heed to him if it were not for the fact that Prince Ostrosky, a very influential and widely respected person in the nation, stood behind him.

The Announcement of the Union of the Orthodox Church with Rome.

However, the metropolitan paid no attention to the protosynkel of the patriarch and his threat. He opened the council of the Church according to the regulation of the ancient church rules, in the presence of the bishops, clergy and representatives of the Catholic Church. The program of the council lasted three days and was completed by a triumphal procession to the Church of St. Nicholas, where a litany of gratitude to the Lord was celebrated for the completed church union. After the litany of gratitude, Herman, the bishop of Polotsk, read the act of union by which the celebration of the union was formally completed. A separate proclamation of the metropolitan announced this important act to the nation.

Right after the council, the metropolitan deprived Hedeon Balaban, the bishop of Lviw, and Michael Kopestensky of Peremyshl of their episcopal power. They were both seriously in the way of the fate of the Ukrainian Church. If they had solidly stood up together with the other Ukrainian bishops and the metropolitan, no foreign influences could have altered the course which had existed for a long time in the Ukrainian metropoly, especially after the Council of Florence. Their inimical stance and condemnation of their own metropolitan had an undeniable influence on the populace, which was not knowledgeable in church matters and was easily swayed by all kinds of rumors, instigations, and foreign propaganda antagonistic to the Ukrainian Church. This propaganda came from all sides which did not accept the union – from the Orthodox east and from the Ukrainian surroundings. The clergy of the newly-formed patriarchate of Moscow did not neglect propaganda either.

In this way, the Church, which needed great order and discipline at this time, became the arena for bickering enmity and various accusations.

Although the Council of Berestya did not herald the excepted salvation of the whole Ukrainian Church and did not renew it as might have been expected, nevertheless it was an important event in its life. Those apprehensions which indicated that, having reached an agreement of union with the Catholic Church, the Ukrainian Church would cease to be the Church of the Ukrainian nation and would be Latinized and lose its rite, proved groundless. On the contrary, its history shows that it not only lost nothing of its Ukrainianism but also brought undeniable riches to the treasury of the Ukrainian culture. The great contribution of the Ukrainian bishops of the end of the 16th century was that they had enough courage to take charge of this not universally popular action. They were aware of those difficulties which awaited them, they knew the power and the influence of Prince Ostrosky, and they also, doubtless, did not completely trust the sincerity of the Polish Catholics, but they believed their action to be honest and sincere and that for this honest action they could expect God's help.

As a result, after the Council of Berestya, matters looked as follows: of all the eight eparchies of the metropoly of Kiev, six eparchies joined the union, including the metropolitan as head of the Church, while two eparchies did not join. The following eparchies joined the union: Kiev, Volodimir-Volynsk, Turiv-Pinsk, Lutsk, Cholm and Polotsk; Lviv and Peremyshl did not join.

The Fight after the Union

Notable is the fact that the eparchies in which Prince Ostrosky's influence was direct and significantly greater than in the southwestern areas of the country joined forces with their bishops and with the metropolitan, while those of Lviv and Peremyshl, where the main anti-union action was led by the fraternities, did not accept the union and showed a great strength of opposition. The fraternity of Lviv, as has been mentioned, was not under the control of the bishop but served the patriarch directly and was on constant inimical terms with Bishop Hedeon Balaban. Balaban, doubtless, took this into consideration when it came time to issue a definite resolution. If he had shown more backbone and courage in his convictions, then perhaps in time the fraternity would have made its peace with the new state of affairs, but he did not show this backbone and in this way the division of the one church organism came about.

With this division, the Ukrainian Church entered the 17th century, an era of prolonged battle, self-destruction, and mutual slanders in spoken and written word. This obviously was neither to the glory of God nor for the good of the Church or the nation. If this energy and activity directed to the weakening or destruction of opponents had been channelled towards the strengthening of the church's organization, the building of schools, the cultivation and development of the church culture, and the spreading of literacy, education and writing, then this decisive moment would have turned the wheel of the history of the Ukraine in a totally different direction than that in which it went because of this unfortunate turn of events.

4. Relations in the Ukraine after the Union

The eastern Patriarchs intensify the Battle

The acceptance of the union alone did not resolve all the difficulties which besieged the Ukrainian Church at the end of the 16th century. On the contrary, new difficulties joined the old ones. Now the Church was divided into two warring camps – the Orthodox and the Uniates. Both sides regarded it their holy duty to defend their position, to defend it with all the means at their disposal. Life became more intense. Persistent preachers appeared, as well as polemicists and writers. The eastern patriarchs, who until this time had been little interested in the Ukrainian Church, now unceasingly wrote messages, letters, and advice in which they encouraged the faithful and the clergy to disobey their bishops, to reject the union and to remain obedient to the patriarch of Constantinople. From one patriarch alone, the patriarch of Alexandria, Meletius Pihas, there were seven messages in a short time. The bishop of Lviv, Hedeon, became the exarch of the patriarch, that is, his representative for the Orthodox Ukrainians. Through his exarch, the patriarch patronized both Prince Ostrosky and the proto-priest, Nestor Kuzmynych of Zabludiw (in Polizia), in order to prevent a complete union of the Ukrainian Church from occurring and to set up all possible defenses against those hierarchs who longed for unity.

There was disturbance also among the monks of Mount of Athos, where Anthony, the founder of the monastic life in the Ukraine, had resided and where monks from all corners of the Ukraine came on pilgrimages. Among them was one of the most interesting figures of that time – Ivan Vyshensky, who played an important role in the overpowering of the union. From Athos he sent messages to the fraternity members in Lviv, to Prince Ostrosky, and to the bishops "of the Orthodox faith who had fled", in which he laid waste to the union and defended Orthodoxy.

The Polemic Literature

At home appeared the messages of Prince Ostrosky and the Bishop Balaban, the appeals of the fraternities, and the polemic writings of Stephan Zyzany, Martin Bronevsky, Clyric Ostrosky, and many other staunch defenders of Orthodoxy. In them the authors accused the Catholic Church of erring in faith and the Uniates of abandoning their ancestral faith.

The Uniates did not remain silent either. On their side they defended the union of Berestya, straightened out accusations made against them, cautioned the faithful against lying slanders, and pointed out the benefits which the Church could have by entering into union with the Catholic Church, at the same time not losing anything of her own ancient rite and traditions.

These polemic writings explained very little but rather deepened the rift which developed after the Council of Berestya. The accusations of the Orthodox polemicists that the Catholic Church seemingly did not preserve the Orthodox faith, were nothing new. These were the same accusations as those against unleavened bread, the "primacy of the pope", fasting, and the procession of the Holy Spirit, which from ancient times the Greeks had cited and which had been definitively resolved and explained at the Council in Florence.

However it is not right to think of the polemicists as people of ill will, driven by base motives or not wishing the good of the Ukrainian Church. They really believed in the issue which they defended and supported, often laying themselves open for great personal hardship. The trouble was that these were people of little or no theological education, who did not understand and could not understand the dogmatic differences between the eastern and western Churches. Nor did they understand the situation of the Ukrainian Church and the situation of the church in the East in general. In the given circumstances, they gave precedence to their emotions and to a blind loyalty to the past, regardless of the fact that this past was leading the Ukrainian Church into an untenable position.

The Front of the Fraternities and the Ukrainian Nobility against the Union.

Prince Ostrosky put his full authority behind the defense of the Orthodox position. Neither the pleas nor the persuasions of the Ukrainian bishops helped. He persuaded delegates to the regional governments to ask for the rejection of the union and the condemnation of the bishops. The fraternities also joined this campaign. Most notable in this campaign were the very influential fraternity of Lviv affiliated with the Church of the Blessed Assumption, the Vilenian fraternity, and in time also the fraternity of the Epiphany of Kiev. Thanks to the influence and activity of the fraternities, the fraternal movement gained new life. Fraternities sprang up in the whole territory of the metropoly, in Mohylev, Minsk, Lublyn, Lutsk and many other smaller cities. Until this time, the fraternities had attracted primarily citizens, but now representatives of the higher social classes began to join them: princes, noblemen, high state officials and the Cossack leaders. In the fraternity of Lublyn, for example, were found such famous families as the Sangushky-Koshyrsky, Chartoryjsk, Chetwertynsky,Drutsky, and Lubetsky families, all of them suddenly showing great zeal in defending the ancient Orthodoxy. But not even one generation had passed before most of them had cooled to such an extent that they rejected not only Orthodoxy but Ukrainianism in general.

What was the reason for this? The reason was that very soon either they themselves or their children became disenchanted. They reached the conclusion that Ukrainian Orthodoxy could not expect any greater or more serious help from the East than just the messages themselves, the encouragements and calls to the defense of the past and to loyalty to the patriarch. And having investigated the matter well, instead of putting all their efforts into a national and church union, they let themselves be swayed by influences, persuasions and propaganda of an environment foreign to Ukrainianism; they dropped the matter which they had recently defended so zealously and became Latins. The Latin rite was foreign to the Ukrainians and a change over to that camp meant a rejection of one's own nationality. The Ukrainian Church in communion with Rome was not attractive to them, even though it was they who had weakened the Church. Now the Church had to wage a continuous battle for her very existence and had to defend herself against the delegations of the Polish Latin clergy who sought to undermine those rights which the conditions of the union of Berestya had guaranteed. In this way the Ukrainian nation lost many of its famous clans in a short time – the very ones who, with their social status, influence, wealth, and education could have put the Ukrainian Church on her feet and created strong foundations for a national rebirth.

The Revival of the Monasteries and their Role in the Battle

Besides the influence of fraternities, a second factor which determined the fate of the Ukrainian Church was the influence of the monasteries. As has been mentioned, at the end of the 16th century, monastic life in the Ukraine had declined sharply. New personalities now appeared who were concerned with the reorganization of church discipline, the deepening of the monastic spirit, the spreading of enlightenment, the printing of books, and a closer contact with the nation.

After the Council of Berestya, most monasteries did not ally themselves with the Ukrainian bishops. The Monastery of Caves in Kiev, the main center of monastic life in the Ukraine, also did not join them. Its archimandrite, Niciphor Tur, proved himself an ardent opponent to the new orientation of the Ukrainian Church and since the authority of the Monastery was unquestionable, other monasteries looked to the monks of the Caves of Kiev for leadership as well. Thus all the more notable monasteries, such as those of Mychayliw, Mykolayiw, Kuryliw, Megyhirskyj, monasteries past the Dnipro and the monasteries of the eparchies of Lviv and Peremyshl remained true to Orthodoxy. Nevertheless, about fifteen monasteries sided with the Ukrainian hierarchy, among them such famous centers of monastic life as the monastery of Vydubytsk, the Holy Trinity in Vilna, The Holy Trinity in Slutsk, the Supralsky monastery in Polissia, the Gydychynsky in Volynia, the Holy Saviour in Kobryn, the Lavryshivsky near Novhorodok, the Lishchynsky near Pinsk, and somewhat later the Dermansky monastery and other smaller ones.

New monasteries sprang up as well: the Fraternal – Epiphany monastery in Kiev, the monastery of the Holy Ghost in Vilna, the Lubensky and Hustynsky monasteries (on the other side of the Dnipro), three new monasteries in Halychyna, founded by Job Knihynetsky, a companion of Ivan Vyshensky, two new monasteries in Minsk in White Rus and some monasteries in other areas, all set up chiefly through the goodwill and loyalty to Orthodoxy of the remnants of the Ukrainian nobility.

The atmosphere of battle, the influence of the delegates from Mount of Athos, and the feeling of support from influential and wealthy Ukrainian nobles all this contributed to a definite renewal and elevation of monastic activity. The printing movement began and as a prerequisite to this, publishing houses were founded. Up until this time, there were few printing houses in the Ukraine – two or three in all. Now a whole row of them appeared, for example in Derman, founded by Isaak Borysovich in 1601, in Pankiwtsi in Podilya (in 1601), in Stryatyn near Rohatyn (in 1604), in Krylos near Halych (in 1605), in Kiev (in 1616), in Pochayev (in 1618), in Rachmanov (in 1619), and with time in other areas as well. As can be seen from the dates they were founded all these printing houses were set up immediately after the completion of the union and this indicates that the orienation of the Ukrainian Church to Catholicism, although making much trouble for the Ukrainians, nevertheless dispelled some of that lethargy which had so recently ruled in the Ukrainian monasteries. Every new book inspired another, every new word, or new idea gave birth to others; the circle of readers grew and literacy spread.

The Benefits of the Polemics

Without a doubt, the printing and publishing movement had one main aim: to fight the opposition. But this could not be circumvented and besides that, any matter is clearer in a public discussion and in the printed word than in whispered propaganda, secret meetings or instigations. For this reason, it was better to discuss delicate matters out loud rather than in secret. When the general results of the printing-publishing activity are taken into consideration, there is not the slightest doubt that the religious-polemic disadvantages were not at all in proportion to the benefits which the Ukrainian nation received from this movement.

The early years after the establishment of the union were relatively quiet. Metropolitan Rohoza was a thoughtful man of quiet temperament who did not force anyone to accept the union. He tried instead to influence others with a good word, with messages, with explanations of matters, and by his own example of an upright and humble life. It was not his lot to do much in the reorganization of the united Church and he died three years after the Council of Berestya in 1599.

After his death, the bishop of Volodimir-Volynsky, Ipathy Potiy, became metropolitan. He was a highly-enlightened man who had received his education in foreign schools before his ordination to the spiritual life. He held high state offices, understood administration, and knew the value of order and discipline. As a zealous supporter of the idea of union, he enlivened this action. Realizing his responsibility for the fate of the Church, he strived to safeguard her future with word and act. A stronger action on the part of the Uniates encouraged, obviously, a stronger counter-reaction.

The means and methods of the fight-mutual occupation of churches and monasteries and summonses before the state courts – became sharper, and this complicated and strained relations between the Orthodox and the Uniates still further.

The Fate of the Eparchies of Lviv and Peremyshl

In 1607, Hedeon, the bishop of Lviv, died. And although the metropolitan, depending on the aid of the king, wanted to assign a bishop united with Rome to the episcopate of Lviv, nevertheless the resistance of the fraternity was so strong that he failed in this. Jeremiah Tyssarovsky, ordained in Moldavia, became the new Orthodox bishop of Lviv. A few years later, in 1610, Michael Kopystensky, the bishop of Peremyshl, died as well. Here the situation took a different turn. Athanasius Krupecky, a Uniate, became the new bishop and from that time the eparchy of Peremyshl came under the jurisdiction of the metropolitan. This does not mean that the faithful changed over as well. On the contrary, here resistance against union lasted for a long time yet. The Orthodox Church also assigned her bishops here, and only from 1692 is there considered a full subordination of the eparchy to the metropolitan.

Why was there such a large opposition in certain circles of Ukrainian society against the union of the Ukrainian Church with the Catholic? Why did the well-organized fraternities, the high noble class, a significant number of monasteries, the Cossak leaders, and the Cossaks in general fight the union so zealously? Why did the post-union times distinguish themselves with these particular methods, including bloodshed?

These are difficult questions and there is no one answer to satisfy them all. The Orthodox claimed that they were defending the true faith, the faith of their ancestors and were also defending the past Ukrainian church culture, traditions and rite. They believed that the changing over to subjection to the pope would bring with it the ruin of the Ukrainian Church; they feared that their church would dissolve in the Latin Church and later would become a means to national assimilation in the multinational Polish state of that time.

Supporters of the union with Rome understood these matters differently. They believed that the change over to subjection to the pope did not touch the foundations of the Ukrainian faith and that the united Church, having safeguarded her own separate rite, past church traditions, rights, hierarchy, even the old calendar, would never be sacrificed to the Latins. Instead they believed that the Ukrainian Church was profiting greatly by having realized its equal value to the Catholic Church in the state. Above all, she would lose her inferiority complex, stem the assault from the Polish nobility, gain state and church holdings, get the opportunity to build up her education, her churches and her monasteries and establish for herself an order and a strong organization similar to churches in Catholic countries. These obviously were strong and persuasive arguments and a great percentage of the clergy and society accepted them.

The Changeover to Latinism was a justifiable Precaution.
The apprehensions of the Orthodox were not without a basis. The Orthodox were witnesses to the fact that everyone who changed over to Latinism became a Pole at the same time. Having accepted Catholicism, the Vyshnevetskys, the Ostroskys (Yanush, the son of Constantine), the Chartoryjskys, the Sangushkys, the Sapyhys and a whole line of others took this path. Now that the Ukrainian Church was coming closer to the Polish Catholic Church and was becoming a sister-Church, the question arose as to how the other (Polish) side would understand this sisterhood. Since the Poles supported the union very strongly, there arose the suspicion that the matter was not completely aboveboard. To influence society with these (forgivable) arguments was both unwieldy and ineffective. For this reason almost all the attention was focused on the theological side of the matter, that is, on the "verity of the faith", on the fear for the salvation of souls, on the resolutions of the councils, and so on. The populace listens to such arguments and believes more in them; such arguments call forth fanaticism and it is known that there is no stronger fanaticism than religious fanaticism. Fanaticism, that is, intolerance of other views, should be foreign to religion, especially to the Christian religion, but the Ukrainian leaders of that time did not subscribe to such a theory. They knew that only by unscrupulous dispute could they achieve their intended goal.

Besides that, the truth cannot be avoided: a significant number of Polish Catholics really viewed the union as a bridge to Latinization. Their true objectives became apparent very soon after the Council of Berestya. The drawing of the Uniates into Catholicism began and there was even open talk to the effect that the united Ukrainian Church should be forced into Latinism and that the Orthodox should be left in peace, and in this way peace would be preserved in the state.

In such extremely difficult and serious circumstances, the Ukrainian Church had to live and develop and defend herself against the encroaching Latinism and against that part of Ukrainian society which did not accept the union. This task was very difficult, all the more so because the pressures from the Polish side were very ably taken advantage of by Moscow which hurried to supposedly help her "brothers in faith". The result of this help will soon be seen. It will also be seen that all the apprehensions which were connected to the union were not realized. This Ukrainian Church survived grave moments and remained the Church of the Ukrainian nation.

5. The Renewal of the Orthodox Hierarchy

After the death of Michael Kopystensky, the bishop of Peremyshl, and the taking of the seat in the eparchy by a Uniate bishop, there remained but one Orthodox eparchy – that of Lviv. Thus there were now seven Uniate eparchies. However, this account did not reveal the true state of affairs. In the eparchies where the bishops were Uniates there remained many priests and faithful who were Orthodox. They were supported above all by the monasteries which had not accepted the union, and also by influential worldly persons, delegates to the local governing bodies, and different eastern hierarchs who continuously resided here or there in the Ukraine.

In the twenty-five years after the Council of Berestya the situation changed little. The battle for possession of the churches was unceasing and in local parliaments discussions on the dispute continued each year but these discussions did not ease matters either for the Uniate or the Orthodox Churches. The Orthodox Church, not having a higher hierarchy, found herself in a very critical position. No help came from the patriarch, only delegations.

The Establishment of the Orthodox Hierarchy

In the spring of 1620, while returning from Moscow, the patriarch of Jerusalem, Theophan, stopped in the Ukraine. The eastern patriarchs often went to Moscow, usually for donations. This time, the patriarch of Jerusalem had journeyed there to institute the patriarch of Moscow, Philotheus, who was Isar Michael's father and the founder of the Romanov dynasty.

In the Ukraine, Patriarch Theophan was welcomed with all honors. Before his arrival in Kiev, he was met by Hetman Sahaydachny and a division of Cossaks and escorted into the city. In Kiev the patriarch took up residence in the Monastery of the Caves and remained there for several months, making use only of letters and messages to the fraternities, to important Orthodox leaders and to the monasteries. The Polish rulers did not create any obstacles for him because at that time the Poles were engaged in a war with the Turks and did not wish to antagonize the Cossaks and the Ukrainian Orthodox populace against themselves. The Poles sorely needed help from the Cossaks.

The Fraternity of the Epiphany was raised by the patriarch to the status of the Holy Cross Society, that is, it was placed under the direct rule of the Patriarch of Constantinople.

Having reached the conclusion that the political situation was sufficiently favourable, the patriarch finally began the actual action: the renewal of the Orthodox hierarchy. Having the Bulgarian metropolitan, Neophitus, and the Stahonian bishop, Abraham, under his control, the patriarch ordained Isaiah Kopynsky, the abbot of the Megyhirsky monastery, as bishop of Peremyshl on the 6th of October, 1620. As has been mentioned in the eparchy of Peremyshl, there was already a Uniate bishop who had been established in 1610. A few days later, the patriarch ordained the abbot of the monastery of Mychayliwsky, Job Borecky, as metropolitan of Kiev and Meletius

Smotrycky as the archbishop of Polotsk. All these ordinations took place in secret, for in accordance with the customs of that time, the sanction of the king was necessary for the establishment of a metropolitan or bishop and the king would not have given his consent in this case.

The hurried Departure of the Patriarch

Having therefore established the bishops, the patriarch left for home. He hurried because such an important event could not long be kept secret and once it became common knowledge, matters could become very unpleasant for the patriarch.

On the way, the patriarch stopped for a short time in Bush, in Podilya, not far from the Moldavian boundary of that time and ordained three more bishops, by which he raised the number of Orthodox hierarchs to six bishops.

Finally he placed an anathema on the Ukrainian Uniate Church, on her bishops and on her faithful because they had rejected the patriarch and gone under the rule of the pope. He read to the Cossacks the "prayer of absolution", that is, he freed them from "mortal sin" which, said the patriarch, they had brought onto their souls because they had gone to fight against Moscow together with the Polish king, and he ordered them "not to march against Moscow any more". From Moldavia he informed the patriarch of Moscow of his success and thanked him and the tsar for the donation and hospitality.

The ordination of Isaiah Kopynsky took place on the eve of the battle at Cecora in which the Poles, together with the Cossack army, suffered a heavy defeat. In this situation the king, so as not to set the Cossacks against himself and disregarding the protests of the Uniate bishops and the even greater protests of the Polish Catholic clergy, accepted the ordination as a completed action and left the Orthodox in peace. Yet none of the newly-ordained bishops had an eparchy. In fact, every one of them resided in some monastery and was regarded as an eparchial bishop in name only.

The Revitalization of the Orthodox Clergy

Metropolitan Borecky evidenced the most vigorous activity. The following year, in 1621, he called a council in Kiev which determined the basic direction for further activity. At this council it was decided that the bishops, archimandrites, abbots, and generally all the clergy would work for the fulfilment and sanctification of life, that a greater attention be paid to leadership, that worthy candidates be ordained to the priesthood, that books and defenses of Orthodoxy be written and spread, that schools and fraternities be founded obviously to keep within the Orthodox church all those who had not accepted the union. The metropolitan published a message to the faithful, calling them to remain faithful in obedience to the patriarch and to the Orthodox Church.

The renewed Orthodox hierarchy and program which was hinted at heralded a stronger fight between the two camps.

The Uniate bishops protested the recognition of the Orthodox hierarchy and turned to the state officials with this matter, but the Orthodox did not neglect the matter either. In their name, a prominent activist, Drevinsky, stepped out very successfully in the local state council and he heartened the Orthodox Ukrainians with his speeches, letting the Poles know that they had to come to terms with the Orthodox Church.

And truly the Poles had to come to terms. In the fall of that year of 1621, a large Turkish army, three hundred thousand strong arrived, and having crossed the Dunay, stopped at Chotyn. Without the Cossacks help, the Poles could not have withstood this large army. The Cossacks helped and the Turks were defeated. Poland came to a peace settlement with the Turks which was very comfortable for Poland. When the danger had passed, all the promises which the king had made to the Orthodox were forgotten and their requests were shunted from one department to the next.

Meanwhile the local battle became very sharp and finally culminated in the killing of the archbishop of Polotsk, Josaphat Kuncevich (in 1623). This event shook the whole Ukrainian Church, both the Uniate and the Orthodox. Many Orthodox Ukrainians condemned this action and began going over to the Uniate side.

One of the most distinguished figures who crossed over to the Uniates after the killing of St. Josaphat was Meletius Smotrytsky. As has been mentioned, he was ordained by Metropolitan Theophan for the Polish eparchy. He resided uninterruptedly in the Vilenian monastery of the Holy Ghost. He was the son of Herasym Smotrytsky, a teacher at the Ostrosky Academy. He received his education at home and abroad and was one of the most highly-educated people of his time. He is credited in Ukrainian literature for the outstanding work "Trenos", in which he showed the tragic position of the Orthodox Church. After the killing of St. Josaphat, Smotrytsky left on a journey to the East to observe the churches of that area at first hand. After his return, upon reviewing the evidence he had seen, he changed his outlook. He immediately made contact with Metropolitan Rutsky and indicated his readiness to enter the union. Residing in the Dermansk monastery in Vilinia, Smotrytsky wrote a book on his trip to the East under the title "A Defense of the Journey to the Eastern Countries" in which he described the true position of Orthodoxy in the East and proved that the united Church erred in nothing by recognizing the "supremacy of the pope". But publicly Smotrytsky did not yet cross over to the Uniates and considered himself Orthodox. He believed that he would be able to persuade other Orthodox bishops to see the truth of his observations and opinions and lead them to union as well. However, he had miscalculated.

The Council of Kiev and the Condemnation of Bishop Smotrytsky

In August 1628, the metropolitan called a council in Kiev. Although the metropolitan himself had formerly shared the views of Smotrytsky, now being the influence of the other bishops and perhaps fearing the Cossacks, he took a different position. The council condemned Smotrytsky and his "Defense", laid the blame on him, and ordered him to withdraw what he had written. Smotrytsky yielded. He seemingly repented, burned his book, and in this way fulfilled the wishes of the fathers at the council. It should be added here that this council, two years after the renewal of the hierarchy, revealed in itself a perceptible power. Besides the metropolitan, the participants included: Isaiah Kopynsky, the archbishop of Chernihiw, the founder of many monasteries on the other side of the Dnipro, Isaaky Boryskovich, the bishop of Lutsk, Peter Mohyla, the archimandrite of the Monastery of the Caves, Job Gelizo, an abbot of Pochauiw, and also representative-abbots from monasteries of Podilya, Volynia, Halychyna, Polisya, Bilirus, and Lithuania. This proves that the new hierarchy was able to quickly enliven her activity and mobilize numerous widespread strongholds of Orthodoxy.

After the council, Smotrytsky withdrew his repentance and wrote a new book, "Parenesis", in which he showed a passionate love for the national question and its correct understanding. He saw clearly now how the Ukrainian national development was being held back by the enmity between the Orthodox and the Uniates and, as a result, how much the nation was losing politically, culturally and religiously. "Parenesis" means advice. In this book he advised, persuaded, and proved the need for union of the Ukrainian Church with the western Catholic world. He warned that the Orthodoxy of Moscow to which the Ukrainian bishops were inclined would bring no benefit to the Ukrainian Church. On the other hand, from union he expected greater easement in the state, the building of schools, churches and monasteries, enlightenment, access to high state offices and occupation of these offices by local powers, and chiefly the resolving of the animosity which the church division called forth. However his persuasions were unsuccessful and he did not live to see the fulfilment of his dreams but died in his prime in the monastery of Derman in 1634.

A few years earlier, in March 1631, Metropolitan Borecky had died. In his place, Isaiah Kopynsky, known as a "pillar of ancient orthodoxy" and an irreconcilable enemy of union, became metropolitan. He was one of the first Ukrainian hierarchs to begin the drawing closer of the Ukrainian Church to that of Moscow. Isaiah was very popular, especially among the monastic orders; he was recognized for his zealous work in the building up of monastic life, his foundation of new monasteries and his strong ties to Orthodoxy. There remains one significant letter from him to Prince Yarema Vyshnevetsky, that nobleman whose parents had donated great estates for monasteries on the left side of the Dnipro. Disregarding the wishes of his parents, Yarema left Orthodoxy, and dispirited by the Ukrainian interchurch battle, converted to Latinism. For this reason, the metropolitan sent him a message. He reminded the prince of the wishes of his parents, instructed him on the superiority of the Orthodox Church to the Catholic and called upon him to return to the faith of his fathers. However, his persuasions were unsuccessful.

The Ukrainian Nobility abandons its Nation and Church

The Vyshnevetsky clan was lost both for the Ukrainian Church and the nation. Others followed it, even those who remained Orthodox, such as the Oginskys, the Solomyretskys, the Puzynys, the Shpakowskys, the Domashevskys, the Kysels, the Stetkevych's, the Kostushkys and many, many other ancient and well-known names. Thus, thanks to its own ignorance and the instigations of foreign powers unfriendly to Ukrainianism, the Ukrainian national organism weakened, ate itself away internally and lost, from the political point of view, her most influential and most qualified social class – her nobility. If this nobility had joined the united church, it can be imagined what kind of power the Church would have stood for and in what direction the Ukrainian national rebirth would have gone. The Orthodox complained, and still complain today, that because of the Uniates, the Ukrainian noblemen converted to Latinism. But these had been Orthodox sincerely bound to Orthodoxy, and for some reason, their ties dissipated and the defenders of obedience to the patriarch were unable to hold them in the Ukrainian Orthodox Church. Those who fled to Latinism cannot all be judged as weak in character. They showed their strength of character for a sufficiently long time. When they saw in which direction the Orthodoxy of Moscow was leaning, they abandoned that church which they had recently so ardently defended.

Another Attempt at Union

There were yet other attempts of the united bishops to reach an understanding with the Orthodox bishops by means of fraternal understanding, exchange of ideas, and common councils. The main driving force behind this movement was the Uniate Metropolitan, Rutsky. Metropolitan Boretsky also sympathized with such endeavours, but he met such opposition on his surroundings that the good and wise endeavours of both the metropolitans came to nothing. With the death of Metropolitan Boretsky, the division took on a sharper course. The Orthodox hierarchy was firmly entrenched. In the metropolitan's cathedral, the Orthodox Church's chief spokesman, Kopynsky, took power. However, he did not remain there a long time. After a year, he was replaced by the archimandrite of the Monastery of the Caves, Peter Mohyla. Mohyla obtained a validating document from the new king, Volodyslav IV, and he took power in the Orthodox Church with a firm hand. This was a key moment in the Church's life and also to a certain extent in the relations between the Ukrainian Churches. For although the personal battles still did not diminish, nevertheless they were not as sharp a character as had been the case previously. The arrival of Mohyla to the metropolitanate dates the rebirth of the Ukrainian Orthodox Church and it must be conceded that this Church owes him a great deal.

6. Metropolitans Rutsky and Mohyla

Two notable figures dominate the history of the Ukrainian Church in the first half of the century – Rutsky and Mohyla. They were both foreigners, not Ukrainian in origin, yet they embraced the life of the Ukrainian Church, both Uniate and Orthodox. The accepted the national interests of the people as their own and sincerely served them to the best of their abilities. Both Mohyla and Rutsky left their marks on the lives of Ukrainians of that time and entered the history of the Ukraine as brilliant figures in that dramatic erea.

An Overview of the Life of B. Rutsky

Rutsky, christened John, came from White Rus from the village of Ruta and for this reason he was called, in the way of the nobles, Rutsky. His parents were emigrants from Muscovy and having settled in White Rus, accepted Calvinism. Young Rutsky was also brought up in this faith. He obtained his education in Prague and later in Rome,where he converted to Roman Catholicism. Before his return home in 1603, he changed from Roman Catholicism to Uniate. At home, Metropolitan Ipathy welcomed him very cooly, not trusting this young person whom he did not know and who in the short span of his life had been both a Calvinist and a Roman Catholic and had now joined the Ukrainian Church, Catholic in faith and eastern rite. For this reason, Rutsky left Vilna and returned to Rome and there again changed over to Latinism.

In 1605, he finally returned to Vilna and here under the influence of Josaphat Kuntsevich, again joined the eastern rite, this time for good. In Vilna he joined an order in the monastery of the Holy Trinity and took the name of Joseph. Velamyn was his parents' family name and Rutsky was the name of the village which his father governed. In 1609, Rutsky, who was more highly educated than many of his contemporaries, became the abbot of the monastery of the Holy Trinity in place of abbot Synchyl who had abandoned the union, gone over to Orthodoxy and thus completed his service. Two years later, Metropolitan Ipathy made Rutsky his aide and after the metroplitan's death, Rutsky took his place in 1614.

The Reform of the Uniate Church

The time of his metropolitanate was very important. Having taken charge of the metropoly, he set himself the goal of reforming both the internal life of the Uniate Church and its external manifestation. Above all, he established permanent councils of bishops which heard every four years and together reflected on Church matters. He brought discipline into the secular monastic clergy, strictly forbade the buying of church offices, organized the property matters of the Church, brought in archives where the given (property) documents were to be kept and finally reformed monastic life. Rutsky, who had lived abroad for a long time as did Peter Mohyla, had had a chance to observe the monastic orders in the Catholic Church.

He understood that the Catholic Church owed thanks for its success in the fight against Protestantism primarily to the strong organization of the

Jesuits. The Jesuits were an army, educated and taught in strict discipline and obedience. On these principles Rutsky thought to build up in the Ukraine the existing order under the rule of St. Thedosius. For this reason in 1617 he called the abbots of the Uniate monasteries to Ruta and established order. From that time monasteries were to be subject to one rule, the protoarchimandrite, who would in turn be responsible to the metropolitan. The protoarchimandrite was to visit the monasteries every year and care for the order and spiritual life therein. Moreover, all the abbots were to gather every four years for a monastic assembly or chapter. The metropolitan made this reform more exact with the Rule of St. Basil which he announced in 1621. This rule was accepted by over twenty monasteries. The metropolitan assigned the abbot of the Vilenian monastery, Leo Krevza, as protoarchimandrite.

Another important act of Rutsky was to urge the building of schools. The fight against ignorance and illiteracy had already been led earlier by Metropolitan Potiy. Now Rutsky set himself the task of training a new type of priest. For this he established, mostly with his own money, several school-colleges which were to prepare the younger generation for higher education. He sent the candidates for higher education abroad, to Prague, Rome, Vienna, Grats, Braunsberg and other important educational centers.

In relation to Latinism, Rutsky was a determined defender of the eastern rite. The Jesuits pulled many of those young people who studied in their schools over to Latinism. The metropolitan protested with letters to the king, to the pope and to the Polish bishops. When the Polish Catholics realized that the Uniates absolutely did not want to go under their rule, that the Ukrainian Church did not intend to break with her traditions and nationality and that she wished to decide her own matters independently, they began to change their attitude towards the union. Almost all the Polish bishops, with the exception of one Vilenian bishop, Volovych, took a negative attitude towards union and some even an extremely inimical one. Rutsky had to defend himself in this with messages, letters and complaints to Rome. Thanks to his untiring activity, the Ukrainian Church came out of this difficult position without any important losses.

The Attitude towards the Orthodox Church

In his attitude toward the Orthodox Church, Rutsky acted with great understanding and patience. He made all efforts to reach some sort of agreement with the Orthodox hierarchy so that this dissent could be fraternally settled, so as "not to divide Rus" and not to weaken her in the Polish state which was unfavorable to Ukrainianism, that is, a state which was largely formed and defended by Ukrainians but in whose government they had no voice. To this end, he called a council in Kobryn in 1626 and in Lviw in 1629, but the Orthodox bishops refused to take part.

The metropolitan took very badly the martyr's death of St. Josaphat to whom he owed his conversion to the eastern rite and whom he had set up as auxiliary bishop in Polotsk in 1617 and a year later made archbishop. In 1637, Metropolitan Rutsky died in the monastery of Derman.

Just as Rutsky defended those united with Rome, so Mohyla played a very important role among the Orthodox. Mohyla came from a prominent Moldavian family. He appeared in the Ukraine somewhere in the mid-twenties of the 17th century. He was already an archimandrite at the Council of Kiev in 1628, the one at which Smotrytsky was condemned. As far as is known, Mohyla obtained his education in western European schools, in Holland and in Paris. During the life of Metropolitan Borecky, Mohyla took an active part in the life of the Orthodox Church. He met with Rutsky and Smotrytsky and together they made plans for a settlement of the church dispute; if the atmosphere had been more amicable, perhaps something would have come of these plans.

The Plan to Form a Ukrainian Patriarchate

During Mohyla's discussions with Metropolitan Rutsky and Smotrytsky a plan for the formation of a Ukrainian patriarchate, independent of Constantinople, came up. This plan was approved by many other Orthodox activists. But the anti-Uniate feelings, chiefly among the Cossacks, were so strong that Mohyla did not risk trying to realize these plans.

After Metropolitan Rutsky's death, Isaiah Kopynsky became metropolitan in 1631. He attained a widespread popularity in the Ukraine, chiefly thanks to his zeal in the organization of monasteries and also because of his unyielding stance regarding union. In the following year, 1632, King Zigmont III died and for this reason an electoral body gathered to elect his successor. The Orthodox Ukrainians took advantage of this opportunity and made all efforts to have the former rights of the Orthodox Church restored. In this gathering, Mohyla, the protoarchimandrite of the Monastery of Caves, also took part. Having widespread contacts among the Polish nobility and relying on the help of other notable Ukrainian activists who were participating in the gathering, Mohyla was able to obtain serious concessions for the benefit of the Orthodox Church. These were the so-called "Articles of Reconciliation" which the king-to-be Volodyslav on the advice of the electoral body's commission, promised to accept and respect.

According to these articles, the Orthodox Church in the Ukraine was recognized as enjoying the same rights as the Catholic or Uniate Churches. Her hierarchy as well, up until this time not recognized, obtained a state recognition. Besides a metropolitan, the articles foresaw four more eparchies and the same number of bishops, that is the Orthodox Church was now to form a recognized church unit in which were included the following eparchies: Lviv, Peremyshl, Lutsk and the newly established Minsk. The Uniate Church also received four eparchies: Polotsk, Volodimir-Volinsk, Cholm and Pinsk.

Neither the Orthodox nor the Uniates were pleased with such a solution. The former wanted the return of all eparchies and churches and monasteries, disregarding the fact that a large part of the Ukrainians and White Ruthenians had long since crossed over to the union side and regarded this Church as their own. Nevertheless, the king ratified these articles in November,

1632, and in this way he greatly helped the Orthodox Church to get back on her feet. The assistance of Mohyla in this event is undeniable.

The Recognition of the Orthodox Hierarchy

Because of the fact that the hierarchy established by Patriarch Theophan did not have official recognition and perhaps for other considerations as well, those representatives of the Ukrainian world present at the gathering immediately elected Mohyla metropolitan. Mohyla obtained the decree and recognition of the king without difficulty. Bishops were also elected: Alexander Puzyna for the Lutsk eparchy, Sylvester Hulevych for that of Peremyshl and Joseph Bobrykowich for that of Minsk. A notable fact is that at the election of Mohyla for metropolitan, the religious clergy did not take part and only wordly delegates elected him. This is explained by the fact that like it or not, the religious delegates had to respect the living metropolitan, Isaiah, whereas the Orthodox lay activists disliked him for his relations with Moscow. Here was outlined for the first time the diversity of views on Ukrainian Orthodoxy. Mohyla and a circle of people who stood by him were for the kind of Orthodoxy which was not responsible to foreign interests but was to arrange its own matters in such a way as the interests of the Church and the people indicated. Isaiah was aware of his pro-Moscow sympathies which obviously were not pleasing to many Ukrainian activists.

Mohyla accepted the ordination as metropolitan in Lviv in the church of the Assumption, on the 28th of April, 1633, at the hands of bishop Tysarovsky, who was also the exarch of the patriarch of Constantinople, and other Ukrainian Orthodox bishops – Abraham, the bishop of Pinsk, Isaak, the bishop of Lutsk and Payisy, the bishop of Cholm. It becomes apparent that in this ordination, Metropolitan Isaiah, the primate-hierarch of the Ukrainian Orthodox Church, did not take part. But there is nothing strange here. The relations between the metropolitan and Mohyla had never been very good. They each represented a different world. Kopynsky was a staunch supporter of the "ancient orthodoxy"; Mohyla educated in the western culture, had very different views. Although he was a non-Ukrainian by origin, he sincerely bound himself to the Ukrainian nation, loved it and wished to apply all his powers, abilities and finances to help it at this hard time.

Now when Mohyla, without the sanction and knowledge of the ruling metropolitan, won the election and ordination to the metropoly, Isaiah understandably could not take part in the celebrations of the ordination.

Mohyla came to Kiev after a few months, having waited for the storm to subside, especially among the Cossacks. He removed Isaiah and locked him up in the Monastery of Caves. He issued a proclamation to the nation and the clergy in which he informed them that he had taken power and would demand obedience. He was not recognized for a long time by supporters of the former metropolitan, least of all by the monasteries under the influence of Kopynsky.

Finally the opposition was broken and Mohyla firmly took power in the metropoly. Now the Orthodox Church had a completely different form for she was recognized by the state rule, and both the Uniate bishops and the Latins had to take this into consideration Neither the former nor the latter were happy to do this. And although the king had given his approval to the Articles, nevertheless he did not want to grant them a council. To this end discussions. continued until 1635.

Again the Matter of a Ukrainian Patriarchate

These discussions again brought up the matter of the patriarchate, a Ukrainian patriarchate independent of Constantinople. This idea was favored by both Rutsky and Mohyla, two leading representatives of Ukrainian Churches. The king agreed to this solution as well, but the opposition in the conservative circles of Ukrainian Orthodoxy was so strong that the matter did not move past planning stage.

Unable to bring about a "general union" as he had hoped, Mohyla now turned his whole attention to the internal development of the Church, and the matter of relations both between the clergy and the monastic orders.

Before he was to be ordained metropolitan, Mohyla had founded a school in the Monastery of the Caves which he bound himself to support in a celebration speech. This school later became the basis for the famous Mohylansky College. How very concerned he was with the enlightenment of the nation generally and the clergy in particular can be seen from his pledge, given on the occasion of the foundation of the school at the Monastery of the Caves. Seeing in the Orthodox Church a great loss in people's souls because of spiritual ignorance and because of the lack of education of the youth, he said, ". . . I wish to remedy this great need" not for his own glory, but "for the glory and honor of the lifegiving Trinity, for the benefit and pleasure of the true-believing nation." A few years later, Mohyla joined the school of the Fraternity, which existed at the Monastery of the Epiphany with the school at the Monastery of the Caves. He brought in good teachers, started up a program of learning on the pattern of higher western European schools and ordered that Latin be taught, that is, the language which was then in use in higher schools, in the state, in politics and in education. He also took interest in schools in other centers, in monasteries and fraternities and in larger cities which were included in the metropoly.

In the second year of his metropolitanship he founded a new school, a part of the College of the Monastery of the Caves, in Vynnytsia, and in 1636, the same kind of school in Kremyanets was affiliated with the fraternity there.

The Renewal of Monastic Life, and Church Fraternities

Thanks to his effort and influence, monastic life was renewed and new monasteries sprang up in Mohylev, Kremyanets and Minsk. Like Rutsky, Mohyla paid careful attention to monastic discipline and tried with all his means to uproot the comfortable and carefee monastic life which in the era of weakened church rule prevailed in the monasteries.

The metropolitan understood the usefulness and power of church fraternities well. By this time, the fraternities had a history behind them and had formed a definite tradition, a tradition as defenders of the faith and the nation. Mohyla strengthened their net work and ordered the formation of fraternities in all the larger churches, monasteries and guilds, assigning them special rights and privileges. Such fraternities now sprang up in Mohylev, Bilsk, Pinsk, Kremyanets and in many other centers. Mohyla encouraged the Ukrainian nobility not to shun the fraternities but to join them and thereby strengthen their power. It must be conceded that his appeal was not in vain for the membership in the fraternities grew and wealthy classes of society joined them, thus forming a strong support for church authority.

Doubtless Metropolitan Mohyla was a sincere pastor of the Orthodox Church. But besides that, he did not give up the idea of uniting the two Ukrainian Churches. He believed that the difference between them were such that they could finally be resolved with goodwill. It is possible that with better relations in the church united with Rome and a longer life for Metropolitan Rutsky some settlement would have been reached. But it was a secret to no one that the Jesuits' colleges were pulling Uniate students over to Latinism, that the Ukrainian nobility was fleeing to Latinism, and that the church in union with Rome could not cope with this situation. All this obviously reduced the inclination of the Orthodox to a "general reconciliation". Latin orders began to push their way into the environment of the Uniate Church — Jesuits, Benedictines and Franciscans, and this aroused the suspicion that sooner or later the union would come to an end and that Roman Catholicism would reign all-powerfully in the Ukraine.

To the achievements of Mohyla should also be added his efforts to renew St. Sophia. Earlier this cathedral had belonged to the Uniate church. Yet for a long time St. Sophia was in a very dilapidated condition. There were no funds for its renovation, and since the metropolitans of Kiev had not resided in Kiev for a long time, nobody cared about renewal of this ancient church. Now Mohyla used part of his family wealth to renew St. Sophia. In 1635 he ordered the ruins of the Church of the tithe to be dug up. During this work, the relics of St. Volodimir the Great were found. This was a priceless treasure to the Ukrainian nation.

The Works and Death of Metropolitan Mohyla

Mohyla also had great merit in the field of publishing. During his archimandriteship many important works were published, mainly for church use. He himself was acclaimed as a good theologian; his "Profession of Orthodox Faith" was known in all the Orthodox Churches of the East. He also published other works — theological, polemic and pastoral writings, letters, messages, and memoranda for the defense of the rights of the Orthodox Church.

Politically, Mohyla was inclined to the West. Before he was tonsured into a monastery, he had served in the king's court, had numerous ties among the Polish nobility and was educated in the western culture. Thus it is not surprising that at first he was not trusted in the Ukraine. He was not trusted primarily in those circles which had long cultivated the idea of yielding to the "care of an eastern tsar". The Cossacks did not like him either. He was accused of Latinism because he brought Latin into the school of the Monastery of the Caves and he was called a Uniate because in accordance with his religious convictions, he always believed that one could talk with people of different opinions, and still respect the human value of the people. After Mohyla had been in Kiev a log time and had fully shown his ability and his character, all the suspicions were dropped and for a while his authority stopped the unhealthy orientation to help from foreign powers and encouraged the Orthodox Church to take charge of her own fate.

Metropolitan Mohyla died in his prime, at the age of fifty on the 11th of January, 1647. With his death, the Orthodox Church lost the same power, or perhaps an even greater power than that which the Uniate Church lost with Rutsky's death. Rutsky had been replaced by other talented metropolitans. It was more difficult in the Orthodox Church. Although the Orthodox lived for a while in the atmosphere of Mohyla's time and had such outstanding metropolitans as Sylvester Kosiw, nevertheless they were unable to create from the metropolitan's seat an authority which would be strong enough to repel the threat that existed at the end of the 17th century, that is, her union with the Church of Moscow and along with this, her complete ruin. Mohyla saw this coming and for this reason his eyes were intently focused on the one possible solution in this situation: the reconciliation of the two warring Churches. It is not his fault that he failed in this. If the political and church activists of that time had shared his thought and orientation, Ukrainian state and church life would have taken a different course.

7. The Mohylian Academy

History shows that those nations which care for schools, education, enlightenment, and upbringing of their citizens play a much more important role in the world than those nations which do not care for these things. There were in the Ukraine many intelligent people who understood this. There were princes, church activists and many lay people, well-educated for that time, who time and again called the people to education and the building of schools.

The Benefits and Losses of Education Abroad

However, building of schools and passion for education on a large scale began in the Ukraine with the growth of the fraternities. With the exception of the Ostrosky Academy, most schools were lower grade schools in which were taught reading and writing with the needs of the Church primarily in mind. For their higher education, the young Ukrainian students went abroad, to foreign, usually Catholic, schools. This had both its good and its bad aspects. The good ones were that the Ukrainian people and the Church gained enlightened people, but the bad effects were that very many of those students did not return to their Church and their people. Having seen now much higher the education was in other countries, these young people lost faith in the future of the Ukrainian nation and fled to foreign service. It was so before the acceptance of the union and not very different after the acceptance of the union. Ukrainian Church activists saw this and they tried as well as they could to prevent it. The Uniates had their own schools and even their own Seminary in Vilna for a time, but these were lower schools. Both the Uniates and the Orthodox sent their students to foreign schools. But with time, when the battle between the Catholics and the Orthodox had intensified, the Orthodox Church was forced to think about having her own higher schools. But for this, both suitable funding and talented, enlightened people were needed. Peter Mohyla was of this type.

In Kiev, affiliated with the Fraternity of the Epiphany, there existed the so-called Fraternity school from as early as 1615. Its first director was Job Boretsky, who was later the metropolitan. Boretsky, who was from Halychyna, had obtained his education at first in the Fraternity School in Lviv and later abroad. But this school in Kiev could not be compared to those schools which Mohyla had seen and at which he himself had studied. For this reason he decided to organize a separate school affiliated with the Monastery of the Caves. He did this in 1631. This school was to open educational possibilities comparable to those of western European universities and give a fuller, more widespread enlightenment than did the Fraternity's school. It was not very pleasing to the fraternity members that the archimandrite of the Monastery of Caves was starting up a separate school at the monastery, especially since it was in the format of the Latin schools. For this reason, a movement against Mohyla and his school began. Finally an agreement was reached between Mohyla and the fraternity members. In 1632, both the Fraternity's school and the school of the Monastery of Caves were joined into one, under the supervision and leadership of Mohyla and a group of teachers whom he chose.

The Mohylian Academy in Kiev

This was the first school of higher learning in the Ukraine. A year later, in 1633, this school obtained the title of college, that is, it was put by the state authorities on an equal footing with other higher schools in the state. From that time it was known as the Mohylian College or Academy of Kiev.

Youth of all classes were accepted at this school, regardless of their social origins — not as was often done in many Polish schools of that time. Thus the children of the Ukrainian nobility, Cossack leaders, rich citizens and also poor ones studied here. For the latter a boarding house was built at the Academy where a few hundred poor students lived.

The program of education included the teachings of grammarians, poeticians, rhetoriticians and dialecticians (who taught public speaking and debate), philosophers and theologians. The teachers also taught history, geography, mathematics, geometry, astronomy and foreign languages, including ancient Hebrew, Greek, Latin, Polish, German and French. The full course of studies at the Mohylian College in Kiev lasted six to seven years. The most outstanding teachers, whom Mohyla found among his own people and among foreigners, taught here. The sytem of teaching and generally the whole school was built on the pattern of the modern scholastic institutions, chiefly the Jesuit and the Piarian. Even the Sasiv goal Mohyla adopted from the West. It is known that at that time, Thomism ruled, that is, the philosophical system of Aristotle, elaborated and applied to the Christian world view by St. Thomas. Almost all the philosophical courses offered in the College were based on this system and textbooks for these courses were published in the West. Many such textbooks were supplied to the library of the Academy.

The College obviously had an outstanding library for which neither Mohyla nor his successors spared any expense. Unfortunately, like many other priceless Ukrainian treasures, this library did not survive but burned down in the great fire of 1780. At that time it contained may thousands of unique books, prints, and Ukrainian and foreign manuscripts and constituted the largest and finest treasury of the printed or written word in the whole European East. It was also the oldest school of higher learning, for the University of Lviv was founded only in 1661 ad in Moscovy education began to develop only in the 18th century, the University of Moscow being founded only in 1755.

Who studied in the Mohylian Academy?

From this school there graduated a multitude of noted church and secular activists, politicians, diplomats, writers, composers and many learned persons. Only a small number of widely-known names will be mentioned. Some of these were church activists such as Lazar Baranowsky, the archbishop of Chernihiw, J. Halatowsky, a prominent Ukrainian church writer, I. Gizel, T. Safonowych, T. Prokopowych, S. Polotsky, and E. Slavinetsky. The Urainian hetmans, for example, Samolylowich, obtained their education here, and also, state activists such as O. Bezborodko or O. Mylodarowych, composers M. Berezowsky, D. Bortnansky and A. Vedel, scholars such as O. Maksymowych and M. Bantysh-Kamensky, the philosopher H. Skovoroda, the writer Hulak-Artrmowsky and a whole line of other prominent figures in Ukrainian history.

Not only Ukrainians obtained their scholarly training here. The history of the College indicates that from its very inception, there were foreign students - Bulgarians, Serbs, Greeks, Moldavians, Moscovites (Lomonosov, one of the most highly-educated Moscovites, studied here) and even Arabs. That so many foreign students came there to study is a sign that there must have been a high standard of education in this college.

The College also distinguished itself by its publishing activity - the printing of books. Here the "Synopsis" of Innocent Gizel (1674) was published and the first history, which was the only history text until the end of the 18th century, not only in the Ukraine but also in Moscovy. Here the works of Halatowsky, T. Safonowych (a historical chronicle), Lazar Baranowych, Kopynsky, Dovhalevsky, Prokopowych and numerous others were published as well.

The Beginning of Ukrainian Drama

The College also rendered a great service to the field of dramatic art. At that time a passion for the dramatic form of writing was flowering in central and western Europe. The teachers of the College, who had mostly themselves obtained their education in the West, brought this passion in with them and seeded it in their own land. Thus these scholarly poetic dramas gave the Ukrainian theatre its begining. The authors of these dramas were usually either teachers of poetics or the more talented students. The actors who were brought forward by these dramas on different occasions were students of the College. The themes of the dramas were varied; there were Christmas and Easter dramas, moralizing dramas, vignettes out of history, and dramas of the people's lives and customs. Famed for the writing of dramas were such authors as Juriy Konysky, Thephan Prokopowych, Yakiw Markowych, Simeon Polotsky (a White Ruthenian), J. Gavatowych, Mytrophan Dovhalewsky, and others.

The Mohylian College played yet another notable role in the life of the Ukrainian Church. This was in the form of a preaching. Without a doubt, there had been some preaching done before the foundation of the College. Now, the teachers brought into the Ukraine the western style of preaching, the so-called scholastic sermon. The study of rhetoric and eloquence had an influence on the development of this style. Now in the sermon the preacher turned his attention not only to the contents themselves but also the the literary form of the development of the theme and its proclamation. Besides being religious, the sermon now acquired a literary flavor. Some outstanding preachers were Dmytro Tuptalenko, Joanyky Halatowsky, Anthony Radywyliwsky, and Lazar Baranowych. Some of them published their sermons and these may be read today with great interest and admiration for the skill and literary flavor of their authors.

The Mohylian Schools beyond Kiev

Based on the pattern of the Mohylian College, other similar schools in the Ukraine and beyond the Ukraine sprang up. It has already been mentioned that Mohyla founded a similar school in Vynnytsia and somewhat later in Kremyanets. Later such schools were to be seen in Pereyaslav, in Chernyhiw, and in Charkiw. On the pattern of the Mohylian school a similar school also sprang up in Moscow. Here its organizers and first teachers were Mohylians, that is graduates of the Mohylian College, or the very teachers of the College themselves. From this it is obvious what a collossal influence this Mohylian College had on the whole, national life of the Ukrainian nation, not just on its church life. It was the center of the whole cultural, literary, political and church life. If it had remained in such good hands after the death of Mohyla, its productive work could have served its nation better than it did.

During Mazepa's time at the beginning of the 18th century, the Mohylian Academy reached its highest development. Then it received the name of Academy and was called the Mohylian-Mazepian Academy for a time. Mazepa valued the weight and significance of this higher school and never spared it any expense. The Academy survived the hard times after the lost battle of Poltava and existed for yet another few years. Only after the abolition of the hetmanate during Catherine II's reign (1764) and later that of the final stronghold of Ukrainian independence, the Zaporizian Sitch (in 1775), did the Academy begin to decline rapidly. Then all the property of the monastery of the Fraternity, by which the Academy had always survived was taken away and distributed among the newly-arrived foreign lords. In this way, the Academy lost its means of subsistence and unavoidable collapse threatened. Although its spirit after the abolition of the hetmanate was not half of what it was during the time of Mohyla, nevertheless it had its tradition and was at least considered a higher Ukrainian school. When the Moscovites took over all life in the Ukraine into their own hands, this school was not wanted.

In 1817 the Moscow rule closed the Academy and in the same year, in place of the Academy, it created a church school-seminary under the jurisdiction and rule of the metropolitans of Moscow. Two years later the seminary was raised to the status of a Spiritual Academy, which existed until 1920, when the Bolsheviks finally closed it. But this Spiritual Academy of Kiev was in no way tied to the Mohylian Academy, neither in tradition nor in spirit, nor in its teaching. Being under the rule of the Moscovite metropolitans, it set itself the task of educating the kind of priests who would help the secular rule of Moscow in its Russification of the Ukrainian nation.

8. Church Relations during the Time of Chmelnytsky

The middle and second half of the 17th century was the most tempestuous period in the history of the Ukrainian Church, both Uniate and Orthodox. With the deaths of Metropolitans Rutsky and Mohyla, there was felt a lack of those eminent individuals who even in an era of great stress and careless polemics tried to find some common language and did not lose hope for union. The succeeding metropolitans, both Orthodox and Catholic, did not have the drive, the understanding of the political situation, and the diplomatic skill which characterized Rutsky and Mohyla. The idea of a Ukrainian patriarchate which Rutsky posed as a means to unite the Ukrainian churches and which was sufficiently favored by the Ukrainian Orthodox circles (especially Mohyla), seemingly persisted and even stirred up an active interest in Rome. However after the death of Metropolitan Mohyla, there was no one to continue the campaign. The metropolitans of the Uniate Church were completely unequal to the tasks of the times and the situation. In addition, after Mohyla's death, the idea of a patriarchate cooled off in Rome, which comforted itself with the thought that sooner or later it would be possible to assign someone with Catholic views to the metropoly of Kiev and thus a patriarchate could be done without. But Rome resolved the matter poorly. In the Orthodox Church there was found greater power of support and welcome than could have been expected.

The Role of the Cossacks

Significant developments among the Cossacks occurred in the first half of the 17th century. At the time of the settlement of the union (1596) the power of the Cossacks was not yet very great nor very well-organized and for this reason the antagonists of the union could not take advantage of it to any great extent. In approximately fifty years, the Cossacks grew into a great power, evolved a strong organizational base, hardened through numerous battles and now became a political factor which had to be reckoned with, even by the Polish kings. Now the commands and orders of the king were not being held to so strictly as before. For example, although metropolitans Boretsky and Kopynsky were not recognized by the king, they were not hindered in their rule of the Church. The king did not dare touch them now for behind them stood the power of the Cossacks and the king reckoned with this power because he needed it.

After Mohyla's death, the attempt of the Uniates to take over St. Sophia and the Monastery of the Caves brought on such a strong reaction from the Orthodox clergy and the Cossacks that there could be no question of these two symbolic centers of Orthodoxy becoming the possessions of the Uniates.

The possessions of the Ukrainian Church at that time cannot be understood without at least a short overview of the internal and external political situation of the state. For this reason, in examining the Ukrainian Church matters of those very troubled times, it will be necessary to touch upon matters which have an indirect relation to the Ukrainian Church, that is, political matters.

The political situation, it can be said, was to a certain extent favorable to the Orthodox. In the first half of the 12th century, Poland waged almost incessant war with Turkey, Sweden, and Moscow and was generally successful. Of course Poland needed the Cossacks' help for this and the Cossacks did not wish to give their help for nothing. For this reason Polish Catholicism, no matter how intolerant it was, had to leave the Orthodox Church in some kind of peace. Mohyla obtained for himself recognition as metropolitan, the right to build schools, and the legal recognition of four eparchies. In this way he forced the Catholic side to consider him an equal partner. Had he lived longer his wish to see the Ukrainian Church relations put in order might have possibly come true.

Poland was disappointed with the Union

Along with this territorial expansion and new conquests, an old illness tormented the Polish state. The overgrown liberties of the nobility constituted an illness which undermined the very foundations of Poland's existence. The Polish kings, elected by the nobility, were forced to indulge and satisfy the nobles' insatiable appetites. The nobility gained increasing power; the enslavement of villages, which in its beginnings reached back to the 15th century, grew to such proportions that life became intolerable. Such enslavement provoked displeasure and even revolts in the Ukraine (Kosynsky, Nalyvayko, Loboda and others). And in such an environment a church battle developed in the Ukraine. Obviously, this battle was not to the liking of the state, which had great plans and for the fulfilment of these plans needed the Ukrainian military force and some sort of internal peace. The union dispersed the Polish plans. There is no doubt that the Catholic Poland imagined union somewhat differently than it really came about. The Uniate Church didn't want to Latinize and become a bridge to Polandization. Nothing came of all the promises which were made at first to the Uniate Church. That church did not gain equal rights with the Catholic Church in the state, Ukrainian Uniate noblemen were refused state offices, and Uniate bishops were not allowed into the senate. Taking advantage of the discord between the Orthodox and the Uniates, Poland put the Uniate Church in a doubly difficult position. On the one hand this Church provoked the resentment and hate of the Orthodox for she was seemingly favored by the Polish Catholics, and on the other hand, not having help from anywhere else, she was forced to repel the encroachment of Latinization as well as to defend herself from attacks from the Orthodox camp. The Polish state, especially the clergy, saw that the Uniate Church did not wish to submit herself to the Polish Catholic rule and did not intend to become an instrument of assimilation but on the contrary, was making all efforts to maintain her own national character. The Polish clergy realized that they were to be disappointed in their hopes. Furthermore, the union, besides having cotributed to internal discord, complicated the tense relations in the state still further. Slowly a campaign was begun to forcibly Latinize and destroy the Uniate Church and in this way to resolve the tangled situation, to neutralize at least one front and then have only the Orthodox to deal with. The solution was simple: those Ukrainian nobles which until this time had remained faithful to Ukrainianism would sooner or later change over, it was thought, to Latinism and the Orthodox Church, stripped of its leading class, would decline. But it happened differently. The nation, having been pushed to exhaustion by the pressures and persecutions and arrogance of the nobles, flared out and destroyed all the enemies' designs. A new era began - the rise of Khmelnytsky.

The Rise of Khmelnytsky

The rise of Khmelnytsky was conditioned primarily by political and social considerations, but it cannot be denied that religious matters played a definite part in it as well. The union too collapsed because of the Cossacks at this time. Many churches and monasteries were destroyed and many parishes became depopulated in the whole area of the Ukraine, with the exception of the eparchy of Kholm which the uprising did not reach. The Uniate Church found herself in a very difficult position. By the agreement of Zboriw (in 1649) between Hetman Khmelnytsky and King Jan II Kazimir, the Orthodox Church was granted certain rights, while the problem of the Uniate Church was left to the decision of the regional parliament. But the agreement was one thing and the realization of its resolutions something else again. When Metropolitan Kosiw came to the regional parliament (the agreement of Zboriw guaranteed him second place in the senate, right after the Polish primate), such a riot sprang up against him that he left parliament and returned home, not having realized his treaty rights. It is true that the agreement of Zboriw was recognized by the parliament after long negotiations and pressure from the king but not one article of the agreement was held to. This contributed to new military actions, to the Cossack failure (thanks to the Tartars who betrayed Khmelnytsky) at Berestechko in 1651, and to the agreement of Bila Tserkva, which was somewhat worse than that of Zboriw.

The defeat at Berestechko gave the political thinking of Khmelnytsky a new direction and by the same token pointed the direction for the Ukrainian Orthodox Church. The victories of the Cossacks over the Poles at Batoh and Gvanets did not fundamentally change the situation and Khmelnytsky began to look to the north. In 1654 the Pereyaslav Pact was reached between Khmelnytsky and the Tsar of Moscow under which the Ukraine came under the "protection" of Moscow. At that time the Orthodox Church possessed four other eparchies besides Kiev, the metropolitan's see. These were Lviv, Peremyshl, Lutsk, and Mohyliw-Mstyslav (or white Rus). It was the fate of the Orthodox Church to play an important role here. When the Hetman decided on such a step, he found no support from the Orthodox hierarchy and this became evident very soon after the Pereyaslav Pact.

Sylvester Kosiw (1647-1657)

After Mohyla's death, Sylvester Kosiw, until now the bishop of Mohyliw-Mstyslav, became the metropolitan of Kiev. Neither the Cossacks nor the bishops turned to the king for permission to elect a bishop, but completed the election on their own with the blessing of the patriarch of Constantinople. The new metropolitan, a person of high culture, had been the closest co-worker of the deceased Peter Mohyla. He had obtained his education in western theological schools and for some time also studied in the Fraternity school in Lviv. As one of the organizers of the Mohylian College, he was a professor there and together with Mohyla, lived through the very difficult beginnings of its organization. By determined effort and by his wisdom he finally earned for himself the full confidence and respect of the Cossacks. At that time in the Ukrainian Orthodox world there were visible two different points of view. One of these views, represented by Mohyla and his supporters, among whom Kosiw was numbered, was more favorably oriented to the West was inclined to take steps towards the making of peace between Orthodoxy and Uniatism. The second point of view, represented by Isaiah Kopynsky, whom Mohyla had replaced as metropolitan of Kiev, belonged to the conservative circles of the so-called "ancient Orthodoxy" who had an unreserved orientation towards Moscow. As Kosiw now took over the direction of the Orthodox Church, it is easy to guess why neither the metropolitan nor any of the higher clergy took part in the Pereyaslav Pact. The metropolitan himself was obviously an unreconcilable enemy of the Pereyaslav orientation. When the administrators from Moscow reproached the metropolitan in Kiev for not giving his allegiance to the tsar, for not asking his help and not taking an oath of loyalty, he answered that he had not taken part in the Pereyaslav Pact, did not approve of Khmelnytsky's action and would not take an oath of allegiance. He kept his word, and however intrusive the representatives of Moscow were, knowing the character of the metropolitan, they preferred to leave him in peace and not try to persuade him to take an oath any longer. He proved a worthy successor to Mohyla and a fearless defender of the independence of the Ukrainian Orthodox Church. If the Ukrainian Church, Orthodox or Uniate, had had more of such bishops, her history could have taken a completely different turn.

The Attack on the Church after Khmelnytsky's Death

Metropolitan Kosiw died in April 1657 and a few months later (on July the 27th), the hetman died as well. After Kosiw's death, the hetman did not notify Moscow that the metropolitanate was vacant. He himself temporarily assigned the leadership of the metropoly to the bishop of Chernyhiw, Lazar Baranowych, and set the date for the election of the new metropolitan as August 15th. But he did not live to see this election.

The funeral of the hetman had not even taken place yet when the Moscow administrators were already taking advantage of the confusion which set in after Khmelnytsky's death and began energetically persuading Vyhowsky not to hold the election for a new metropolitan without the "blessing" of the patriarch of Moscow. They stirred up a strong reaction among the clergy, chiefly the monastic, by exhorting the latter to obtain the "tsar's favor" for themselves by recognizing and submitting to the rule of Nikon, the patriarch of Moscow. But their efforts were unsuccessful. The election of the metropolitan took place in December 1657, without the patriarch's blessing and Dionysius Balaban, the bishop of Lutdk, was chosen. How very interested the overseers from Moscow in the Ukraine were in subjugating the Ukrainian Church is shown by their letter to the tsar in which they ask what to do:

". . . and when they (the bishops) gather in Kiev and begin to elect a metropolitan, what are we, your servants, to do? Are we to reproach them for electing without your tsar's edict and without the patriarch's blessing. . ."

But the metropolitan was elected without "blessing". It seems that the answer from Moscow was to "reproach", for immediately after the election, the administrators began asking by what right he had become metropolitan, without the tsar's agreement or the patriarch's blessing. The metropolitan answered from the beginning of Christianity in the Ukraine, the bishops had elected the metropolitan of Kiev, that they accepted the blessing of the patriarch of Constantinople, and that he would not accept the blessing of the patriarch of Moscow.

Balaban and Vyhowsky's Policies

Vyhowsky, who held the hetman's mace after Khmelnytsky's death, did not continue in the policy of his predecessor. He immediately came to an agreement with the Poles and set up the Hadatch agreement with them (in 1658) on approximately the same terms on which the Zboriw agreement had been reached. The legality of the Orthodox Church was guaranteed and all her bishops were to have seats in the senate. It was agreed that the union would be abolished and that those Uniates who would not wish to return to Orthodoxy would be placed under the jurisdiction of Latin bishops. Metropolitan Balaban's sympathies were completely on Vyhowsky's side and he even took part in the agreement. But Vyhowsky could not obtain the needed support among the Cossacks and especially among the wide masses. The masses of the nation had suffered so much misfortune from the Polish lords and from so many unfulfilled promises from the king that they did not trust the nobility's word any more.The Poltavian colonel, Martin Pushkar, and the chief of the Zaporozhian Sitch, Barabash, started a revolution against Vyhowsky. While Vyhowsky succeeded in squashing the uprising, he did not remain hetman. The leadership was again taken by pro-Moscow circles and this led to the second Pereyaslav Pact (in 1659), which was to confirm the articles of 1654 and besides that to decide the fate of the metropoly of Kiev. At this council, the young hetman, George Khmelnytsky, understood perhaps the mistake of his father, for although he agreed with the articles of 1654, nevertheless he wished to maintain the independence of the metropoly of Kiev at all costs. For this reason he made the stipulation that the metropolitan of Kiev would remain under the jurisdiction of the patriarch of Constantinople, not Moscow. But he was unable to reach this goal.

The Pressure of the Moscovites

Influence from Moscow grew in these few years and more Pushkars and Barabashes, greedy for Moscow rubles and furs, were found. They outvoted the resolution that in the future the metropolitan of Kiev should have "the blessing" of the patriarch of Moscow who had already assumed the title of patriarch of "the Major and Minor and White Rus". From this it can be seen how quickly after Pereyaslav the true aims of Moscow became evident. The patriarch of the foreign church, disregarding the resolutions of Ecumenical Councils, had already claimed the title and right to rule an independent church for himself, and this at a time when the clergy of that church were defending themselves with all their strength against his protection and blessing.

137

There was no higher clergy at this second Pereyaslav Pact and the fate of the Church was being decided by secular people. Having realized their mistake, the Cossack leadership demanded in that same year the annulment of this resolution as unlawfully decided upon but the tsar stood his ground. Then Metropolitan Balaban left Kiev and went to the territory on the right bank of the Dnipro, where the Moscow influence did not reach. Not deliberating long, the Moscow administrators installed Baranowych as the leader of the metropoly. Yet Baranowych made no haste in making concessions to Moscow and selling out his Church. Along with this, there was great discord in the Church of Moscow at the time. Patriarch Nikon, who wished to be as great a master in the Church as the tsar was in the state, fell into disfavor with the tsar, was locked up in a monastery, and the patriarchate was ruled by Metropolitan Pytyrym, who was faithful to the tsar's commands. This Metropolitan Pytyrym, not trusting Baranowych, found a different candidate to conduct his plan. The eparchy of Mstyslav in the metropoly of Kiev was then vacant. Not consulting anyone, he ordained the Niginian archpirest, Maxim Filimonowych, who took the name of Methodius and ordered him to take charge of the metropoly. Metropolitan Balaban who resided in the territories on the right bank of the Dnipro, removed Methodius from power at once, denied his right to the eparchy of Mstyslav, and ordained JosephTukalsky, a Ukrainian patriot, as bishop of Mstyslav in his place. The Ukrainian clergy came to hate Methodius and also refused to obey him. Even Patriarch Nikon, either sincerely or because he wanted to take revenge on the tsar, condemned the interference of Metropolitan Pytyrym in the affairs of the metropoly of Kiev as uncanonical and placed an anathema upon Pytyrym. The patriarch of Constantinople placed an anathema upon Methodius and Moscow was again unable to set up its own candidate in Kiev.

The Death of Metropolitan Balaban in 1663

In May, 1663, Metropolitan Balaban died and his successor was Joseph Nelubowych-Tukalsky, who also resided on the right banks of the Dnipro, within reach of Polish rule. The king did not want to recognize him until 1675, nor was he recognized either in Kiev or on the left Bank. The recently excommunicated Methodius, from whom the patriarch of Constantinople contrived to remove the anathema, again became the leader of the metropoly. Methodius continued in his zealous service to Moscow, and to gain for himself even greater favor, he sent denunciations of Hetman Brukhovetsky (1663-1668). But Brukhovetsky had also been sent in by Moscow and to revenge himself on Methodius, he suggested in Moscow in 1665 that Methodius be removed and a metropolitan from Moscow be sent. When this became known in the Ukraine, it so enraged the clergy and Methodius himself that he, together with the clergy, would sooner have accepted death than a metropolitan from Moscow. Obviously the situation was serious. Even the administrators from Moscow (Sheremetev) wrote from Kiev that it would be better not to send a metropolitan at that time for a strong reaction could be expected.

The Peace of Andrusiv of 1667

Meanwhile there was a constant war being waged between Poland and Moscow for the Ukrainian and White Rus land, with changeable fortune for one and then the other side. Finally in January 1667 Poland signed an agreement with Moscow at Andrusiv (a prince of Smolensk) in which the Ukraine was divided. Moscovy obtained the left Bank with Kiev and besides that a large share of the White-Rus land, and Poland was left with the territories on the Right and south-western White-Rus. This was a heavy blow to the Orthodox Church. Now that the resistance of the clergy of Kiev had been weakened, the metropoly was formally dismembered. Lazar Baranowych, the bishop of Chernyhiw, who until now had been trying to decide where he was to go, hurried to Moscow to obtain the title of archepiscopale for his eparchy, expecting to make it the center in the event that the metroplitan of Kiev with the eparchies under Poland could not obtain jurisdiction over the eparchies under Moscow. There was no possibility that the metropolitan would be able to obtain these rights, for Metropolitan Tukalsky was a decisive opponent to all ties with Moscovy. He ordered that the tsar of Moscow not be mentioned in churches, but only the hetman (Peter Doroshenko). The bishop Methodius fell into the hands of the metropolitan who deprived him of his rank and sent him to an Umanian monastery.

But the hetman on the right bank of the Dnipro, Peter Doroshenko, did not survive. He did not fare well either in the alliance with Poland or in the alliance with the Turks. The Turks devastated the territories of the Right Bank and this angered the populace and further strengthened the actions of a pro-Moscow orientation. At this tragic moment for the Orthodox Church, Metropolitan Tukalsky died on July 26th, 1675. The metropoly was orphaned. Again Lazar Baranowych went to the top and thus, for the third time, he was the leader of the metropoly of Kiev, this time for 10 years, until 1685.

The Uniate Church after the Death of Metropolitan Rutsky

After Rutsky's death, the Ukrainian Uniate Church found herself in a difficult position. As has been mentioned above, the Uniate church did not wish to become an instrument of Polish state ambitions, but wanted to be a separate, national Church for the Ukrainian nation. This interfered with the ambitions of the noblemen and for this reason Poland began to re-examine its relation to her. It even went so far as the Hadatch agreement in which it was stipulated that the union would be completely abolished, leaving only the Catholic and Orthodox Churches in the state. It is not known what the outcome of this resolution would have been had it not been for the fact that the years immediately following changed the whole system of relations.

The era of Khmelnytsky, undoubtedly, seriously weakened the Uniate Church. The contemporary metropolitan, Anthony Selava (1642-1655), who at first had to withstand a strong offensive by the Latin clergy, could not find a way, either by himself or with any of his close co-workers, to convince Khmelnytsky that the Uniate Church was not an affiliate of Poland but a true Ukrainian Church close to the people's hearts. His one talented co-worker, bishop Terletsky, died in the very heat of events, in 1649. Two years later in 1651, after the death of bishop Krupetsky, the eparchy of Peremyshl went back to Orthodoxy. In the administrative districts of Kiev, Bratslav,Chernyhiw and partly in Volynia, that is in the areas where the events of the insurgence took place, the Uniate Church even ceased to exist for a time. The metropolitan, not receiving shelter from anyone, wandered from one place to another, being a sorrowful example of the decline of that Church which he headed. Only Yakiw Susha, the administrator of the eparchy of Cholm after it had become the possession of the Orthodox, did not lose faith or hope, and to a great extent the Uniate Church owes him thanks for the fact that she finally arose from the ruin, recovered her strength, and stood once again. Metropolitan Selava died in 1655. While on his deathbed, the metropolitan indicated the archbishop of Polotsk Gabriel Kolenda, a Basilian, as his helper with the right to the succession to the metropolinate. But neither the Basilians nor the Polish king wanted to agree to Kolenda's candidacy, for the nomination had taken place without their consent. The Basilians did not want to recognize Kolenda as metropolitan because every metropolitan was also a protoarchimandrite of the order and for this reason the Basilians required that their agreement be given for any nomination. The king refused to recognize Kolenda so as not to antagonize the Cossacks; otherwise, Poland didn't have any interest in the Uniate Church. Even in Rome there were those who willingly listened to Polish persuasions that it would be better to neglect the union and uphold the Latinization of the remaining members of the Uniate Church.

Yakiw Susha - Efforts in Rome

In this uncertain situation, Yakiw Susha, the administrator of the eparchy of Cholm of that time, went to Rome in 1664. Here he submitted the basic memorandum about the condition of the Uniate Church, about the zeal and loyalty of faith which the faithful and the clergy showed, about the deeds of the martyrs and finally he dispelled all illusions that the Uniate Church would ever Latinize and come under the rule of the Latin bishops. He was able to push through many of his suggestions, including one indicating that Rome should recognize Kolenda as metropolitan. This recognition took place in 1666. Besides that, Rome sent the Polish king Jan Kazimir a letter in which he was forbidden the use of the union in political trading. The metropolitan received a place in the senate but he (as predecessor before him), did not answer to the needs of his time and did not even take advantage of his position in the senate.

Cyprian Zokhowsky

Kolenda died in 1674. His place was taken by Cyprian Zokhowsky (1674-

1693), a person of indubitable talents, who had until now been the deceased metropolitan's helper, holding the title of Bishop of Vitebsk and Mohyliw. The era of his metropolitanate may rightly be called a turning-point in the Uniate church. Above all, he stepped out decisively against all attempts at Latinization and pointed out clear and unambiguous goals for the Church in order to obtain the trust of the large masses of people and become closer and dearer to them. In this he was slowly successful. After a few decades of chaos and ruin, he brought the Church to a clear path. His success was all the easier because those in the left Bank territories had already become convinced of what the protection of the tsar of Moscow and the blessing of the patriarch really meant. After the Andrusiw division of the Ukraine (in 1667), the Uniate Church recovered all its lost churches on the Right Bank. It methodically joined together even those eparchies which had been Orthodox until now, without persecutions, without unnecessary legal processes and without polemic battles, all of which had characterized her beginnings. Zokhowsky began to write a new page in the history of the Uniate Church.

The activity of Metropolitan Zokhowsky distinguished itself in two directions: the building up and spread of the Church and at least partially the ordering of internal relations. As has been mentioned, Zokhowsky took over the Uniate Church after uncommonly unsettled times in a much weakened state. In the final quarter of the 17th century, after the peace agreement of Andrusiw, somewhat more peaceful times were ushered in.

The Attempt at a Union of Prayer
In Poland, Jan Sobeski (1674-1696), who was sufficiently favorably inclined toward the Uniates and also tolerant toward the Orthodox, came to power. This created a beneficial atmosphere for the exchange of thoughts. At that time, on the Left Bank, there was a strong attempt by the Church of Moscow to bring the metropoly of Kiev under its jurisdiction, under a strong opposition from the Ukrainian clergy. These two factors, the more peaceful times on the Right Bank and the attack of the Church of Moscow, contributed to the fact that between the Uniates and the Orthodox in Poland there sprang up the idea of reconciliation, of healing the ancient enmity and attempting to reunite the two Ukrainian Churches. Thus in 1680 there was held the Council of Lublyn (so-called from the latin "collegium lublinense"), at which the Uniate bishops along with Metropolitan Zokhowsky and representatives of the monastic life took part. From the Orthodox side, Bishop Shumlansky of Lviv, Svyatopolk-Chetvertynsky of Lutsk, Archimandrite Varlaam Sheptytsky of Uniw, representatives of other monasteries, and also delegates of the Holy Cross Society of Lviv came to the Synod. The fact that the recently fighting sides had gathered to examine their differences in a Christian manner speaks well of the Ukrainian bishops of that time.

Possibly even then an agreement could have been reached were it not for the fact that the papal nuncio in Poland took a negative view of this dialogue and in this way defeated the purpose of the congress. On the Orthodox side, only the Bishop of Lutsk Gideon (Svyatopolk-Chetvertynsky) did not show any great desire for agreement, but his later activity and orientation explain why he took an inimical stance against alliance with the Uniates. It was his unenviable fate to subjugate the Ukrainian Orthodox Church to that of Moscow in 1685, only five years later. Another reason why the congress failed was that, as some historians speculate, the Latin clergy were not in favor of the growth of the Uniate Church and for this reason they tried to disband the congress. This is entirely possible, for the hatred which the Polish clergy felt for both the Uniates and the Orthodox had even in those times a well documented history.

Internal Reforms of Zokhowsky

The second action which the metropolitan undertook was the improvement of internal relations in the Church. The most important role in the Uniate Church of that time was played by the Basilians, the only Ukrainian order of that time, which after Rutsky's reforms (1617) grew into a significant power. Almost all the schools were in the control of the Basilians. They held the most important church offices and the most influential parishes, and from among their ranks bishops were chosen. There would not have been anything wrong with this if not for the fact that many Polish noblemen, greedy for comfortable church positions, had entered the Basilian order in the course of the 17th century. While it is true that they changed from the Latin rite to the eastern, they in fact brought many Latin elements into the Ukrainian rite. In this way, the ancient rite of the Ukrainian Church became slowly polluted by Latin practices, lost its distinctness, and gradually became closer to the Latin.

Besides using the Latin language in schools, the Basilians used Polish at school and at home, and this conflicted with the interests of the Ukrainian Church. Against this background, frequent disagreements and misunderstandings arose between metropolitans and Basilians. Such disagreements had existed during Selava and Kolenda's time and also during Gokhowsky's. In accordance with the customs of the eastern Church, every metropolitan was also the protoarchimandrite of all the monasteries. But this disturbed the Basilians, for they wanted to have an archimandrite (or protoarchimandrite) of their own choosing. Metropolitans, however, did not wish to grant the Basilians this right for they themselves would lose all control over the monasteries and would be giving the Basilians a free hand in their church politics. This dispute became very sharp during Gokhowsky's time. The metropolitan required that Basilians leave all the innovations in rite alone in order to stop Latinization. Together with other bishops Gokhowsky referred to Rome and requested that the pope order the Basilians to preserve a pure eastern rite.

Metropolitan Gokhowsky also cared for the enlightenment of the clergy. He set for his theologians, who studied abroad, the task of learning well the old Church slavonic language, for under the influence of the Basilians, the clergy had begun to neglect this language.

The metropolitan died in 1693. He lived to see the eparchy of Peremyshl change over to the union in 1692. In this, his service and that of his close co-worker, the bishop of Cholm, Yakiw Susha, were significant.

9. The Joining of the Ukrainian Orthodox Church to the Patriarchate of Moscow.

The Fight for Distinctiveness

After the division of the metropoly of Kiev (in 1458), church life in these two parts of the once great Christian society went various ways. The Ukrainian Church, although remaining true to orthodoxy, adopted many new ideas from the West. Ukrainian theologians studied primarily in higher western schools - Polish, German, Czech, Italian and other - and in this way brought the archivements of western education to their native land. Such was not the case in Moscovy. Here the western influences did not penetrate. There was almost no contact with the Catholic world, there were no schools, theological education was on a very low level, priests were treated like slaves and all new thoughts, whether in theology or in rite, were treated as heresies and were strictly suppressed. In the course of two centuries these differences between the Ukrainian and Moscovite Orthodoxy were quite significant and provoked among the Ukrainian clergy a distrust of the church of Moscow. In the Ukraine it was said that in Moscow there existed as many faiths as there were villages and as there were houses in the villages; it was said that in their lands faith consisted of not shaving one's beard and not smoking tobacco.

At the beginning of the 17th century, when the Ukrainian Orthodox Church found herself in a difficult position, some Ukrainian bishops began to look to the north, to the "Orthodox tsar", expecting help and protection from there. But these were only individuals; most of the Ukrainian clergy, especially those in higher offices, feared Moscow and that slavish life which the clergy of Moscow was used to living. In this way, two points of view appeared in the Ukraine; one was the so-called "ancient orthodoxy" which would have been glad to come under the rule of the Church of Moscow, and the other, the more progressive, was the group which wanted to maintain the complete independence of the Ukrainian Church under the nominal rule of the patriarch of Constantinople, as had been the case for a long time, but did not lose hope for a reconciliation with the Uniate Church. So long as the Ukraine was indepedent of Moscow, these pro-Moscow tendencies did not amount to anything concrete. But after Pereyaslav, the situation changed. Although in Khmelnytsky's articles there was no mention made of the subjugation of the Ukrainian Church to that of Moscow, nevertheless this did not prevent the clergy of Moscow from entertaining such pretentions and attempting to reach for the Ukrainian Church. The stronger the pressure which came from Moscow, the greater was the reaction of the metropolitans of Kiev against subjugation.

It is known from history how strongly the Ukrainian clergy opposed the Pereyaslav Pact. Metropolitan Kosiw didn't even hide his inimical stance to the administrators from Moscow and when the later began building fortifications in Kiev not far from St. Sophia, the metropolitan became decisively opposed to this and threatened to use force if they continued building. To the order that he should pledge allegience to the tsar and influence the clergy to take the oath, the metropolitan answered that the Pereyaslav Pact had occurred without his consent, that he would not take the oath, and that he would not enslave the clergy, who were free people. Immediately after this agreement, the metropolitan sent the monk, Krynytsky, to Lutsk so that the latter could write a protest under his name and the name of the archimandrite of the Monastery of the Caves against the joining of the Ukraine to Moscow.

A Change in Tactics

The decisive action of the clergy of Kiev stopped the attacks of Moscow on the Ukrainian Orthodox Church for a time. Moscow saw that the whole Church could not be undermined at once. For this reason it changed its tactics. Having undermined White Russia in 1654, that is, the eparchies of Polotsk, Mohyliw and Smolensk, Moscow immediately began imposing her own order there. The patriarch took the title of patriarch of Major, Minor and White Russ. In this way violating the ancient rights of the metropolitan of Kiev, and without asking whether the metropoly of Kiev wanted his supremacy or not.

How much Moscow wanted to undermine the Ukrainian Church is shown by the fact that in the liturgical books of Moscow was printed at that time a special prayer to Alexei, the patron of the Church of Moscow, which implored that the "throne of Kiev (that is, the metropoly) be united to the altar of Moscow which had been set up by God". As has already been mentioned, the times after the death of Metropolitan Kosiw (in 1657) were very hard for the Orthodox Church. After the short hetmanate of Vyhowsky (1657-1659), the hetman's mace was taken by Bohdan's son, Juriy Khmelnytsky, who at first was inclined toward the interests of Moscow. But when in 1659 the Moscovites passed the so-called Pereyaslav Articles (at the second Pereyaslav congress) which severely limited the rights of the hetman and placed the Church under the rule of the patriarch of Moscow, he left Moscow and entered into an alliance with the Poles. And although he and the Poles defeated the Moscovites at Chudnov, nevertheless he was unable to unite all the Ukrainain lands and in 1663 he gave up his mace. From that time on there existed two hetmans in the Ukraine, one on the left Bank, under the protectorate of Moscow, and the other on the Right Bank of Dnipro, under the protectorate of Poland. On the Left Bank, during Bruchovetsky's rein (1663-1668), the influences of Moscow strengthened significantly. On the Right Bank under Poland the hetmans changed one after another and this benefited neither the state nor the Church.

Peter Doroshenko (1666-1676)

The most brilliant figure of Ukrainian history of that time was Peter Doroshenko, a Chercassian colonel, who was elected hetman at a Cossack council at Chyhyryn in 1666. His first goal was to free first the territories of the Ukraine on the Right Bank from the Poles and then those on the Left Bank from the Moscovites. Guessing Doroshenko's plans, the Poles came to terms of peace with Moscow at the peace agreement of Andrusiw (in 1667) and divided the Ukrainian lands among themselves. This trading off of Ukrainian lands provoked inimical attitudes on both sides of the Dnipro. Uprisings began against Brukhovetsky and when in 1668 Doroshenko appeared on the Left Bank, the whole nation pledged its sympathy and loyalty to him. For some time Doroshenko had again united the Ukrainian lands. When the Polish army came in on the Right Bank territories of the Ukraine, Doroshenko named Damian Mnohohrishny as the substitute hetman on the Left Bank and he himself returned to the Right Bank to repel the Polish advances. The Left Bank did not survive and Mnohohrishny, under pressure from pro-Moscow circles, decided to recognize the protectorate of Moscow. Doroshenko ruled in the territories on the Right Bank of the Ukraine. In 1668 he signed a pact with Turkey with quite comfortable terms for the Ukraine and with the help of the Turks he took back from the Poles almost all the Ukrainian lands up to Lviv. By the Buchatsky agreement (in 1672), Poland gave up all claims to the Right Bank territories. But the populace, irritated by the Turks-Tartars sackings, did not support Doroshenko. In the following year, the war between the Turks and the Poles again sprang up and the Moscovites, taking advantage of this, invaded the Right Bank territories (in 1674). Almost all of Doroshenko's divisions went over to the Left Bank, to Hetman Samoylovych.

Times of Ruin

Doroshenko repelled the Moscow army and again took power on the Right Bank but finally, after long discussions, passed on his mace to Samoylovych in 1676. A year earlier (in 1675), Doroshenko's closest co-worker and friend, Metropolitan Tukalsky, had died, and the metropoly remained without a leader until 1685. The bishop of Chernyhiw, Lazar Baranowych, managed the metropoly for the third time in twelve years. After Samoylovych's occupation of the Right Bank territories, the dissenting Turks again set up George Khmelnytsky and together with him began a war against Samoylovych. They won over the Right Bank (in 1679), but the war created such havoc among people and property that the survivors preferred to relocate in the Left Bank territories where life was more peaceful. The territories of the Ukraine on the Right Bank became almost depopulated and the central and southern areas around the Kiev province and southern Podilya became an unpopulated desert for many years.

It is necessary to examine this historical period carefully and describe it more fully in order to understand the difficult circumstances in which the metropolitans of Kiev were forced to defend the independence of their Church. As long as hope prevailed that the Ukraine, at least in the Right Bank territories, would be able to maintain her independence from Moscow, the metropolitans of Kiev did not yield in their position. In those uncommonly difficult tragic times, they were a key support for those hetmans, for example Vyhowsky, Teterya, or Doroshenko, who saw Khmelnytsky's error and tried with all their power to correct it. Having to deal with such pastors, Moscow preferred to wait for a more opportune moment to enslave the Ukrainian Church. Such a moment came and suitable people were found as well.

Hetman Samoylovych and Patriarch Yakym

Ivan Samoylovych (1672-1687), a hetman of the Left Bank, earlier the chief judge during Damian Mnohohrishny's hetmanate, understood very well what weight and influence the metropolitans of Kiev had. He also knew their attitude to his pro-Moscow policy. For this reason, when Metropolitan Tukalsky was gone, he applied all efforts to have a metropolitan set up in Kiev, who would fully support his political views. In Moscow the patriarch at the time was Yakym, formerly a soldier, a person without education, semi-literate, brutal, and stubborn as well. History records that this Yakym, when he was still a monk, was suspected of unorthodoxy. He was taken for interrogation and examination of his orthodoxy began. Not concealing anything, Yakym replied: "I know no faith, neither the old or the new, but whatever the leaders wish, I am ready to do and will obey them in all things." After a few years (in 1674) he became the patriarch.

Hetman Samoylovych sought to develop closer ties with this patriarch, and soon opportunity for this arose. In 1683 the archimandrite of the Monastery of the Caves, Innocent Gizel, died and Samoylovych immediately hurried to the patriarch and the tsar to inform them of this and asked them to give their blessing to the new archimandrite which the monks were to elect. Of course both the patriarch and the tsar gladly agreed and the patriarch even expressed the wish to ordain the new archimandrite. But the clergy guessed where Samoylovych and the patriarch were headed and by an independent election elected Varlaam Yasynsky archimandrite. Yasynsky did not have any intention of going to Moscow for ordination. He accepted his ordination to archimandrite from Lazar Baranovych, the temporary leader of the metropoly of Kiev.

The battle for the metropoly of Kiev would have lasted much longer, perhaps, had it not been for the fact that disorder came up in the Orthodox hierarchy itself. The bishop of Lviv, Joseph Shumlansky, began to make evident his pretentions to the properties of the Monastery of Caves. This frightened Archimandrite Yasynsky so much that he hastened to write to Patriarch Yakym asking for an edict for the archimandracy.

This action was an indirect recognition of the patriarch of Moscow and his authority in the matters of the metropoly of Kiev. Meanwhile the metropoly

146

was still without a leader, for a suitable candidate had not been found. Now this candidate had been found.

Directives from Moscow

In 1684, a relative of Hetman Samoylovych, the former bishop of Lutsk, Gideon Svyatopolk-Chetvertynsky, came to the hetman's capitol. He left his eparchy, he said, because the Poles were doing him mischief and even threatening his life. Thus the bishop decided to protect his own life; he abandoned his flock and left to find a better place. Gideon immediately wrote meek letters to Moscow. Samoylovych was ordered immediately to elect the metropolitan of Kiev and along with this it was made unambiguously clear that the new metropolitan was to recognize the patriarch of Moscow, not of Constantinople, and that after his ordination he was to come to Moscow. The election for metropolitan was set for July the 8th, 1685.

This time the hierarchy did not live up to the trust placed in it. Very few clergy attended the election. Even the temporary leader of the metropoly, Baranowych, was not there. The clergy, considering such an election to be unlawful, requested a postponement. Nevertheless, the hetman's delegates and supporters of his policies did not agree to the postponement and elected Gideon as metropolitan of Kiev.

After this election the hetman notified Moscow, but it seems that both he and Gideon had a pang of conscience. The hetman in his letter maintained that the rights of the Ukrainian Church should not be violated while Gideon, who twenty-five years before had pledged his loyalty to the patriarch of Constantinople, did not know what to do with this oath now that he was to pledge his allegiance to the patriarch of Moscow.

The clergy of Kiev, seeing these electoral torments, gathered for another congress, protested the election, and notified the hetman of this. Along with this, the fathers of the congress asserted that the matter of the subjection of the metropoly of Kiev to the patriarch of Constantinople could be decided upon only by the clergy of the metropoly in agreement with the metropolitan. The Ukrainian Church, they wrote, in attaching herself to the patriarch of Moscow, would lose her ancient rights, to the great detriment of the Church and the nation. They pointed out the new order which the Church of Moscow had established in the eparchy of White Rus where a priest, for nonpayment of his dues of the bishop, was "beaten about the thighs with a stick", where the liturgical services were altered to the Moscow style, and where other illegalities had been brought in. But this protest was unsuccessful. A mandate came from Moscow that Gideon should come for his blessing with all possible haste.

The Subjugation to Moscow

In October 1685, the newly-elected metropolitan went to Moscow and accepted the patriarchal ordination on November the 8th. Here he placed an oath of allegiance to the patriarch of Moscow and to his successors. After his ordination, Gideon received two documents, one from Tsars Ivan and Peter and their sister Sophia and the other from Patriarch Yakym. In their document the tsars reaffirmed the ancient rights of the metropoly of Kiev, recognized the metropolitan's judgement to be the highest court, insured the free election of the metropolitan and the supremacy of his dignity among other metropolitans, and recognized other rights which the metropoly of Kiev had gained over the centuries. But the patriarch's document was somewhat different. He now called the metropolitan of "Kiev only the metropolitan of Kiev, Halych, and Minor Rus", thereby placing him on the level of an ordinary hierarch under his jurisdiction. In this way the final act of the subjection of the Ukrainian Orthodox Church to that of Moscow was completed.

Trades in Constantinople

Having taken over the Ukrainian Church, the patriarch nevertheless feared the possible effects of his action. Moscow had already tried to persuade the patriarch of Constantinople to give it power over the metropoly of Kiev earlier, but the patriarch had refused. In December 1684, when the candidate (Gideon) was already hinted at, the tsars sent the patriarch of Constantinople a generous gift of two hundred rubles and asked him to give the Ukrainian Church over to the patriarch of Moscow, claiming that this was the wish of the nation itself. The patriarch refused. Now, after the ordination and oath of Gideon, the tsars again sent a delegation to Constantinople with rich gifts. In Adrianople, the delegates met with Dosytey, the influential patriarch of Jerusalem, and began to persuade him to support their cause before the patriarch of Constantinople. But Dosytey was unyielding. He told them that "even for a greater sum" he would not give his blessing to such an unlawful act and condemned the Moscow patriarch's act as contrary to church canons. At that same time, Dionysius, the newly-elected patriarch of Constantinople, arrived in Adrianople to ask the sultan for approval for his election. After finding out about the delegation and its purpose, Patriarch Dionysius also refused to give it his approval. Then the delegates from Moscow, having realized that they would not receive satisfaction from the patriarchs, turned to the Turkish authorities asking that they order the patriarch to give the Ukrainian Church over to the patriarch of Moscow. Turkey then found herself in a difficult situation. Peaceful relations with Moscow were very important to her and for this reason the grand vizier called the patriarch and ordered him to yield the metropoly of Kiev to Moscow. While up to this time Moscow's behaviour had been unlawful and the takeover of the Ukrainian Church was a breach of law, now everything was canonical.

In May, 1686, Patriarch Dionysius wrote out six decrees: two to the tsars and one each to the patriarch of Moscow, to the metropolitan of Kiev, to the hetman and to the Ukrainian nation.

In the decree to the patriarch of Moscow, Patriarch Dionysius wrote the following terms: The clergy of the metropoly were to freely elect their metropolitan of Kiev according to their ancient right. It was not necessary that the metropolitan go to Moscow for ordination and as for liturgical services, the metropolitan of Kiev was to mention first the patriarch of Constantinople and only then the patriarch of Moscow. For the surrendering of the Ukrainian Church to the patriarch of Moscow, each of the eastern patriarchs, Dionysius and Dosytey, received a "favor" of two hundred rubles from Moscow. This was quite cheap in comparison to the thousand rubles which Mazepa, two years later, paid to Prince Golicyn for the hetman's mace.

The Ingratitude of Moscow

Who benefited from this trading off of the Ukrainian Orthodox Church? First of all, Turkey seriously miscalculated when she thought that she could buy herself peace with Moscow by paying the price of surrendering the Ukrainian metropoly to the patriarch of Moscow. The tsar's delegates had not even had time to cross the borders of Turkey when Moscow declared war on Turkey. The first to pay for this was the Patriarch Dionysius. The Orthodox clergy of the Constantinopolitan patriarchate, stirred up by the Turks, called a council, condemned Patriarch Dionysius for breach of church cannon and took the patriarchate away from him. Patriarch Dionysius, grieved bitterly, complained to Moscow in letters, asking that the promised "favors" be sent him for he, had done a great service to the tsars by having surrendered the Ukrainian Church to them. Patriarch Yakym replied that the surrender of the metropoly of Kiev was such a trifle that it did not merit special thanks or favor.

Hetman Samoylovych, who had contributed most to this action, wandered to Siberia for an unsuccessful campaign against the Turks and died there in exile in 1687. His property was confiscated and his son, who stood in his father's defense, was beheaded. This was how "faithful service" was repaid in Moscow.

A similar fate awaited Bishop Methodius. From the Umanian monastery, he was taken to Moscow and there he was condemned to life imprisonment in the Novospasky monastery, where he died in 1690. He was condemned because, having finally matured, he had come out against Brukhovetsky's efforts to obtain a metropolitan for the church of Kiev from Moscow.

Metropolitan Gideon did not enjoy his new metropoly for long. Soon after, the Monastery of the Caves and the Mezyhyrian monastery, the two most important centers of the metropoly, slipped from his grasp, for the patriarch of Moscow had given them the right to self-rule and had placed them under his direct control. The metropoly lost almost all of its church properties while the angered clergy refused Gideon the respect which it had always given its metropolitan. Gideon died on April 6th, 1690. He had had only four short years as metropolitan, but these four years sufficed to destroy the cultural gains of the Ukrainian Church acquired after many long years. With this cunning and deceit, Moscow took possession of the Ukrainian Church.

The Tsardom of Moscow spread with Orthodoxy

Who benefited by this? During the deliberations of the patriarch of Constantinople, Moscow wrote him that the metropoly of Kiev was too distant from Constantinople, that it was difficult for the metropolitans to communicate with the patriarch and finally that the Ukrainian nation "tearfully wished" to be under the blessed rule of the patriarch of Moscow. Moscow assured him that under its rule the Ukrainian Church would enjoy the same rights she had had up to this time and that she would develop better and work more successfully for the glory of God and the salvation of souls.

The early years had already indicated how false these assurances were. The archeparchy of Chernyhiw was joined directly to the patriarchate of Moscow; the wealthiest monasteries the patriarch removed from the metropolitan's control and placed directly under his own; the same order of enslavement was brought in as existed in Moscovy and in this way the positions of the metropoly of Kiev and its hierarch were made insignificant and without honor.

This was the time when the idea of the so-called Third Rome held sway in Moscow. Ancient Rome, the oldest center of Christianity, had served its purpose and when the capitol of the empire had been transferred to Constantinople, the New Rome had sprung up there. When Constantinople, along with the empire, had fallen under the advance of the Turks, then Moscow had inherited the right to be the third Rome. This third Rome, it was thought in Moscow, should be the center of all Christianity, for this was where the most powerful tsar resided. It was of no consequence that in this third Rome there were patriarchs such as Yakym, for example, who could barely read and write.

In truth, the tsars of Moscow and their patriarchs were not worried about Christianity. In the mid-17th century (in 1666), a council took place in Moscow at which the Moscow fathers expressed their Christianity and the mission of their Church in the following way: "that the tsardom of Russia, protected by God, spread by the use of Orthodoxy from generation to generation", that is, Christianity and Orthodoxy were made an instrument to widen the boundaries of the empire and enslave neighboring peoples. The fathers of the council hardly realized in what direction they were leading the Church of Moscow, but no one doubts that they spoke exactly as they thought.

According to this plan, the first sacrifice was the metropoly of Kiev, the greatest and most important center of Christianity in eastern Europe, a center of Christian education, art and monastic life. It had survived the difficult times of the Tartar evil, the times of the decline of the principate, the Polish advance, times of ruin and up until this time had been able to maintain its dignity and importance. It fell during the difficult times of Ukrainian national degradation under the attack of violence and deceit.

10. Orthodox Metropolitans of 1620-1690

It is true that after the signing of the union of Berestya (in 1596) the Orthodox Church continued to exist, but her hierarchy was greatly weakened. Two bishops were all that remained; the bishop of Lviv, Gideon Balaban and the bishop of Peremyshl, Michael Kopestensky, had not accepted the union. The fact that these two eparchies so strongly defended Orthodoxy in the western Ukrainian lands should not be explained solely by the individual characteristics of the hierarchs of those two eparchies. As has been mentioned, Balaban was one of the first initiators of the action for union. The fact that he, like the bishop of Peremyshl, remained true to Orthodoxy finds its explanation primarily in the fact that the Orthodox clergy, like the laity, having been in continual contact with Latinism, had such an aversion to Polish Catholicism that they trusted neither the union nor the promises of the Polish kings. This shows instead the positive traits of the bishops. Faced with the dilemma of which direction to take, they chose the more difficult path for themselves and for the eparchies which they led. If they had accepted union, they would have rid themselves of many worries, pressures and troubles, but they nevertheless decided to remain true to Orthodoxy, well understanding that they would be compelled to fight relentlessly for their Church. They counted on the help and support of the still-numerous Ukrainian nobility and of the monasteries, chiefly the stronger and more influential ones such as the Monastery of the Caves, of Dermansk, Pinsk, Suprasylsk and others. Yet there was too little of this support, for the most important support, that of a metropolitan who would lead the hierarchy, ordain new bishops, and indicate the direction of Church activity, was lacking.

The leadership of the Hierarchy

This temporary condition in the Orthodox Church lasted until 1620. In that year, Patriarch Theophan of Jerusalem, returning from Moscow, stopped in Kiev and here ordained Job Borecky, the abbot of the monastery of Mykhayliw, as metropolitan of Kiev, as well as five bishops - Meletius Smotrytsky, Isaiah Kopynsky, Ezekiel Kurtsevych, Isaac Boryskovych and Payis Ipolitovych. This was a very important event in the Orthodox Church. Now the hierarchy was strongly fortified, all the episcopal cathedrals were at least nominally manned (since most of the cathedrals were led by Uniate bishops) and the most important fact was that the Church had received a primate - a metropolitan.

Following is a list of Orthodox metropolitans of Kiev who ruled the Church until the end of the 17th century, that is, until the time of her subjection to the patriarch of Moscow.

Job Borecky

Job Borecky (1620-1631) came from Birch in Halychyna. As a young man, he studied at the Fraternity school in Lviv in which he was later appointed rector (in 1604). When a Holy Cross Society school was founded in Kiev, he took control there (in 1615-1616) and in 1618 became the abbot of the monastery of Mykhayliw. He remained in this position until his ordination as Metropolitan in 1620. An upright and highly educated person, Borecky, although not in favor of the union, nevertheless did not lose hope for a peaceful resolution of the internal dispute in the Church and took an understanding attitude towards the Uniates. He compiled the "Protest" in 1621 as a defense of the Orthodox Church and a year later put out the "Justification," another important work on the history of Church relations of that time. When Meletius Smotrytsky, afer his journey to the East, changed his views regarding union and decided to accept it, the metropolitan shared Smotrytsky's thought. Only after the Council of Kiev in 1628, which condemned Smotrytsky's "Apology" did the metropolitan, having considered the deciding attitude of the Cossacks, refuse to go along with Smotrytsky. In 1629, the metropolitan held yet another council at which it was decided to publish a catechism for the faithful. In that same yar, through his representatives, Borecky also took part in the common council (with the Uniates) in Lviv, whose goal it was to begin friendly talks for mutual agreement. Before his death he still founded a printing press at the monasteryof Mykhayliw (where he himself resided). He did in 1631.

Isaiah Kopynsky

Isaiah Kopynsky (1631-1633) was ordained archbishop of Smolensk and Chernyhiw in 1620 and took over the metropoly after Borecky's death in 1631. He was an unreconcilable enemy of union and led the so-called conservative circles of the Ukrainian Orthodox Church. The man himself was holy and sincerely dedicated to church matters and gained a distinct popularity for his development of the monastic life, chiefly on the Left Bank territories. From these monasteries he also had his greatest support and following, primarily from the Hustynian monastery. He wrote several works, among them the "Spiritual Letter" (about monastic life) and the "Spiritual Alphabet". Peter Mohyla removed him from the metropoly in 1632 and there is little information on his later life. Some sources record the year of his death as 1634.

Peter Mohyla

Peter Mohyla (1663-1647) was one of the most brilliant figures of Ukrainian Church History. He came from a family of Moldavian princes, obtained his education in western universities (in Paris and perhaps in Holland as well) and some sources indicate that he also studied in the Fraternity schools in Lviv. In 1625 he appeared as a monk in the Monastery of the Caves of Kiev and after the death of Zachary Kopystensky, became its archimandrite. Having attended the electoral congress for the new king (the Polish King Gyhmont III, died on April 30th, 1632), Mohyla gained himself such respect with the representatives of the Ukrainian nobility and clergy that, disregarding the fact that the metropoly of Kiev was already occupied, he was elected metropolitan and King Volodyslav IV confirmed this election. After his return to Kiev, he dismissed Kopynsky, pacified the opposition and took control of the metropoly. His most important action was the foundation of a higher school in Kiev which began to be called the Mohylian College in his name. This was the first higher school in the Ukraine on the pattern of the western European universities. Mohyla belonged to that type of Ukrainian Church activist who looked far into the future. Having been educated in the western culture, he was also oriented to the west. He maintained relations with the Uniate Metropolitan Rutsky and together with him considered the possibilities of the union of the Ukrainian Churches and a separate patriarch for the Ukraine. He raised the prestige of and respect for the metropoly of Kiev, chiefly through his work in the area of education and development of schools (in Vynnytsa in 1634, which school was transferred to Hoshcha in 1639 and in Kremyanets in 1636). An outstanding theologian and writer, he enriched Ukrainian literature with numerous works, among which the most important were: The Gospels for Teaching, Antologion, the Orthodox Profession of Faith, the Trebnyk, the polemic work, "Litos," and a number of sermons. He died at a young age in the fifty-first year of his life in 1647.

Sylvester Kosiw

Sylvester Kosiw (1647-1657) was of one mind with and the closest co-worker of Mohyla. He came from the Vitebskian eparchy and together with Mohyla, was a founder of the Mohylian College. In 1635 he was ordained bishop of Mstyslav, Mohyliw, and Orshansk and in 1647 was elected metropolitan. During his metropolitanate came the Pereyaslav agreement, to which he was a definite and unyielding enemy. He refused to take an oath of loyalty to the tsar of Moscow and subject the metropoly of Kiev to the patriarch of Moscow. All the efforts of the Moscow leaders, both secular and spiritual to unite the Ukrainian Church with that of Moscow, were unsuccessful. Like Mohyla before him, he was a supporter of a western orientation. His best known works are the "Didaskalia" (a teaching about the Holy Sacrament) and "Exegesis" a work in which he described the difficult beginnings of the Mohylian College. He died in April 1657.

Dionysius Balaban

Dionysius Balaban (1657-1663) came from a well-known noble family, known since the 15th century, which had great estates in Volynia and Halychyna. In the 16th and 17th centuries, three bishops came from this family - Arsen Balaban, Gregory, and Gideon. They entered into the monastic order which took control of the eparchy of Lviv during the lifetime of their father-bishop (1566-1607) who was noted for his activity in the field of education and the establishment of schools (in Lviv in 1585 and in Stratyn in 1596) and publishing houses.

Dionysius Balaban also belonged to this family. At first he was an administrator in Volynia in the see of bishop of Lutsk and Ostroh, until Kosiw's death. Having been elected metropolitan of Kiev, Dionysius received the blessing of Parthenius, patriarch of Constantinople. For this reason the church did not want to recognize him in Moscow and the metropolitan of Moscow of that time who, after the removal of Nicon, ruled the patriarchate, gave the administration of the metropoly of Kiev over to Bishop Methodius, whom he had earlier unlawfully ordained. Like his predecessors, Dionysius was an enemy of Moscow and when in 1659, at the second congress of Pereyaslav, the tsar's noblemen passed the resolution about the subjection of the metropoly to the patriarch of Moscow, the metropolitan left Kiev and went to Corsunia. He was a supporter of the politics of Vyhowsky and probably had an influence on the resolutions of the agreement of Hadatch reached between Hetman Vyhowsky and the Poles, according to which the Orthodox church was to get back her lost eparchies and equal rights with the Catholic Church in the state. But the resolutions of that agreement never went into effect. In October 1659, Vyhowsky stepped down and in 1661, a Polish state assembly rejected the agreement of Hadatch. Metropolitan Balaban died in Corsunia on May 10th, 1663. It must be added that although the metropolitan resided outside Kiev, nevertheless the clergy of Kiev as well as that of the Left Bank territories did not recognize the imposed temporary Bishop Methodius but rather the legal Metropolitan Dionysius, who possessed great authority.

Joseph Nelubovych-Tukalsky

Joseph Nelubovych-Tukalsky (1663-1676). After the death of Dionysius Balaban, the representatives of the Ukrainian Church and the Cossack leaders could not agree on who the next metropolitan was to be. This led to a division and two metropolitans were elected - the bishop of Mstyslav, Joseph Tukalsky, and the bishop of Peremyshl, Anthony Vynnytsky, a companion of Hetman Tetara. Both candidates received the approval of the king, which obviously was not to the benefit of the Church. A year later, the Poles imprisoned Tukalsky, suspecting him of activity against Poland and he remained imprisoned for two years. He was freed only after an attack on Hetman Peter Doroshenko. Tukalsky ruled the eparchies in the Right Bank territories, White Rus, and Latvia while the eparchies of Lviv, Peremyshl and Lutsk recognized Metropolitan Vynnytsky. Tukalsky was a fiery Ukrainian patriot, was favored by Doroshenko, and was his closest advisor for this reason, he was not liked either by the Poles or the Moscovites. Nevertheless, even historians inimical to the Ukrainian Church cannot deny that in the person of Tukalsky, the metropoly of Kiev was led by a very distinguished individual. His authority in the Church was great. The metropolitan died on the 26th of July, 1675 at the monastery of the Holy Trinity in Chyhyryn.

Metropolitan Vynnytsky outlived Tukalsky (he died in 1679), yet he was unable to unite the metropoly, for the king had given the title of administrator of the eparchy to the bishop of Lviv, Joseph Shumlansky. In this way the Poles wished to weaken internal church discipline and to make impossible the normalizing of church relations in the metropoly. After Tukalsky's death, Moscow again assinged Lazar Baranowych as temporary metropolitan and he fulfilled his obligations until 1685, that is, until Gedeon Svyatopolk-Chetwertynsky, with the support of Hetman Samoylovych, was elected metropolitan.

Metropolitan Vynnytsky was the last metropolitan "of Kiev, Halych and all Rus" who was subject to the patriarch of Constantinople. With him broke the line of metropolitans which, except for small breaks, had been in union with the patriarch of Constantinople for seven hundred years.

Lazar Baranowych

Lazar Baranowych (1620-1693). Although Baranowych was not the metropolitan of Kiev, his relation to the metropoly is nevertheless so close that in discussing the succession of metropolitans one should also mention him. He was a "permanent candidate" to the metropolinate and thrice carried out the functions of a substitute in the metropolitan's see. He was a noted hierarch of the Ukrainian Church of that time, a good theologian and writer, a preacher and a politician as well.

Baranowych received his education first in a Kievan school and later in Vilna and Kalish. After the completion of his studies he became a professor at the College in Kiev and in 1650 became its rector. In 1657 he was made bishop of Chernyhiw, having received his ordination from the Moldavian metropolitan at Yay. In 1668 he received the title of archbishop from the eastern patriarchs and the eparchy of Chernyhiw was raised to the status or archeparchy. He did not sympathize with the Pereyaslav politics of Khmelnytsky, although he did not come out strongly against the hetman. His contemporary, St. Demetrius (Daniel Tuptalenko 1651-1709) said about Baranowych that, by his clever politics, he had been able to win for himself the sympathy of Moscow while at the same time defending the independence of the Ukrainian Church with all his means. Realizing the value of the printed word, Baranowych established a printing house, at first in the Novhorod Siversky, and in 1679 he transferred it to Chernyhiw. During his lifetime, the press published over fifty books, which was quite a number for that time. Baranowych especially loved singing and kept the best singers (who were gladly snatched away by Moscow) at his cathedral. He was an outstanding preacher and brought the best preachers in to his eparchy. He wrote two collections of sermons: "The Spiritual Sword" (in 1666) and "The Trumpets of Preached Words" (in 1676) - of his poetic works, today there remain the "Lute of Opollo" (in 1671) - about fifty poems for the glorification of God, the angels, and the saints, poems about storms, spring, and the war against the Turks and Tartars. In these latter poems there shines through a great love for his native land and nation. Baranowych was also a polemicist and wrote an interesting work called "A New Dream of an Old Faith" (in 1676) in defense of the Orthodox Church. He is doubtless a very prominent figure in the history of the Ukrainian Church. If along with his talents, he had had a somewhat more emphatic political worldview, he could have played a very much greater role in his times. Baranowych died in 1693.

Gedeon Svyatopolk-Chetwertynsky

Svyatopolk-Chetwertynsky (1686-1690) was an ancient royal family from which came many Turovo-Pinskian princes. Gedeon earlier the bishop of Lutsk, having been deprived of his eparchy by Joseph Shumlansky, the bishop of Lviv, came to Baturyn, the hetman capitol in 1685. The hetman then was Samoylovych, who was related to Chetwertynsky and who was loyal to Moscow. Gedeon arrived just in time. Samoylovych had long sought a suitable candidate for the metropoly of Kiev which had been vacant since the death of Tukalsky. Perhaps Lazar Baranowych knew Gedeon well, for when he learned of his arrival, he commented jokingly: "What sort of eparchy can I give him unless it's the metropoly?"

Thanks to Samoylovych, Gedeon was in fact elected by the hetman's followers (in the absence of higher clergy) as metropolitan and on the 8th of November he received his ordination in Moscow at the hands of Patriarch Yakym, pledged an oath of allegiance and subjected the metropoly of Kiev to the Church of Moscow. In this way, in his old age, a descendant of a famous royal family ruined the flock which had been entrusted to him and became the executioner of the hitherto independent Ukrainian Orthodox Church.

Two years later, Patriarch Yakym sent a "questioning document" to Gedeon and Lazar Baranowych: "Do you not hold to the Council of Florence there?" The problem was that the smallest differences in rite made Moscow suspicious of unorthodoxy. Gedeon died on the 6th of April, 1690 and Moscow assigned the duties of administrator of the metropoly to Chryzanthus, the Greek bishop sent from Moscow. In this way the sad era of the succeeding history of the Ukrainian Orthodox Church began.

11. The Uniate Metropolitans, 1596 - 1713.

A 100-year Test

In this section silhouettes are given of those leading hierarchs of the Uniate Church who stood in her command from the end of the 16th century, that is, from the Council of Berestya, until the beginning of the 18th century. In this century the Uniate Church went through a severe test of time, protected her right to exist, proved that she was a national Church and at the end of this period, gained the two new eparchies of Lviv and Peremyshl and finally a stronghold of Orthodoxy in Western Ukraine - the Holy Cross Society of Lviv.

These leading churchmen and the metropolitans were part of the history of the Church. Among them were exceptional individuals, hierarchs of great form, while others were little known. Not all of them answered the requirements of their times; they allowed themselves greater or lesser mistakes and perhaps they used methods not to our taste, but in evaluating their activity, we should not measure them by present day standards but by the standards of the times and the conditions in which they lived and acted. It must be remembered that that which is clear and self-explanatory today because of the historical perspective of the centuries was not at all clear or self-explanatory in those uncommonly unpeaceful times. While the political conditions changed unceasingly, the kings and hetmans changed and their attitude to the Church changed as well.

To give objective characterization of the metropolitans of that time is a very difficult thing to do and for this reason the characterizations will be short and bounded by facts known through history.

Michael Rohoza (1589-1599)

Rohoza came from White Rus nobility, from the district of Minsk. He was ordained metropolitan by Jeremiah, the patriarch of Constantinople, in 1589. Just at that time, the patriarch, travelling through the Ukraine, approved serious violations of church canons, removed Metropolitan Onysyphor, and set up Rohoza. At that time Rohoza was the archimandrite (since 1579) of the Elevation of the Cross monastery in Minsk. Somewhat later, he also took control of the Slutsky monastery of the Holy Trinity and another Slutsky monastery (Morotsky) in 1589. He must have been obviously a popular figure and respected by the monks. There is little known about his younger years. There are surmises that he studied in Jesuit schools, but this is hardly probable for at the beginning of his metropolitancy he showed no evidence of distinct sympathies towards Catholicism. After some indecisiveness, he joined Potius and Terletsky in the action for union in 1594, only shortly before the Council of Berestya. Both Orthodox and Catholic historians characterize Metropolitan Rohoza as a person of weak will and little education, as one who was indecisive and unprincipled. There are inadequate foundations for such an evaluation. First of all, if Patriarch Jeremiah established him as metropolitan (in 1589), it must be assumed that he did not do this lightly but that he must have had some knowledge of his education and character. And if he had all the requirements to carry the great honor of metropolitancy in 1589, then why would he have changed so much in those few years? That the metropolitan hesitated and only joined the action for union in 1594 is not necessarily proof of weak will or lack of principles. He doubtless was well aware of the importance of the action and of all the difficulties which came up with it and for this reason he deliberated his future step long and hard. Instead, this hesitation gives evidence to his benefit, showing that he did not eagerly rush into major decisions. Understanding his great responsibility for the fate of the Church which he led, he gave his decisive word when he was sure that union had a chance of success. For this reason, a negative evaluation of him as a person and of his actions is harmful and unfair. Metropolitan Rohoza died in 1599.

Ipaty Poty (1600-1613)

The successor to Metropolitan Rohoza was the bishop of Volodimir Ipaty Poty, the most active figure in the completed union. Poty came from a wealthy Volynian Ukrainian nobility. He obtained his education in the Academy of Kracow. After its completiton, he remained for a time in the service of the Lithuanian Prince Radzivil. As a young man, Poty was not sympathetic to Catholicism, even though he had studied under the watchful eye of the

Metropolitan Ipaty Poty
(1600-1613)

Jesuits of Cracow. In Lithuania he converted to Calvinism but in 1574, he had already returned to Orthodoxy. In 1580, he was a secular judge in Berestya and in 1589, an administrator of Berestya. There is nothing strange in the fact that Poty was a Calvinist for a time. At that time, the Orthodox in Lithuania, seeing the decline of the Orthodox Church and not having any support from their pastors, were massively converting to Protestantism. Among them was Poty, but not for long. He did not find there what he sought and returned to the faith of his fathers. Now he began to seek other assistance for his Church - in union with Rome. In 1594 Poty was widowed (he had been married to the daughter of the Volynian Prince, Theodore Holovni-Ostrogetsky), took the monastic tonsure and in the same year became a bishop of Volodimir, after the death of Bishop Khrebtovych. In the following year, together with Bishop Terletsky, he journeyed to Rome in the hope of possible union.

He was fated to live through the most difficult times of the Uniate Church - her beginnings. In all the time of his metropolitancy, he was obliged to fight a zealous battle for her very existence, a battle on two fronts, against the hidden ambitions of Polish Catholicism and against his own people who were inimical to the union.

As a polemicist, Poty distinguished himself with quite a sharp style. From his pen came works which characterize the atmosphere of that time and are source materials for the history of the Ukrainian Church, her theological thought and her literary genre. The most important of these works are: "The Union of Greeks with the Church of Rome" (in 1605), "Antirresis" (in 1598), prepared by his order, "The Harmony of the Eastern Church with the Church of Rome" (in 1608), a list of sermons, published after his death, and several letters to Prince Ostrosky. Metropolitan Poty died in 1613.

Joseph Velamin Rutsky (1613-1637)

Mention has already been made of Rutsky earlier. Here it will be added that even during his predecessor's rule he had quite an important voice in church policy, especially in the latter years of Poty's metropolitanate. Rutsky decided to develop the Church from the inside. He saw very clearly how great a power was manifest by the Jesuits; thus he decided first of all to reorganize the monastic order of the Basilians. He wished to create a stronghold of the Uniate Church, an early defense against Latinism and a force attractive to the Orthodox monasteries and monks. This reform of monastic life and administrative centralization, begun in 1617, must be regarded as one of his most important achievements. The Uniate monasteries at that time found themselves in conditions which were possibly even worst than those of the Orthodox monasteries. Many Poles were joining the order, superficially accepting the eastern rite but remaining whoever they were in their souls. Slowly they began to bring in Latin practices in the monasteries, removing altars, iconostases, in a word, reforming the rite in a Latin way. Understandably, a worse service to union could not be thought up. For this

Metropolitan Joseph Velamin Rutsky
(1613-1637)

reason Rutsky took to making repairs with all his energy. In 1616 he set up the novitiate in Byten and three schools (colleges) in Vilno, Minsk, and Novhorodok. For higher theological studies he sent the students to foreign universities abroad and when they were forcibly drawn to Catholicism there, he protested with such force that finally even Rome forbade such practices. The forbidding of the pulling over or voluntary going over from the Uniate Church to Catholicism (Decree of Urban VIII, 1624) called out a moment of anger in Poland and further strengthened the hatred of the Uniates.

In 1626 the metropolitan called a council at Cobryn which concerned itself with the internal matters of the Church. From that time on the bishops were to gather every four years and together deliberate on the matters of the Church. Eparchial archives were begun, discipline and order among the clergy was brought in, and finally a serious vice of the Church was condemend. This vice was simony, that is, the obtaining of church offices for money.

These two matters, the reform of the monasteries and the ordering of the internal life of the Church, were the most important actions of Rutsky. If not for this, then the flight of clergy and laity to the foreign camp would have brought the Uniate Church to an unavoidable end.

The Orthodox metropolitan Rutsky's contemporary, was Borecky. Then in the 1620's, for the first time, the idea of a patriarchate of Kiev came up, gaining for itself the support of Borecky and other Orthodox bishops. Then the rector of the college at Kiev, Cassian Sakovych, joined the cause of union (and later went over to the Latins) along with Cyril Tranquilion Stavrovetsky, a professor of the Fraternity school in Lviv and Meletius Smotrytsky, the Polotsk archbishop, to name just the more prominent activists of the Orthodox world. The cause of union was unsuccessful, but Rutsky continued in it until the end of his life. In 1629 he tried his luck at the common council with the Orthodox in Lviv, but here the papal nuncio interfered, being against the common council. The succeeding years brought heavy losses to both the Uniates and Orthodox. In 1632 Metropolitan Boretsky died and a year later Smotrytsky died. With the election of Volodyslav IV as king and his "Articles" (of 1632) about the interrelations between the Uniates and the Orthodox, the plans for Ukrainian church union became unrealistic. Nevertheless, Rutsky maintained quite friendly relations, for example, with Puzyna, the bishop of Lutsk (1636) with Drevynsky, with Peter Mohyla, and with others. Metropolitan Rutsky died in Derman in Volynia in 1637.

Raphael Korsak (1637-1642)

Korsak, with the title of bishop of Lviv, was a helper of Rutsky's since 1626. Somewhat later he was the bishop of Pinsk and after Rutsky's death, he became metropolitan. He tried to follow and continue the policies of Rutsky but he could compare with him neither in learning nor in talent. He died in Rome, where he had gone concerning matters of his Church, and was buried there in 1642.

Metropolitan Raphael Korsak
(1637-1640)

Anthony Selava (1642-1655)

After Josaphat Kuncevych's death, Selava became the archbishop of Polotsk. Earlier he had been the abbot of the Vilenian monastery and in the 1620's took an active part in religious polemics. During his lifetime the insurgencies and wars of Khmelnytsky with Poland took place. As has been mentioned, the Uniate Church, in the face of wartime events, suffered significant blows. But this was not the end of the disaster. The worse matters went for the Poles at the front, the more determinedly the Polish clergy tormented the Uniate Church, seeing in her one of the reasons for the agitation in the state. The Latin hierarchs refused the Uniate bishops their titles (they could not endure the fact that the Uniate bishops wanted themselves called, according to their tradition, "ever-more-brilliant"), demanded that they pay them (the Latin bishops), the respect of a title, denied them the right of separate spiritual seminaries and schools, and allowed themselves other chicaneries.

Selava defended himself against these attacks as well as he could, with memoranda to Rome, to the nuncio in Warsaw and with urgings to his bishops to stand in battle until the end and not let themselves be swallowed up. A key role in this battle was played by Methodius Terletsky, the bishop of Cholm. A man of good education, with important contacts abroad and besides that an ardent pastor - he actually carried the main burden of battle on his own shoulders.

During Selava's rule, the matter of a patriarchate again came up. As has been mentioned, in that period even Metropolitan Mohyla had certain hopes for the success of such a solution and had given a projection of his own to Rome along with conditions for agreement. But the matter was put off in Rome and when the pope turned to Selava for more detailed information, it was already too late, for Mohyla had died.

The metropolitan had no sympathy with the monks. The Basilians elected him protoarchimandrite only when he promised that in the future his successor would have no pretentions to the protoarchimandriteship and that they would be able to elect their own protoarchimandrite with free votes.

Gabriel Kolenda (1655-1674)

Before his death, Selava, without consulting the Basilians, assigned as his successor, the Polish archbishop Kolenda. Immediately after the death of the metropolitan, Kolenda obviously made pretensions to the protoarchimandriteship. In answer, the Basilians called an assembly of representatives of all monasteries in Torokany (in 1656) and elected Benedict Terletsky as provincial for two years (instead of protoarchimandrite). But Kolenda did not even want to hear of this. Gathering an assembly of representatives of monasteries favorable to him, he held his own election in Suprals. The opposition, with Terletsky as provincial, protested the metropolitan's deed (at an assembly in Vilna in 1661) and sent delegates to the nuncio with a complaint about the unlawful seizing of power in the order by the metropolitan. For this Kolenda anathematized Terletsky.

Metropolitan Gabriel Kolenda
(1655-1674)

After Terletsky's death, the order held a new assembly in Gyrowytsi (in 1661) and here elected Jacob Susha, the bishop of Cholm, as protoarchimandrite and gave him the task of going to Rome for a definitive resolution of the matter. To resolve the matter somewhat, the pope made Kolenda (up until now administrator) metropolitan but rejected both of the previous assemblies of the order and ordered a new election of protoarchimandrite to take place. The assembly took place in Suprasl (in 1665) but now the election again favored the metroppolitan, which was contrary to the will of the pope who had ordered that the protoarchimandrite be elected from among the ordinary monks. Hearing of this, the nuncio declared the election invalid and began to call a new assembly in Berestya-Lytovsk (on the first day of March, 1666). When the nuncio at this assembly declared that Rome's conditions be respected and that the metropolitan not be elected protoarchimandrite, he was told that the good of the Church and the order required that there be but one Church authority and not two. Even Susha now agreed that only the metropolitan could bring back harmony and order within the order. The metropolitan was elected protoarchimandrate but he had taken an oath of loyalty to the order and he guaranteed the Basilians the right to a free election of the protoarchimandrite in the future.

Kolenda really did not spare any effort and until the end of his life he tried with all his powers to restore monastic life and bring in some sort of discipline. He taxed the monasteries for new novitiates, ordered an exact adherence to the monastic rule, encouraged the archimandrites to reject all types of kingly privileges, which they had obtained without the agreement of the order, and he carefully watched over the fulfilment of his orders. Generally speaking, Kolenda does not receive the sympathy of Ukrainian historians; however this era is still too inadequately known about to allow a definitive judgment to be rendered. Kolenda died in 1674.

Cyprian Zokhowsky (1674-1693)

Kolenda's coadjutor, with the right of succession, was Cyprian Zokhowsky, the bishop of Vitebsk and Mohyliw. He was an important figure in the history of Ukrainian Church. He obtained his theological education in Rome, was naturally well-gifted, of strong will, and had a clean slate. Zokhowsky was more suited than anyone else to the difficult post of metropolitan. But the twelve years in which he controlled the Ukrainian Church were an unceasing battle, not so much with a foreign camp as with his own Basilian order. Although Kolenda had given his word that the succeeding metropolitan would have no pretensions to the protoarchimandriteship, nevertheless Zokhowsky considered himself the legal successor both in the metropoly and in the order. In 1675, at the assembly of Zyrowytsi, it is true that, under pressure from the Basilians, he agreed to the election of Pakhomy Ohylevych as protoarchimandrite. However, he immediately saw that the Basilians' ambitions did not end there. They elected a line of other pretensions, which, if approved, would bring the metropolitan's control of the

Metropolitan Cyprian Zokhowsky
(1674-1693)

order to virtually nothing. Examining the situation more carefully, the metropolitan saw that practices were springing up in the monasteries which were very different from those imposed by the rule.

The Fight with the Basilians

Disregarding the deficiencies in the character of the administration, the monasteries began to bring innovations into the rite, to change liturgical services, remove iconostases and show a tendency to free themselves completely from dependence on the metropolitan. The metropolitan could not endure this. In 1683 he called an assembly in Minsk and here the supporters of the purity of the Ukrainian rite elected Zokhowsky as protoarchimandrite, disregarding the protests of the Latinizing wing of the order. Zokhowsky's opponents sent a complaint to Rome and Pope Innocent XI nullified the assembly at Minsk and returned the former protoarchimandrite his rights. For this, Zokhowsky called a new assembly to Novhorodok, the capitol of the metropoly of that time, and the fathers present, having confirmed the former assembly of Minsk, again turned to the metropolitan with the "humble request" that he accept the rule of the protoarchimandrite and in this way avoid the anarchies in the Church.

When Rome found out that the assembly had once again elected the metropolitan as archimandrite, it decided once and for all to push the metropolitan out of this office. The Novhorodok assembly was nullified and a new one called (in 1686) under the direction of the Jesuit, Thomas Uyeysky. Joseph Petkevych, the secretary of the order of a faction antagonistic to the metropolitan, was elected protoarchimandrite. A separate resolution guaranteed the protoarchimandrite great powers. Without his consent the metropolitan did not have the right to assign any hierarchal honors, that is, to ordain new bishops. When the assembly elected bishops (after Lev Zalensky's death), first the administrator of the metropoly and later (in 1708) Metropolitan George Vynnytsky, then the superior of the Basilians of that time, protested this election as illegal and only with his agreement (in 1709) could this government begin to act. Until the end of his life, Zokhowsky had many difficulties with the Basilians, including the complaints before the Polish tribunal.

The success of the Basilian order in establishing its rights did not help the interests of the Uniate Church. A danger was that the Uniate Church would lose the national character which her leading hierarchs at that time, especially Zokhowsky, cared so much for.

Having so many troubles with the Basilians, the metropolitan nevertheless found enough energy for the growth of the Church, for the foundation of schools and publishing houses, for the improvement of religious life, for contact with the Orthodox, and finally, for at least a partial cleaning up of the rite which had been polluted by the Basilian innovations.

An Attempt at Dialogue

In January 1680, with the agreement of King Jan Sobesky, a conference of

Orthodox and Uniate Bishops took place in Lublyn. The situation at the time was such that hopes could be placed on the successful outcome of this "dialogue". The metropoly of Kiev (Orthodox), after the death of Tukalsky, was subject to great pressure from Moscow. The clergy of Kiev defended itself against Moscow with all its strength, and having in mind Zokhowsky's beneficial actions as a fighter for the national outlook of the Church, evidenced a favorable attitude to an understanding. Unfortunately again in this instance the papal nuncio opposed a common council. It was postponed to a later date but in the end it never took place. Zokhowsky lived to see (and to a great extent this was due to his own efforts) the eparchy of Peremyshl transfer to the Uniates (in 1692).

Leo Zalensky (1694-1708)

Leo Zalensky is a little-known figure though he held not only the post of metropolitan but also the eparchy of Volodimir, the archeparchy of Polotsk and the abbotship of Derman and Budno. This mound of positions and duties did not give him any opportunity to apply himself more fully to the duties of metropolitan. It is true that the Uniate Church spread during his rule; the eparchy of Lviv joined the union in 1700 and two years later so did that of Lutsk and finally (in 1708) that of the Holy Cross Society of Lviv. However, this was more due to the efforts of Zalensky's predecessor, who had created suitable conditions for this spread.

Zalensky had an active interest in the politics of that time and even took part in it somewhat. This was the time of the so-called Northern war. When Karl XII conquered Poland, he set up Stanislav Leshchynsky (in 1704) as king. Through Mazepa, Zalensky kept continuous contact with this Leshchynsky during the gathering of an anti-Moscow coalition (of Mazepa, Karl XII and Leshchynsky). It is possible that had the battle at Poltava (in 1709) been successful, the future of the Ukrainian Church would have been very different.

The consolidation of the Uniate Church, after difficult times of battle during development and formation, formed itself during a definite era. It was close with the Holy Cross Society's acceptance of union (in 1708). Having survived the beginnings of sharp polemic attempts at Latinization, destruction during war in the mid-17th century, the Uniate Church finally took root and became a strong body in all the Right Bank territories and western Ukrainian Lands, including the region beyond the Carpathians.

In an overview of the metropolitans of that time, stronger and weaker characters can be found, yet one thing characterizes them all - the desire to protect the church's ritual and national distinctness. They were successful in maintaining this distinctness (remembering the Latinizing tendencies of several Basilian monasteries). And this was important, for with this gain the Church would enter the following century, a century in which she would meet Moscow's "favor" face-to-face.

12. The Transfer to Union of the Western Ukrainian Eparchies.

The Church in Carpathian Ukraine

The organization of the Church in Carpathian Ukraine took place at the end of the 14th century. Doubtless, by this time Christianity was widespread and there were churches and monasteries there, but there is no definite information about the beginnings of the church organization. In all probability, the control of churches until the establishment of episcopates fell to the monasteries on the eastern side - the Hrushiwsky monastery, which received its independence in 1391, and in Mukachiv, the monastery of St. Nicholas. The bishops of Peremyshl had jurisdiction over the western section and fulfilled this duty until the end of 15th century.

Contributing much to the organization of church life was King Theodore Koriatovych who, being persecuted by Olgerd, the great Lithuanian prince, left his principate in Podilya and went to Carpathian Ukraine as a vassal of King Ludwig of Hungary.

The first episcopate in Carpathian Ukraine is connected with the name of King Volodyslav II (of the Yagellos) in the year 1490. The first bishop of the eparchy of Mukachiw was John, who was subject to the patriarch of Constantinople. Some historians speculate that there existed an episcopate here significantly earlier, at the time of the council of Florence, but there is no definite proof of this. How long John was bishop and what his eparchy was like is also not known. The problem was that Carpathian Ukraine, after all, like all of Hungary, changed hands repeatedly in the beginning of the 16th century. After the conquest of the Turks at Mohach (in 1526), the northwestern part of Carpathian Ukraine went under Austrian rule, the eastern part was joined to the Semyhorod principate, and the central and eastern section of Hungary was occupied by the Turks. Perhaps the episcopate of Mukachiw was not occupied for long after this, for the succeeding bishop appeared only in 1551. The Austrian emperor, Ferdinand, set up his bishop, Basil. The Hungarian prince Zapolia, who ruled the Semyhorodian principate, set up Ilarion, his own separate bishop in the Hungarian monastery. From the 16th century the bishops of Mukachiw, Evthemy, and Amphilokhy, are known. Archimandrite Matthew took part in a Council of Berestya (Orthodox) through Amphilokhy, being a monk of the monastery of St. Panteleymon of Mount of Athos.

In the beginning of the 17th century the bishop of Mukachiw was Sergius (1601-1616). During his rule the bishop of Peremyshl visited the eparchy of Mukachiw, attempting to bring in union there. According to records, he found many supporters here among the clergy but the people opposed any innovations and thus this first attempt was unsuccessful. The next bishop about whom there is any information was Ivan Hryhorowych (1627-1633). He was noted for the fact that he first began to establish national schools affiliated with the churches. The inducement for this was the Jesuit order, which set up its own schools wherever Jesuits were found. The Jesuits attributed their successes to their schools. When they appeared in Carpathian Ukraine, they immediately (in 1612) established their own school, which they later transferred to Uzhorod, in Humenno. In this way Hryhorowych realized that schooling was an important activity and adopted this idea in his own Church.

The Transfer of Union

His successor was Basil Tarassowych (1634-1648), ordained in Yassy. He immediately became a supporter of the union and developed secret ties with the Egerian Latin bishop. Yet the action of transfer was not easy. Prince Rakochy, a Calvinist and great enemy of Latinism, ordered him arrested (in 1646) and although he set him free on the intervention of the Austrian emperor under the condition that he not maintain any contact with the bishops of Halych, finally banished him from Carpathian Ukraine completely.

Disregarding these persecutions, the clergy of Mukachiw held a council on the 24th of April, 1646 in Uzhorod under the direction of the Egerian Bishop Yakushych, and 63 priests agreed to accept the union. As conditions, they placed the inviolability of their rite, the free election of bishops, and the equality of rights with the Latin Church. A new bishop, Partheny Petrovych (1648-1670), was also elected at this council. Earlier he had been the auxiliary to the former bishop. Immediately after his election, Partheny made the statement of Catholic faith to the Hungarian primate, Liptay, but for his ordination he went to Bilhorod and accepted the imposition of hands from the Orthodox bishop, Shymonovych. With this craftiness, Partheny hoped to safeguard himself against the persecutions of the Calvinists and also to prevent Rakochy's widow from setting up another (Orthodox) bishop. In January 1652, he called a council in Uzhorod for the bringing in of union to the whole eparchy. But the matter was not so simple. First of all, Rome did not recognize him as a bishop because, after his statement of Catholic faith, he accepted ordination from the Orthodox hierarchy, and secondly because a great part of the clergy, especially that of Semyhorod, was not in favor of union. Nevertheless, about 400 priests accepted the union at this council, representing over 300 churches. The Basilian monasteries, with the exception of that of the Hrushiwsky (in Marmaroshchyna) also accepted union. But the majority, about 450 priests, mostly from Marmaroshchyna, remained true to Orthodoxy. The latter accepted union only in 1721, about fifty years after the Hrushiwsky monastery, that stronghold of Orthodoxy, had ceased to exist. The matter raised by Bishop Partheny dragged on in Rome until 1655, and only then did Rome pronounce him free from irregular practice and assign him full jurisdiction.

After Partheny's death, a great danger threatened the Uniate Church in Carpathian Ukraine. In Rome they wished then to cancel Mukachiw's episcopate and give the faithful and the churches over to the rule of the Latin bishops. Kolenda was then metropolitan and Rome had much trouble with him because of misunderstandigs with the Basilians. It is possible that this circumstance was of consequence. The bishop himself made an unintelligent move in this direction by giving over his churches on the Spish (on the boundary of Slovakia) to the jurisdiction of the Latin bishop.

All this created an unnecessary disturbance in the Church and after the death of Peter, the priests began to return to Orthodoxy and the succeeding bishop, Rakovetsky, received his ordination from the Suchawsky metropolitan.

Finally, Metropolitan Zokhowsky took this matter into his own hands and advised Rome to set up as bishop of Mukachiw Joseph de Kamiles, who was probably from White Rus and who had been the representative of the metropolitan in Rome. Thus after Ratoshynsky's death, Rome set up de Kamiles (1690-1704) as bishop. It became evident that Zokhowsky's choice was a good one. Kamiles sincerely dedicated himself to the work for his eparchy, mainly in the increasing of knowledge and building of schools. He sent his theologians to good theological schools and from under his hand came noted church and secular activists of Carpathian Ukraine, such as Olshawsky, Bachynsky (both later bishops) and others. When the Barbareum was founded in Vienna, Kamiles sent his students here as well. A very important achievement of his was the procurement from Emperor Leopold of a decree which freed the priests from serfdom (in 1692). To a great extent, this influenced the priests in neighboring Marmaroshchyna to go over to the union. A number of them went over in 1716 and the remainder a few years later (1721).

The Eparchy of Peremyshl (1692)

Innocent Vynnytsky ruled the eparchy of Peremyshl at the end of the 17th century (1680-1700). Next to that of Lutsk, this was the largest and perhaps the most influential eparchy in the whole metropoly. It was called the eparchy of Peremyshl, Sambor and Sanick because at various times the bishops had had their sees in these cities. It encompassed about 1,500 churches and over a million faithfull. As has been mentioned, the bishops of Peremyshl had jurisdiction over even the Carpathian churches until about the end of the 15th century. There were three Vynnytskys as bishops at the cathedral of Peremyshl: Anthony, an Orthodox bishop (1650) who was later metropolitan of Kiev (1667-1679), Innocent, and his brother George (1700-1708), who was later metropolitan (1708-1713). Innocent Vynnytsky, immediately after his election as bishop, expressed the desire to go over to the union and already in 1681 in Warsaw, having come to a secret agreement with Shumlansky, made his statement of faith. This was entirely due to the efforts of, Zokhowsky, who had been able to persuade not only Vynnytsky but also the archimandrites of the monasteries of Uhniv and Ovrutsk that the Uniate Church was not Polishizing or Latinizing but was a separate national Church. Vynnytsky nevertheless realized that to bring over the whole eparchy without preparation would not be easy. For this reason he worked for ten years in that direction, brought in order in the Basilian monasteries, discussed the matter at eparchial conferences, and when he believed the groundwork to be sufficiently complete, he went over to union publicly with his diocese in 1692. A year later he reformed the Basilian order in his eparchy and persuaded the Basilians to accept Rutsky's reform and elect his brother Varlaam (Vynnytsky) as archimandrite.

He was an active bishop. Two years after the union he held an eparchial synod in Sambor at which 22 more deaneries that had earlier remained Orthodox joined the union and at which many beneficial reforms. At that synod, the eparchial assembly or chapter was renewed in order to help the bishop in his direction of the eparchy. Vynnytsky died in Lviv on the 24th day of February, 1700.

The Eparchy of Lviv (1700)

More than a century passed after the Council of Berestya before the eparchy of Lviv joined the union. Although Balaban, the bishop of Lviv of that time, was one of the first to apply himself to the matter of uniting the Ukrainian Church with Rome, nevertheless, shortly before the council, he changed his mind and became the basic Orthodox opponent. His successor, Jeremiah Tyssarowsky (1608-1641), despite all the efforts of Poty (Poty had ordained Rutsky as bishop of Halych although the latter never had any power there), was able to remain bishop in the capitol. After Tyssarowsky, the bishop of Lviv was Arseny Geliborsky (1641-1658) and after him his brother, Athanasius Geliborsky (1658-1667). After the latter's death, a dispute sprang up between the Holy Cross Society which had elected Eustachy Svystelnytsky as bishop and a party which was supported by the royal court and which elected Joseph Shumlansky. Nevertheless Svystelnytsky was approved as bishop of the eparchy and only after his death (in 1676) did Shumlansky take control of the eparchy (1676-1708). Together with Vynnytsky, he made his statement of faith in Warsaw but he did not rush to make a public acceptance of union. Besides that, in 1678 he tried to procure from the patriarch of Moscow, Yakym, the renewal of the metropoly of Halych. A few years later (in 1696), he again spoke of union, but now he needed three more years to decide. Finally, in 1700, he accepted union along with his entire diocese and remained in union until his death.

There remained only the Holy Cross Society of Lviv, along with its bishop, which did not accept union and only after Shumlansky's death (in 1708) did this bastion of Orthodoxy in the western Ukrainian lands fall and go over to the union. In the following years (1709) Pope Clement guaranteed the Holy Cross Society its ancient rights by a special decree and placed it directly under his authority. After the conversion of the Holy Cross Society, only Skyt Manawsky remained Orthodox and he remained true to it until his death in 1785.

The Eparchy of Lutsk (1702)

From the very beginning, the eparchy of Lutsk was the most active theatre in the battle between the Uniates and the Orthodox. Its hierarch at the time of union was Cyril Terlecky, one of the chief promoters of union. but prince Ostrosky lived in the eparchy of Lutsk as well and the Ostrosky Academy was here. Here were gathered the most talented Orthodox polemicists. After Terlecky's death, the eparchy was without a leader for a time and only Rutsky was able to set up a bishop, Jeremiah Pochapiwsky, in the eparchy of Lutsk (in 1621). This eparchy was assigned to the Orthodox by the Articles of King Volodyslav IV. A year later (in 1633) the Orthodox bishop, Athanasius Puzyna, arrived here and after Pochapiwsky's death, he took the whole eparchy into his own jurisdiction. In the 17th century the following bishops were still here: Joseph Chaplits (1651), Dionysius Balaban (1656), Gedeon Svyatopolk-Chetvertynsky (1660), Athanasius Shumlansky (1684) and finally Dionysius Zabokrytsky (1700). But Uniate bishops were also assigned to this eparchy although they had no power here and did not reside here. The title of bishop of Lutsk was carried by Niciphor Lasowsky (1637), Procopius Khmelowsky (1660) and Metropolitans Kolenda, Zokhowsky and Zalensky. Of all the churches in the eparchy only about one hundred seven monasteries held to the union, the rest being in the jurisdiction of the Orthodox bishops.

In 1702 Dionysius Zaborkrytsky went over to union with his whole eparchy. This so angered the tsar of Moscow, Peter I, that he ordered the bishop arrested and sent in chains to Moscow, where he died in 1715; After Zabokrytsky's arrest, Cyril Shumlansky, a Basilian, temporarily took control of the eparchy. Shumlansky however immediately reached an understanding with the Orthodox and received his ordination to the eparchy of Lutsk from the metropolitan of Kiev. Because of the protest of the pope and the Polish King August II however, he did not command the obedience of the clergy and after Zabokrytsky's death, the Uniate bishop, Joseph Graf Vyhowsky, was assigned to the eparchy (1716-1730).

In this way, at the end of the 17th and at the beginning of the 18th century, the Uniate Church united all the eparchies in the Right Bank territories of the Ukraine and in the western Ukrainian lands and in Carpathian Ukraine. This was an important accomplishment and great efforts were required to achieve it but it shows that the nation believed in this Church and stood by it.

13. The Synod of Zamosk (1720) and Succeeding Events

It may seem that the consolidation of the Uniate Church at the turn of the 18th century had conquered all the difficulties of her future growth. But this was not the case. The territorial expansion itself and several reforms brought in by Zokhowsky in the metropoly or by individual bishops in their eparchies did not guarantee the Church her independent development. This became evident early. The Orthodox Church, having been undermined, now began to slowly attack the church of the Uniates.

The Growth of Moscow
Under pressure from Moscow, Poland agreed to renew the episcopate of Mohyliw for the Orthodox and (in 1720) through this action created for the

173

plans of Moscow a comfortable contingent base for the battle against Uniatism. Over this episcopate and other Orthodox islands in the Right Bank territories, Moscow obtained an original right as a protectorate, which gave it the right to interfere in both the Church and the political matters of Poland. The Orthodox parishes in the Right Bank territories were led by priests of the jurisdiction of the metropolitan of Kiev, who after the joining of the metropoly of Kiev to the patriarchate of Moscow (in 1686), came more and more under the influence of Moscow policies of both Church and State. The change-over to Orthodoxy gradually increased, the power of Orthodoxy grew stronger and whole towns, having been subjected to propaganda, changed over to Orthodoxy. The church question increased in gravity and was touched upon more and more often at state councils. The representative of Moscow in Warsaw, with his interference in church matters, finally called out such a hatred among the Polish noblemen that they formed a confederation in Barr as a mouthpiece of the anti-Moscow policy.

The Haydamaka Period

The haydamaka movement complicated the matters of religious relations no less than did the Russian interference. It began in the first quarter of the 18th century, primarily as a protest against the oppression of the Polish lords; thus it was a social action. But the religious question played quite an important role in it as well. This movement gradually became stronger and in 1768 it took on a universal character. Along with the Polish nobility in the Ukraine, the haydamakas also moved against the Uniate Church, seeing it as a Church seemingly under the protection of the Polish government. Many hundreds of Churches and schools were destroyed and many priests suffered. When this haydamaka movement seemed to Moscow to have outlived its usefulness, Moscow sent its armies (under general Rumyantsev) to the Right Bank territories and giving Poland its assistance, helped crush this movement with much bloodshed. Moscow assured all that it was going to the defense of the Ukrainian populace in the Right Bank territories, for the establishment of harmony and order and for the protection of the rights of Orthodox Church, but the alert reader will see that the same occurred when the Moscow government came to liquidate the remains of Ukrainian statehood in the Left Bank territories. In 1764, the hetmanate was abolished and a few years later the Sitch was done away with, along with the final autonomous rights of the Ukraine.

With these political conditions it became very hard for the Uniate metropolitans to uphold that which the Church had gained for herself in the preceeding century. Besides this external danger, the Church had difficult internal problems as well. One of these was the slow process of the Latinizing of the Ukrainian rite, against which the metropolitans continuously waged war. Nevertheless, they were unable to preserve it completely, for the schools, almost exclusively, were in the hands of the Basilians and they showed no great opposition to Latinization. It is known that schools had and have a great influence on the formation of church life. The greatest services in the field of preservation of the purity of the rite were rendered by Metropolitan Zokhowsky, but when he finally procured a prohibition from Rome against the going over of Uniates to Latinism, this threw the Polish Latinizers into such a rage that they definitely resolved to destroy the union.

It is known that there was a plan for the "Destruction of Rus" (1717). According to this plan, all the Uniates were to be forcibly transferred to Latinism and as means to this end it was proposed: 1. remove Ukrainian lords from state offices, 2. set up candidates favoring Polish policies as bishops, 3. forbid the building of schools, 4. keep the priesthood ignorant, 5. bring in the rule of Polish bishops over them and finally 6. have Jews push the Ukrainian citizens out of the cities.

The Synod of Zamost of 1720.

In such difficult times the leadership of the metropoly was taken by Leo Kyshka (1714-1728), a bishop of Volodimir in 1711, earlier the protoarchimandrite of the order (in 1703), a White Rus by nationality, educated in Rome. Immediately after his establishment, Kyshka, knowing very well the conditions in the Ukrainian Church and depending on the support of the Basilians, decided to bring in a fundamental revision of the whole situation in the Church. In 1715 he procured from the pope permission to hold council and this council took place in Zamost (in the province of Kholm) in 1720. It took place at the same time as the enemies of the union were preparing to bring into force the previously mentioned plan for the destruction of Rus".

Although the Uniate Church had, generally speaking, preserved her ancient rite, nevertheless, in the course of a hundred years, such a large number of innovations unapproved by the church authority were brought in that it could not regard itself as the true Ukrainian Byzantine rite which the Ukrainian Church had had until her acceptance of the union. The situation was such that the Sacrament of Baptism, for example, was performed differently in different eparchies. Thus this council set itself the task of bringing in primarily the unity of rite, of publishing liturgical books and catechism and of deliniating certain directions for church policy regarding Orthodoxy. This was an important event in the life of the Uniate Church. Taking part in it were Metropolitan Leo Kyshka, Florian Hrebnytsky, the archbishop of Polotsk, Joseph Graph Vyhowsky, the bishop of Lutsk and Ostroh, Athanasius Sheptytsky, bishop of Lviv, Halych and Kamyanets, Joseph Lewytsky, the bishop of Kholm and Bels, Eronim Ustrytsky, the bishop of Peremyshl, Sambir and Syanick, Theophil Godebsky, the bishop of Turiw and Pinsk, Lawrence Drutsky-Sokolynsky, the bishop of Smolensk, Anthony Zavadsky, the protoarchimandrite of the Basilian order, 8 archimandrites and 129 representatives of white or black clergy.

The Resolutions of the Synod

The synod proclaimed its decisions in the form of "Decrees" and its main resolutions were: the primacy of the pope was recognized in agreement with the teaching of the Tridentine Council (1545-1563); "and Son" was brought into the Creed; the commemoration of the pope in liturgical services was brought in; the Uniates were forbidden to obtain spiritual assistance from Orthodox priests; the reading of anti-Catholic books was forbidden; one format for the Sacraments of Baptism and Confirmation was established; exact prescriptions for the giving of Holy Eucharist to the sick were given; giving the Eucharist to children was forbidden; prescriptions about the conferring of the other Holy Sacraments were drawn up; it was ordered that the offertory be completed before and not during the Liturgy; the reading of low Mass was permitted; and bells and various other changes in rite, similar to the Latins, were brought in.

This Synod also concerned itself with matters pertaining to the rule of the Church, her administrative divisions (dean's offices), the rights and obligations of a pastor, church properties, spiritual seminaries, the prescribing of fasts, prescriptions regarding relics, miracles, veneration of saints, simony, and finally with one more important matter - monasteries and monastic life.

One of the most important resolutions of this Synod was the one which guaranteed to the clergy of the Basilian order the executive right to the office of bishop. As future history was to show, this resolution brought in much more harm than good to the life of the Ukrainian Church. It was put through seemingly because the Basilians considered themselves the most enlightened clergy, the best organized and the most faithful to union. There is no doubt that the Basilians had many educated monks, conducted schools, and evidenced in themselves a definite power, but the same education was available to secular theologians from the Basilians or from schools abroad as well. This differentation - in today's language, discrimination, - called out great displeasure among the white clergy and became the reason for a new dispute for the hierarchal rule in the Church. The Basilians were able to hold this privilege for themselves for a full 60 years and only in 1780 was P. Bilansky able to obtain ordination as bishop of Lviv even though he was not a monk.

Generally speaking, the Council of Zamosk was an important moment and even perhaps a turning point in the life of the Uniate Church. It brought in, exactness in rite, even if not completely favorably. It deliniated for the clergy the basic principles upon which the union with Rome stood and ordered the Church disciplinarily and administratively and this had a great significance for the Church in the face of future events.

The Attempt to Liquidate the Union

These events have been mentioned before. The Synod, having deliniated the exact position of the Church and having consolidated her forces, was seemingly the answer to the project of the "destruction of Rus". Before the advance of the Moscovite Orthodoxy, not that of Kiev any more, the Uniate Church stepped out with a suitable preparation. This did not save her from losses which she suffered during Peter I's rule or during that of his successors, chiefly Catherine II, but here the moral power and worth of the clergy, faithful to their Church, became evident. After the intervention of Moscow in the haydamaka insurgence, the soldiers of Rumyantsev began to "defend" Orthodoxy in the Right Bank territories. In a short time the prisons of Uman, Bila Tserkva, Berdychiw, and other cities were filled with Uniate priests and monks. During this action, about 1200 churches were taken away from the Uniates and hundreds of priests were arrested. This was the time of the so-called "confessors of Berdychiw", priests who suffered for long years in the prison in Berdychiw and who could be helped neither by the intervention of the nuncio nor that of the Polish king. Only thanks to the efforts of Maria Teresa, the Austrian empress, did Catherine II agree to free them (in 1783). But they did not return to their former positions. In all, only 600 churches remained Uniate in the Right Bank territories of the Ukraine.

14. The Division of Poland and the Fate of the Uniate Church

The anarchial spirit of the Polish nobility, which had long undermined the foundations of the state, finally brought this state, built upon lawlessness, injury and opressions of subjugated nations (the Ukrainian and the White Russian) to ruin. In the mid-18th century, two camps sprung up in Polish politics: one, which made advances to Moscovy and by these advances tried to gain the favor of its insatiable neighbor, and the other, represented by the conference of Barr, which took a very inimical stance towards Moscovy and to its own opportunistic leadership as well. To tame the powers of the conference of Barr, Poland requested the help of the armies of Moscow, to which Moscow, obviously happily agreed. But this did not save Poland. Having come to an agreement with Wustria and Prussia, Moscow proceeded to abbreviate the boundaries of Poland. In this way Poland's first division occurred in 1772.

The First Division of Poland in 1772

The first division only nicked Poland. Moscovy received the bordering White Rus lands and the eparchies of Polick and Mystyslav; this was comparatively little. Prussia occupied the land on the Baltic (Varmia, a part of Kuyavia and of central Poland), while Austria gained the largest portion - Halychyna, the palatinate of Belz, and significant portions of the palatinates of Volynia, Podilya, Kholm and Kracow, and two years later it took Bukovyna from a Moldavian noble as well.

This division of Poland made the rule of the Church very difficult for the Uniate metropolitan. Under Austrian rule were the eparchies of Lviv, Peremyshl, Kholm and a part of that of Lutsk. There were no special problems here, for Austria did not trouble the Uniate Church but rather assisted her. It was a different matter in the eparchies under Russian rule. Here even the Latin clergy came to help the Russians, chiefly the Mohyliv Polish archbishop, Sostrgyntsevych, who would have been happy to take possession of the Uniates under his own jurisdiction. Unfortunately the large eparchy of Polotsk did not have any suitable bishops at that time. A few years after the division of Poland, there was a Basilian Archbishop Smogogewsky, who did not care very much for his eparchy. In 1780, when he was elected metropolitan, he left in his place Bishop Maxim Ryllo whom Catherine II approved in Polotsk. But Ryllo resigned from the eparchy and left to go to Poland. After this, the eparchy was for a time without a leader and the Consistory ruled it until 1784, when Heracles Lissowsky became the Uniate bishop. In that time the eparchy realized great losses, due to the conversion of the higher clergy to Latinism under the pressure of the Polish bishop and to Orthodoxy under the pressure of the Moscow leaders. The eparchy lost over 800 churches in that time and over one hundred thousand faithful.

The life of the Church under Austrian rule became normalized even more and with time the actual center of her activity was over there. Austria was an ordered state, and although it was Catholic, as was Poland, nevertheless Austrian Catholicism did not have such chauvinistic tendencies as did the Polish. Austria took the position of equal rights in both of the Churches, the Catholic and the Uniate, and to distinguish one from the other, the use of Greek-Catholic to mean Uniate Church was instituted. Leo Sheptytsky (1749-1779) was then in the eparchy of Lviv at the end of his life (1778-1779) and was also the metropolitan of Kiev, while in Peremyshl, Athanasius Sheptytsky (1762-1779) ruled. To raise the educational level of the clergy, both bishops began to apply their efforts towards the establishment of a seminary. In 1776 Maria Teresa opened the so-called Barbareum in Vienna, that is a seminary where theologians from Carpathian Ukraine, Croatia (the eparchy of Križevci), and from Halychyna lived and completed part of their studies. But there was too little of this and in 1783 Joseph II founded the "Stadium Ruthenum in Lviv, a seminary whose first rector became Anthony Anhelowych, later the first metropolitan of Halych. A year later (in 1784) the Barbareum was closed and only reopened in 1803. The Studium Ruthenum existed until 1817. In that year the University of Lviv, with a faculty of theology, was renewed, or rather organized, and for this reason there was no further need for a separate theological school.

The Second Division of Poland in 1793

After the first blow, the division in 1772, a part of the Polish society came to its senses and began bringing in order and reform. To finish off the feudal anarchy, Poland accepted the Constitution on the 3rd of May, 1791, with the goal of bringing in order and returning to Poland her former power. But the new constitution was not favored by the Polish noblemen and once more they called to their aid Moscovy, which had just then completed a successful campaign against the Turks and had taken control of Crimea. Eager to help, the armies of Moscow occupied Warsaw, ordered a state assembly be called, nullified the Constitution and returned the old order. For this help, Moscovy exacted compensation in the form of the province of Kiev (after the first division, Kiev had remained under Polish rule), Podilya, part of Volynia, and the White Rus lands. The Polish state assembly humbly signed this bill. At this opportunity, Prussia also became richer, having occupied Gdansk, Torun, the remainder of central Poland, Kuyavy, and Mazovia. Only Austria did not take part in this division. Thus Poland became a small state from a large one. But even this small one did not last long. As protest against the docility of the Polish government and this parcelization, an insurgence began (in 1794) against Moscovy and Prussia, whose goal was to recover the lost lands.

The Third Division in 1795

With the common forces of Moscow and Prussia, the insurgents were put down and Poland was brought to an end. Moscow took the Ukrainian and White Rus lands which still remained under Polish rule (except for the province of Kholm and Pidlasha) and the neighbors, Austria and Prussia, divided the remainder among themselves. These associates once again divided among themselves the Polish lands in 1815, at the Congress of Vienna, after Napoleon's fall. The White Rus lands found themselves under Moscow, the Ukrainian lands under Moscow and Austria and the Polish lands were divided among Austria, Prussia and Moscovy.

Before the division, Poland controlled great territories, 780,000 square kilometers. After the first division there remained 554,000 square kilometers and after the second, 254,000 square kilometers. The neighboring states divided this remainder among themselves in the final division.

Such a development in the political situation was very significant to the further history of the Uniate Church. Under Russia was White Rus with all the White Rus eparchies and of the Ukrainian lands, the province of Kiev and a significant part of Podilya and Volynia. Just before the division of Poland, the Uniate Church in the territories on the Right Bank again begam to become more lively and many churches which had gone over to Orthodoxy returned to the jurisdiction of the Uniate metropolitan. The Russifying policy of Catherine II made an end to this. In 1795, a holy synod of the Russian Church called a special commission for the turning of Uniates to Orthodoxy. Missionaries went from village to village and either persuaded or made threats to the Uniate priests to force them to convert to Orthodoxy. In that same year an edict was issued that all Churches which had ever been founded by Orthodox believers were to be returned to the Orthodox. The Uniate episcopate did not find anywhere support for its Church and only the one bishop, Peter Bilansky, bishop of Lviv and Kamyanets Podilsky, went to the Kamyanets eparchy to defend the Church. He was ineffectual and the Russian rule removed him at once. After the third division of Poland, in Podilya there did not remain even one Uniate Church and in the provinces of Kiev, Bratslav and Volynia there remained a few tens of churches in all. In total, about 2,300 Churches, about 1,500 priests and over a million faithful converted to Orthodoxy. This was the final balance of the Uniate Church under Russian occupation.

It was a similar situation in White Rus. After the first division of Poland, the eparchy of Mstyslav converted, according to the agreement with Poland, to the patriarchate of Moscow and only the archeparchy of Polotsk remained Uniate. Smogogewsky, who ruled it for a year after 1780, did not care for it much and when the opportunity to become metropolitan came up, he gladly took advantage of it. His successor, Ryllo, abandoned this eparchy and when Lissowsky arrived here (in 1784), he found it in no better condition. He remained here until his death, (in 1809) but he never regained the lost churches. After his death, this eparchy survived for thirty years more and was finally swallowed up by the Church of Moscow in 1839. As a result of these events, the following eparchies went over to the Russian Orthodox Church: Smolensk (in 1778), Volodimir (in 1795), Lutsk (in 1795), Turiw-Pinsk (in 1795), and Polotsk (in 1839).

After the death of Catherine II (in 1796), her successor, Paul I, showed more tolerance towards the Uniate Church and she revived a little. He returned several churches and monasteries to the Uniates and the life of the Church improved a little. His successor Alexander I (1801-1805) was little interested in church matters and gave in to the persuasion and intrigues of the Latin clergy, this to the detriment of the Ukrainian Church. The Uniate Church was finally liquidated in the eparchies under Russian occupation in the final quarter of the 19th century, in 1875.

The Uniate Church (which was now called Greek-Catholic) slowly took control of the whole spiritual inheritance of the long battle under Austrian Rule and having received the support of the secular government, became the main support of Ukrainian society within the boundaries of the Austrian Empire.

15. The renewal of the Metropoly of Halych (1808)

Immediately after the first division of Poland (in 1772) it was evident that the Uniate metropolitan would have serious difficulties in the rule of the Church divided between two states. Bachynsky, the bishop of Mukachiw, soon realized this and he turned to Maria Teresa requesting that she renew the metropoly of Halych and join to it the eparchies of Carpathian Ukraine. The Austrian government took a favorable attitude to this proposition and it is possible that the matter would have been succesful even then if not for the fact that the Hungarians became very opposed to the erection of a metropoly. It was not in their interest that infleunces from Halychyna penetrate Carpathian Ukraine and by this weaken the Hungarianization of the Ukrainians in the territories beyond the Carpathians.

A second difficulty of canonical order in the formation of the metropoly was the fact that Rostotsky, the Uniate metropolitan of Kiev, still lived and he did not wish to give up his rights to the eparchies under Austrian rule. In 1803, the Austrian government began the ordering of Church matters in the state and the matter of a metropoly of Halych again became an active issue.

But protesting against this now were the Polish bishops of Lviv and Peremyshl, demanding that the Greek-Catholic bishop-ordinands be done away with and their eparchies be subjected to the latin hierarchs, that is to themselves. There was a danger that the Austrian government would agree to this, for the territorial government in Halychyna (Gubernia) where the Poles had a considerable influence, favored such a solution. For this reason Bishops Skorodynsky and Harasewych, the latter a highly-educated person with good contacts in the capitol, went to Vienna and frustrated the efforts of the Polish bishops.

The Matter of the Metropoly is Put Aside
The position of the metropoly soon improved. In 1805, Metropolitan Rostotsky died; therefore there was no opposition from that quarter. It also happened that at that same time, the bishop of Kholm, Porphiry Vagynsky, died (in 1804) and also the bishop of Lviv Skorodynsky (on the 23rd of May, 1805) soon after his return from Vienna. The populace of Halych pressured Vienna to order church matters and assign someone to the eparchies as soon as possible. But in Vienna they had other worries. Then the war with Napoleon was in progress and it was going very unfavorably for Austria (which was defeated at Austerlitz on the 2nd of December, 1805), and for this reason the matter of the Ukrainian Church was put aside. Finally thanks to the efforts of Michael Harasewych, the vicar general of the Eparchy of Lviv, the emperor sent a letter to Rome (in 1806) in which he requested the renewal of the metropoly of Halych. Along with this he sent the condition that the future metropolitan would have the same rights as did the metropolitan of Kiev, rights which had been guaranteed at the establishment of the union at Berestya. The emperor nominated Anhelowych, the bishop of Peremyshl, as metropolitan.

The Conditions of the Basilians
Rome did not immediately agree to this. The matter dragged on because (according to the historian bishop Pelesh), the Basilians demanded that the resolutions of the Synod of Zamosk be respected and that the bishops and the future metropolitan be drawn from the Basilians according to the resolutions. In this direction, the chief procurator of the Order in Rome, Jordan Mitskewych, also did his work. Among other things, it was pointed out that after Rostotsky's death, Heracles Lissowsky (who had no jurisdiction over the eparchies under Austrian rule) had become the new metropolitan of Kiev, that there already was a metropoly (Latin) in Lviv, and that the Basilian general would be "shocked". The Austrian government demanded from Anhelowych an exploration of the afore-mentioned conditions by Rome, and having obtained it, renewed its plea in 1807. This time Rome agreed and the pope, with a special bull, set up the metropoly of Halych in that very year, with the rights of the Uniate metropoly of Kiev in the provinces of Halychyna and Kholm. The pope also agreed to the person of Anhelowych, but under the stipulation that the Basilians still retain their

rights to elect the bishops and that Anhelowych inform Lissowsky the Uniate metropolitan of Kiev of the establishment of the metropoly of Halych.

Nevertheless, Austria did not want to agree to the stipulation set by Rome and did not give its consent to the establishment of a metropolitan under these conditions. There was no other course, and Rome finally agreed to the erection of a metropoly and to a candidate for metropolitan without any conditions. Metropolitan Anhelowych took the see of the metropoly of Halych in September, 1808.

16. The Uniate Metropolitan of Kiev, 1780-1838

The Estrangement Between Kiev and Halych

The Uniate metropolitans of Kiev of the 18th century lived through an era of great growth in trust in the Church, of intense warfare and finally of her forcible breakup and division in half. The political conditions and international relations were not favorable to her spiritual development, to the spreading of education, to the cultivation of a new type of priest and the safeguarding of that tradition which her great activists and hierarchs touched upon and which that church, in somewhat quieter intervening times, had evidenced. Nevertheless, notwithstanding these unusually tempestuous times, the Church, although much weakened, was able to survive, and having transferred the center of her activity to a righteous state, gained new life, shook the foreign slime off herself and became dear to the nation.

The metropolitans of this century did not have a permanent capitol but usually remained in the see of their eparchy. Among them there were very dedicated pastors, as for example, Leo Kyshka, but there were also those who did not enrich the history of the Ukrainian Church. The division of Poland severely complicated the rule of the metropoly and this finally caused the creation of a new metropoly, that of Halych. With the exception of Rostotsky, who until his election as metropolitan was a bishop of Kholm, all the metropolitans were hierarchs of the eparchy under Russian rule. This slowly caused their estrangement from those eparchies which had fallen into Austrian hands and weakened their defense against the invasion of Moscow and the intrigues of the Latin clergy. From 1708 to 1833 there were eleven of them in all and of these there were nine who carried the title of metropolitan of Kiev of the Uniate Church (up to 1805), and three which were regarded as papal delegates for the faithful united with Rome within the boundaries of the Russian empire.

George Vynnytsky (1708-1713)

The brother of bishop Innocent Vynnytsky was established in the cathedral of Peremyshl after the death of his predecessor. When still a bishop, he founded in Peremyshl a spiritual seminary and in 1704 he procured from the king a release from war duties for the clergy. Elected metropolitan (in 1708), he continued to rule the eparchy of Peremyshl and after Shumlansky's death

Metropolitan George Vynnytsky
(1708-1713)

Metropolitan Leo Kyshka
(1714-1728)

also that of Lviv for a short time. He set up Archimandrite Varlaam Sheptytsky as bishop of Lviv (in 1710) and a year later Leo Kyshka as bishop of Volynia and Berestya and Joseph Lewytsky as bishop of Kholm.

In 1710 he sent a protest to Rome against the practices of several Latin bishops who were pulling the faithful of the Ukrainian Church over to Latinism. In 1713 he took part in the chapter of the order in Vilna, but after his return he became ill and died on the 22nd of January, 1713. He was buried in Lavrov (near Sambor).

Leo Kyshka (1714-1728)

At first he was the Basilian abbot in Vilna (in 1703), later the bishop of Volynia and Berestya and finally metropolitan from 1714. During his metropolitanate, the afore-mentioned "project for the destruction of Rus" was begun. Kyshka, with other bishops, immediately referred this matter to the pope and demanded that the Decree of Urban VIII (of 1624), which forbade the pulling over into Latinism, be respected by the Latin bishops. This had its effect and in the following years, several Polish bishops (for example, Brogostowsky of Vilenia and Skarbek of Lviv) forbade their clergy, under the pain of excommunication, to turn the Uniates away in such a manner. Kyshka's most important action was the completion of the Synod of Zamosk (of 1720) which brought in a change in rite in the Church, regularized monastic life, brought in administrative order locally (in parishes and deaneries) and accepted for the future the resolution about the exclusive right of the Basilians to the bishops' sees. The final years of his life he gave to the tasks of effecting the resolutions of Zamosk and improving spiritual education (a seminary in Volodimir in Volynia). Before his death he assigned Athanasius Sheptytsky as his aide. He died in 1728.

Athanasius Sheptytsky (1729-1746)

Athanasius Sheptytsky was at the same time the bishop of Lviv from 1715. He gave himself over primarily to the realization of the resolution of the Synod (in 1720), the unifying of the rite and to one other very important matter - the relation of the Basilians to the secular clergy. There is no doubt that the Basilians had merit in the spreading of union, but their privileged position, the occupation of the highest offices in the Church, the condition that they give their agreement to the nomination of bishops or metropolitans and to a certain extent, their independence from the metropolitan, created unhealthy relations within the Church. In 1743 the metropolitan joined the two provinces, those of White Rus and the Ukraine, into one congregation under one protoarchimandrite and along with this set them the task of giving more attention to the education and enlightenment of white clergy. A second matter with which the metropolitan was concerned, a matter as old as the union itself, was the problem of conversion to Latinism. Again in 1731 there was an order from the pope, mainly to the Polish confessors, to decisively stop this practice. It must be mentioned here that the Decree of Urban VIII

Metropolitan Athanasius Sheptytsky
(1729-1746)

(of 1624) about the attraction of Uniates into Latinism was never announced in the Polish state. This stealing of souls continued for a long time and consequently there were later papal commands or constitutions (in 1742, 1743, 1755, 1756 and others).

Athanasius Sheptytsky especially cared about the education of white clergy. Thanks to his efforts, Uniate theologians received 20 places in the Vilenian (papal) seminary and about the same number in that of Lviv (Teatinian). He also cared for churches, and for the building of the church of St.George, he left a large sum (116.820 guldens), which was however, later used for the seminary of Lviv and a cathedral tax was imposed (by the eparchial Synod in Perehinsko in 1750). He also brought through the proclamation of the miracle-working icon of the Blessed Virgin of Gyrovytsi (on the 19th of September, 1730). In his person, the metropoly had in those difficult times a dedicated and caring pastor.

Florian Hrebnytsky (1748-1762)

After Sheptytsky's death, the metropoly was without a leader for a full three years. The reason for this was a dispute between the Basilians and the bishops on the one hand and the Polish government on the other about who had the right to nominate metropolitans. Finally, the Uniate clergy won and brought in its own candidate, the archbishop of Polotsk, Florian Hrebnytsky. Hrebnytsky is known for his activity against Latinization. There is a list of protests from him to the pope and to the king against the persuasions of the Latin clergy to convert the Uniates to Latinism. The situation was such that at a conference of the bishops (at Novhorodok on the 6th of August, 1761), the bishops decided to "buy" themselves a ruling from the king, who would strictly forbid the Latins to pull the Uniate souls over to themselves. They paid a large sum (127 thousand Polish guldens). soon after this, King August III promised the pope that he would put an end to this stubborness of the Latin clergy. The metropolitan lived in a more peaceful relationship with the Basilians than did his predecessor. He appointed Jason Smogogewsky as his aide in the archeparchy of Polotsk and the Basilian bishop of Kholm, Philip Volodkowych, as coadjutor of the metropoly. Florian Hrebnytsky died in 1762.

Philip Volodkowych (1762-1778)

For these very difficult times, the Ukrainian Church received a metropolitan of no great cast. These were the times of the forcible invasion of Moscow, which finally came to the first division of Poland. The Polish king was a nominee of Moscow, Ponatowsky, who wanted to keep the favor of Moscow at all costs, and for this reason he did not favor the Uniate Church. When Volodkowych obtained the approval of the pope for a Synod in Berestya (in 1764), so that a plan of defense in the face of the coming threat could be agreed on, the king opposed him and the Synod did not take place. This was the time of serious disturbances in Poland, the time of confederations (that of Radom, pro-Moscow and that of Baar, anti-Moscow) and finally of the haydamaka insurgence. All these events seriously harmed the Uniate Church. Many priests and faithful suffered and hundreds of Churches and monasteries were burned.

The metropolitan was unable and did not know how to resist. He was already quite old and had numerous enemies in the royal court. Nevertheless he left no effort untried to help the afore-mentioned "confessors of Berdychiv" (1773). After the first division of Poland, which he survived, the metropoly was divided into three parts: under Polish rule there remained the metropolitans eparchy and the episcopates of Volodimir-Berestya, Lutsk, Pinsk and part of Kholm. Under Moscow went the archepiscopate of Polotsk and under Austrian rule the eparchies of Lviv, Peremyshl and part of Kamyanets, Lutsk and Kholm. The metropolitan died in his 81st year in 1778.

Leo Sheptytsky (1778-1779)

Earlier he was the bishop of Lviv (1749-1779). Sheptytsky had no difficulty in stepping into the leadership of the metropoly and both Austria and Poland recognized him. Moscow did not deny him his rights to the archeparchy of Polotsk but bound them to the extent that all the directions to the eparchy should go through the Russian government. The metropolitan, himself a Basilian, had no sympathy for the Order. At his enthronement, when the Basilians requested a place of honor for themselves in the procession, he did not let them participate at all. Later, he had trouble all his life with the Basilians because of the Cathedral school. In the place where today stands the church of St. George, in ancient times there stood a forest and already in the beginnings of Christianity the monks had their caves there. The Volynian prince, Vasylko, the brother of King Danylo, (1204-1270), also lived out the final years of his life in those caves. Later, a monastery sprang up there and for this reason the Basilians considered that this place rightfully belonged to them. But in 1539, when the episcopate of Lviv was established, the church became a cathedral and remained one until the times of Shumlansky. Only Shumlansky allowed the Basilians to take St. George's. The old Church of St.George had been built in 1347 (by Abbot Euthymius); Athanasius Sheptytsky ordered it taken down (it was unusable) and began to raise money for the building of a new one. The conflict with the Basilians continued for a long time and was only successfully ended for the metropolitans of Halych in 1817. The money which his predecessor had left for the building of a Church, the metropolitan used to build a seminary and named a separate tax for the Church, through which in ten years a considerable sum was gathered (147 thousand guldens). He also built the metropolitan's palace of today. In 1762 Sheptytsky became the coadjutor of the metropolitanate (Volodkowych) and in 1768 the administrator of the metropoly (Rome had suspended Volodkowych for his neglect of his pastoral obligations). Shortly before his death, the metropolitan set aside two villages, Mshana and Malchyci near Lviv, and assigned their incomes to the building of a new Cathedral

**Metropolitan Florian Hrebnytsky
1748-1762**

Metropolitan Philip Wolodkovych
(1762-1778)

Church. The metropolitan died in his 65th year, in Radomyshl, on May 24th, 1779.

Jason Smogozewsky (1780-1788)

Smogozewsky had been the archbishop of Polotsk earlier (1762-1780). His greatest service was that he, like his predecessor, cared about the secular clergy, whose support he gained for himself. Along with that, at the time of his metropolitanate, there came a more vigorous opposition from the government of Mocow in the archeparchy of Polotsk, and the metropolitan had continuous difficulties with this.

Theodosius Rostotsky (1788-1805)

This was the last metropolitan of the metropoly of Kiev-Halych. He was the bishop of Kholm at the same time (1785-1790). As a young man, he entered the order, studied in Rome, was later a professor (of philosophy and theology) and from 1778 he was the provincial of the White Rus province. After his taking the metroplitan's throne he sincerely applied himself and urged his bishops to take care of the education of the clergy and by all his efforts he opposed the fleeing of faithful to the Latin Church. He also procured for himself a place on the senate, which nevertheless did not benefit him for long, for a few years later, Poland was destroyed. After the final division of Poland, all the Right Bank territories, the eparchies of Berestya, Pinsk, Volodimir, Lutsk and part of Kholm and about 800 Churches which belonged to the eparchy of Lviv went under Russian occupation. This division sealed the fate of the great metropoly of Kiev-Halych (which numbered 12 million faithful at that time).

In Russia, planning the organizational actions now began against the Uniate Church. People nominated by and favorable to the policies of Moscow obtained appointments as metropolitans, terror and oppression began along with imprisonment and banishment, persuasion and deceit, and after forty years of "conversion" of this kind, the Uniate Church was joined by Polish Catholics on the side of the government of Moscovy (in particular the Mohylian Archbishop Sestrzentsevych) as well as the college (founded by Alexander I in 1801), which was to look after Catholics and Uniates. Members of the college harassed Uniates wherever they could. Metropolitan Rostotsky's jurisdiction, by order of Catherine II, was taken away and he was removed to Petersburg where he lived for ten years. He died on January 25th, 1805.

The Uniate Metropoly in Russia (1806-1838)

After Rostotsky's death, the archbishop of Polotsk, Heracles Lissowsky, asked Tsar Alexander I to re-establish the metropoly. Although both the afore-mentioned Sestrgentsevych and the holy Synod opposed this with all their strength, nevertheless Alexander I agreed and in 1806 he appointed Lissowsky metropolitan and conferred upon him all the rights and privileges of the former metropolitan but under a different title (Metropolitan of Uniate

Metropolitan Leo Sheptytsky
(1778-1779)

Churches in Russia). Now the metropolitan's province was composed of three eparchies: Polotsk, Lutsk and Berestya. Before his death, Lissowsky assigned as his successor Kochanowych, the bishop of Lutsk and the tsar confirmed him. Kochanowych died in 1814. Neither he nor his predecessor had the confirmation of Rome; only the final metropolitan of this province, Josaphat Bulhak, received confirmation as an Apostolic Legate. But he was the last metropolitan. Nicholas I, the successor of Alexander I (who had been quite tolerant to the Uniates) completed the deed of the destruction of the Uniate Church begun by Catherine II. In 1839 the Uniate Church in Russia ceased to exist, for she had become united with the Orthodox Church of Moscow.

17. The Orthodox Metropolitans of Kiev (1686-1799)

After the joining of the Ukrainian Orthodox Church to that of Moscow, the Orthodox Church did not lose ground for a long time. In this Ukrainian Church for yet another few decades the old traditions of Mohyla, Kosiw and Tukalsky lived on. The Mohylian College still existed and enlightened the church and social activists continued to graduate from it. At the beginning of the 18th century, about twenty years after the joining of the metropoly of Kiev to the patriarchate of Moscow, almost all the episcopal cathedrals were led by Ukrainians, graduates of the Mohylian College. This was a sign of the theological ignorance within the Church which was preparing to give her blessing to the metropoly of Kiev. Until the end of the 18th century, Ukrainian metropolitans sat on the throne of the metropoly of Kiev. After this the metropoly lost her Ukrainian character, became staffed primarily by foreigners and became one of the eparchies of Russia. The metropolitanate of Gedeon Svyatopolk-Chetwertynsky - came at the time of the fall of Hetman Samoylowych (1686-1690). This metropolitan has already been mentioned before. Here it will only be added that after the fall of Hetman Samoylowych (in 1678), by the authority of his nominee, the metropolitan also collapsed. In the following year, on the 27th of January, 1688, an order came to Gedeon not to use the old title, "Metropolitan of Kiev, Halych and all Rus", but Metropolitan of Kiev, Halych and Minor Russia". This was the first act of the stripping down of the dignity of the metropolitan of Kiev. It was not necessary to wait long for other such acts.

Varlaam Yasinsky (1690-1707)
A graduate of the Mohylian College during the times of Metropolitan Kosiw, Yasinsky later also studied at the university of Kracow (where he received the title of Doctor of Philosophy). As the archimandrite of the Monastery of the Caves, he was one of the first to protest the efforts of Gedeon Chetverynsky. After the latter's death, he was elected metropolitan. He turned almost all his attention to the College. He defended it materially and obtained new properties to which Mazepa lent a generous hand. during his

reign the College gained the title "Academy". The Academy began to gather books and built up a library. Mazepa also turned a careful scrutiny on the character and quality of the studies in the Academy. There are two curious edicts from the Russian tsars of that time about what should be taught in the Academy and how it should be taught. The first edict came in 1694 from "Tsars Ivan and Peter" (Peter was then 21 years old) proclaiming the fact that at the Academy, its own prefects, professors and teachers and not "strangers" were to teach and that philosophy, rhetoric and theology should be taught (as if they did not know this in Kiev) and that the teaching should in no way differ from the teaching of the "Holy Eastern Church" and above all that the teaching be "pious, Christian and Eastern". It is clear that in Moscow, what was being taught in Kiev was very much feared, for in 1701 a new document arrived of similar content. Yasinsky was a sincere supporter of Mazepa and without a doubt shared his political plans.

Joasaph Krokowsky (1708-1718)

Until 1693, Krokowsky was a professor of the Mohylian Academy and later its rector (1693-1697). During his lifetime, Metropolitan Yasynsky had wanted to ordain him bishop to be his aide, but to the patriarch of Moscow, Krokowsky did not seem worthy of confidence and permission for ordination never came. Nevertheless, after the metropolitan's death, Krokowsky was unanimously elected and this time he was approved in Moscow. Krokowsky showed the care of his predecessor for the Academy and himself taught theology and diligently guarded education. He wrote a prayer of praise to St.Barbara which the patriarch allowed him to publish under the condition that it be translated into the Russian language. After the battle at Poltava (in 1709) he survived for a while yet. Later, suspected of supporting Mazepa, he was banished to Tver where he died on the first of July, 1718.

Varlaam Vanatovych (1722-1730)

Of Halychanian origin (from Yaroslav), Vanatowych wandered to a Tykhvynian monastery (near Novhorod) for some reason. Later, he was the spiritual advisor of Archbishop Theodosius of Novhorod, the hieromonk of the fleet, and finally the archimandrite of the afore-mentioned monastery. In 1722 he was ordained "archbishop" of Kiev. Thus the hierarch of Kiev was now no longer called a metropolitan. In this year the eparchy of Pereyaslav was also removed from his jurisdiction and in this way the metropoly of Kiev was reduced to being one of the eparchies of Russia. In that same year the so-called Russia Minor College was established in the Ukraine. This college had the highest authority in its hands. Vanatovych had to suffer the painful reduction of status of the metropolitan of Kiev. He turned his attention to the renewal of churches. On the 2nd of August, 1730, he was called to Moscow, together with the cathedral council. There a secret tribunal took place and he was relieved of not only his see as archbishop but of his priesthood altogether and he was banished to a Bilozersky monastery for life imprisonment. All the members of his council were set free, but their offices were taken away.

Metropolitan Jason Smogozewsky
(1780-1788)

The reason for this secret tribunal is not exactly known. Kopynsky postulated that the reason was a denunciation by a Moscovite monk named Sukhanov, who roamed across the Ukraine and observed what was happening there. He reported that the Ukrainian clergy had "degenerated the old Russina faith and had become diseased with the damned Latinization", that when they baptized in the Ukraine, they did not immerse but sprinkled, that they sang "either with Roman or Italian notes" in the churches, that the bishops and the metropolitan wore crosses on their mitres while this was allowed only for the tsars, and so on. This was enough to relieve the metropolitan of his priesthood and condemn him to slow death. He remained in that prison for eleven years. The new tsarina, Elizabeth, appeared to have an attack of conscience and he was freed. She even wanted to give him his archbishop's see back, but he refused it and asked that he be left in peace. In his old age he lived in the same Tykhvynian monastery where he had spent his youth. He died in 1751.

Raphael Zaborowsky (1731-1747)

A Halychanian by birth, Zaborowsky came from the province of Lviv. At first he studied in Jesuit schools, later in the Mohylian Academy. In 1723 he became "over-hieromonk of the fleet" by command and was later the archimandrite of the Wverian monastery and an assessor of the holy Synod. In 1725 he was ordained bishop of Pskow and Narva, where he founded the first school in that eparchy. In 1731 he received an order to be the archbishop of Kiev. The Mohylian Academy owes much to Zaborowsky. He was an unusually talented person and a Ukrainian patriot. Being bounded to the eparchy of Kiev, he bent all his efforts, talents and personal money towards building up the Academy, beautifying it and to raising its standard of education even higher. He also built the Church of the Anunciation, the Great Dormitory, the archpirest's home and others. In what high esteem the Academy was then held is shown by fact that even from abroad requests came for its teachers. In 1732 Seyadnovych, the metropolitan of Serbia, asked Zaborowsky to send him ten "learned men", while the Moscovite governor in Kiev, Semen Sukyn, received an order from Moscow in 1737 to send there "a brilliant translator of Latin and Polish writings", because there was no one there with those qualifications. But this did not stop Tsarina Elizabeth from again sending Zaborowsky a "decree" that "the education should be of pious, Christian and Eastern confession". In 1743 the title of metropolitan of Kiev was returned to him. He died on October 22nd, 1747, and before his death he still wrote an Instructional-statute for his beloved Academy, a statute which it was to uphold. The time of his metropolitanate was a time of the greatest flowering of the education in Kiev and of the Academy.

Timothy Shcherbatsky (1737-1757)

Shcherbatsky came from Trepilya in the province of Kiev from a Town household. He was a graduate of the Academy of Kiev, abbot of the monas-

Metropolitan Theodosius Rostotsky
(1788-1805)

teries of Kiev (Mharian, Vydubian and Mychayliwan), and the archiman-drite of the Monastery of the Caves of Kiev (in 1747). In 1748 Joseph, the Moscovite archbishop, died and Shcherbatsky was called to Moscow as a candidate to the cathedral of Moscow. But at that same time (in March) Raphael, the metropolitan of Kiev died as well. Thus, without consulting anyone, Shcherbatsky was ordained metropolitan of Kiev in Moscow. In the decree he was ordered to diligently guard his flock from heresy, from errors and from "wolves in sheep's clothing". In the Ukraine at that time there were neither wolves nor heresies; perhaps the decree had Uniates in mind and this would mean that either there existed such sympathies among the clergy of Kiev, or, if there were no such sympathies, in Moscow they obviously feared this very much and did not trust the people of Kiev. It should be re-membered here that at that particular time, a multitude of heresies were started by the "dividers" (in the mid-17th century) and many other kinds of interpretations.

The functions and rights of the metropolitan of Kiev were very much bounded and for this reason, almost every metropolitan primarily turned his attention to the Academy. During Shcherbatsky's rule, student public de-bates were brought in (formerly there were only class discussions in the scholastic style). The debates were of a high level and reached many listen-ers in the city. In 1755, a university was founded in Moscow (120 years later than in Kiev with the Mohylian College) and students were brought over there. An important action of Shcherbatsky was the renewal of the printing house (the press of the Monastery of the Caves of Kiev had burned in 1718) for which it was very difficult to obtain permission. That permission came in 1753 but with the warning that in the printed books "there would not be the slightest disagreement or discord with the Orthodox Greek-Russian Church". The metropolitan also built the bell-tower of the Holy Cross Soci-ety of Kiev. Angered by the interface of Moscow in the smallest matters of the metropoly, the metropolitan sent a document to the holy Synod with the request that he be relieved of his duties as metropolitan. Instead of that, he was transferred to Moscow, to the eparchy of Moscow, and ordered to serve there. The metropolitan died in Moscow on the 18th of April, 1767.

Arseny Mohylansky (1757-1770)

After Shcherbatsky's transfer, the tsarina (Elizabeth) appointed Arseny Mohylansky, from Reshetylivka (in Poltavshchyna) to be metropolitan of Kiev. After the completion of his studies at the Academy, he was commis-sioned to teach at the Moscow Academy. In 1744 he was appointed archimandrite of the Trinitarian-Sergius monastery and later bishop of Pereyaslav-Zalisk. In 1752 he resigned from the eparchy and entered the monastery. But he was taken from here in 1757 and appointed metropolitan of Kiev. Along with his zeal for the Academy, Arseny assigned great impor-tance to preaching. In this he patterned himself on the writings of Ioanicius Galatowsky, one of the finest representatives of scholastic preaching in the

Ukraine. Mohylanski died on the 8th of June, 1770 and was buried in the Church of St. Sophia.

Gabriel Kremenetsky (1770-1783)

Kremenetsky came from Nosov (in the province of Kiev) and obtained his education at the Academy and at the College of Chakiw. Later he was a professor and rector in the school of the Alexander-Newsk Caves, archimandrite of the Novospasky monastery, the bishop of Kolomensk (in 1749), the bishop of Kazan (in 1755) and metropolitan of Kiev (in 1770). During his rule the division of Poland (in 1772) took place and White Rus consisting of 1200 Churches and about one and a half million faithful (earlier under the jurisdiction of the metropoly of Kiev), was joined to the Church of Moscow. Besides that, when the eparchy of Kherson was founded in 1775, a part of the metropoly (eparchy) of Kiev was assigned to it and also subjected to the patriarch. Kremenetsky took care of the Academy and its library (he donated 58,425 rubles in silver to the Academy) and gave shelter at his residence to about ten eastern bishops and metropolitans from Greece, Asia Minor and others.

Samuel Myslavsky (1783-1796)

A son of a priest in the village of Poloshky in the country of Hlukhiw, a student, professor and rector of the Academy, Myslavsky was archimandrite of the Fraternity monastery in 1761. In 1768 he was transferred to duties in Peterburg; later he was the bishop of Bilhorod, later bishop of Krutyts and in 1776 bishop of Rostov. After Kremenetsky's death he was sent to the throne of the metropolitan of Kiev. His first achievement was to bring the Russian language into the Academy (as the teaching language) while relegating Latin to a lesser position. He ordered the Academy to include among its teachers a student of theology from Moscow, Dimitrius Sigirevych, and set him up as the teacher of poetry with rights "conferred by Moscow". This was the beginning of the decline of the Academy of Kiev, famed in all Europe. He brought in a strict supervision of the professors, limited the learning of foreign languages and those which were permitted were to be learned "under the guidance of that pronunciation which was applied in Great Russia". It is not surprising that this was the time of the liquidation of the remnants of Ukrainian independence: in 1764 that of the hetmanate, in 1775, the Sitch of Zaporize, in 1781, the regimental organization of the Ukraine, in 1783, the institution of serfdom, in 1785, the liquidation of the Ukrainian nobility (the remnant was transferred to the Russian court) and in 1786, the secularization of monastic properties. Any comment is superfluous here. This pastor died on the 8th of January, 1796. A Russian historian says that the archpriest of the Church of St. Sophia, Ioan Levanda, proclaimed: "Come and pay your last respects to your teacher."

Jerotius Malytsky (1796-1799)

Malytsky was born in Chernyhiw and received his education at the seminary there. Later he was an abbot and archimandrite of the monasteries of

Chernyhiw. In 1778 he was appointed bishop of Chernihiw and in 1796 metropolitan of Kiev and archimandrite of the Monastery of the Caves. Now Levanda again proclaimed "Be glad, kiss hands . . ." After the final division of Poland, the territories of the Right Bank were formed into yet another eparchy and the eparchy of Kiev was enlarged, but these territorial changes did not have any significance for the metropoly. The basic task of Metropolitan Malytsky was the institution of "truly Russian education". He made no great efforts and died in the third year of his reign on the second of September, 1799.

With this, the overview of the metropolitans of Kiev may be ended. Beginning in 1783, the metropoly lost its strict character of a Ukrainian Church. The two last metropolitans were able, in fifty years, to destroy that which the metropoly had gained in ages. There is a certain tragedy in that either a graduate of the Mohylian Academy or another son of the Ukraine was used for this destructive work.

The succeeding metropolitans such as Banulesko (a Rumanian), Alexandrovsky, and others were foreigners, well tried and faithful servants of the Russian Empire, and they had nothing in common with the Ukrainian Church or ecclesiology. Nothing remained of the rights which the metropoly of Kiev had had and with which the patriarchs of Russia were not to interfere (or so they claimed when enticing others to their "favor"). The Church became a tool of the imperial rule.

A similar fate greeted the Mohylian Academy, which had been the one center of education in Eastern Europe until the foundation of the Jesuit college of Lviv (in 1661) and the university of Moscow (in 1755). After the liquidation of everything, the Academy remained an eyesore to the looters. Then the Academy was closed -such was the reward for the hundreds of learned people who had graduated in Kiev. In its place a spiritual seminary for the cultivation of "true Russian education" was opened. It was reformed in 1819 into the Academy of Kiev, an institution of Moscow in the Ukraine.

18. The Liquidation of the Union in the Eparchy of Kholm

After the liquidation of the union in White Rus and in the Ukraine (in 1839), the eparchy of Kholm, which belonged to the rule of Congressional Poland (the Congress of Vienna in 1815 granted Poland, which was under Russian occupation, certain autonomous rights) still remained within the boundaries of the Russian Empire. This was a well-organized eparchy having several industrious bishops and, being closer to the metropoly of Halych, was thus able to remain in existence longer. But its turn came as well.

The Role of the Polish Clergy
The Poles, having lost their state, could not of course forget this. They mobilized their national masses, reminded them of the former greatness of their state, showed them the degradation and enslavement of that time, and

in this way prepared themselves for discussion with Russia. The Polish clergy, regarding this as their patriotic duty, also took part. It is known that the clergy can have a very great influence on the formation of national spirituality. To this end they also enlisted the support of Uniate clergy, which did not need much persuasion as to what a blessing Russia was for the Uniate Church. The Polish clergy did not have much success but nevertheless a small handful of Ukrainian clergy was convinced by Polish statements. As we know, there were many monks of Polish origin in the Basilian order who, although they had seemingly accepted the eastern rite, remained Poles in their souls.

Having fired the nation patriotically, the Poles raised their first rebellion against Russia in 1830, which ended unsuccessfully for them and gave the Russian rule a good opportunity to hasten the liquidation of the union in the eparchies in the Ukraine and White Rus (in 1839). An invasion by force took the eparchy of Kholm. In their ignorance, the Poles, having an influence on the Uniate clergy, tried to Latinize and Polonize the eparchy with all their might. In the Churches, Ukrainian priests began giving their sermons in Polish, singing Polish church songs and litanies, changing the internal appearance of the Church to the Latin form and even bringing in organs. This was not pleasing to the Russian rulers and they ordered that sermons be spoken in Ukrainian and not in Polish and that no changes be made in the rituals. Bishop Kalinsky answered that his clergy could not speak Ukrainian and so they would not preach in this language. If he is to be believed, then the process of Polonizing had made large advances. Up until now, the rule of Moscow had not interfered with the relations between the Catholics and the Uniates and it seems, was even glad when the Polish clergy suppressed the Uniate Church. The relations between Russia and Catholicism were completely adequate. In 1779, after the first division of Poland, Catherine II had invited the Jesuits to Russia and after seven years they already had 6 colleges and 178 members of the teaching profession (monks) there. In 1801, after the final division of Poland, there were already 262 of them there and in 1811, 347.

Between the Hammer and the Anvil

Paul I, who in church matters was more tolerant than any other tsar, had even renewed three Uniate cathedrals (Polotsk, Lutsk and Berestya). Alexander I set up diplomatic relations with Rome. This, if the warring Polish Catholicism had been somewhat more human towards the Ukrainian Church and had left her in peace, it is possible that relations could have become more fruitful. Now, however, when the Poles had set themselves the goal of subjugating the Church to themselves at all costs, they inspired rage among the clergy in Halychyna and by this aided the Moscow cause in a definite part of the secular and spiritual intelligentsia. The rule of Moscow wiesly took advantage of this Polish stupidity. By defending the Ukrainians, it gained for itself the sympathies of both the local clergy and the clergy of Halychyna. And these sympathies were very much to the advantage of Russian politics.

They had only to be supported by the sympathizers and embraced more closely; their circle widened and the final effect of this agreement came in to play on its own. In addition, at that time the relations between Russia and the Vatican were much cooler; the concordat which Russia had made with the Apostolic See in 1847 was broken after the second Polish division (in 1866) and now the Russian rule left itself more free and proceeded more unceremoniously.

All these missals, litanies, Polish translations of the Bible, Polish sermons, side altars and so on did not agree with the foundations of the Russian empire but were an outstanding opportunity to put the Uniate Church and the Ukrainian populace, "under protection". They made observations and gave warnings to Kalinsky, but this did not help in the least.

At the end, the Russian rule imprisoned Kalinsky and with him his closest helpers and exiled him to Vyatka (1866) where he soon died. Then a priest named Voytsitsky took control of the eparchy, surpassing all the expectations of the Russian rule. To help clean up the rite, he brought Russian into the Church and school. Naturally, such a method of purifying the rite was not suitable but it did serve to bring the Church very close to that of Moscow. Voytsitsky surrounded himself with his supporters, set them up in the higher church offices, appointed them as teachers in seminaries and schools, and in this way he slowly did his work. Rome interrupted this work and separated (suspended) him from the rule of the eparchy.

Michael Kuzemsky (1868-1871)

The Russian rulers agreed to set up as bishop, a canonist of Lviv, Michael Kuzemsky, a noted social activist who, among other things, had made efforts in the anti-alcohol movement in Halychyna. The clergy and faithful of Kholm accepted him warmly. But Kuzemsky fell into conflict with the supporters of Voytsitsky who were supporters of Moscow (among whom there were foreign priests from Halychyna). These accused him before the Russian government and Kuzemsky was forced to leave the eparchy (1871) and return to Halychyna.

Markyl Popel (1871-1875)

In Kuzemsky's place, the Russian government appointed Markyl Popel, a priest from Halychyna, a noted author of school textbooks and editor of the Moscow-supporting paper, "Sunday". Popel treated the matter simply - he abolished several feastdays (which were not on the Orthodox calendar), forbade mention of the pope, ordered the holy Synod mentioned, brought liturgical books in from Moscow, forbade kneeling in Church and so on. The populace and priests were disturbed by this. Some converted to Orthodoxy, others went over to Latinism, and still others decided to persevere until the end. Mass arrests and repressions followed. Popel forced the priests to sign a declaration of conversion to Orthodoxy and when he had gathered a certain quantity, he sent the tsar a letter asking that the eparchy be accepted in the

Metropolitan Anthony Angelovych
(1808-1814)

Orthodox Church of Moscow. Naturally, the tsar agreed. He only asked that a delegation of two deacons be sent to him from each parish and understandably, Popel mobilized such a delegation at once and sent it off and on the 11th of May, 1875, the official "uniting of the Uniates with the Orthodox Church" took place. According to the count in the eparchy of Kholm at the end of 1874, there were 330 Churches with 246.146 faithful there. The Orthodoxy, which had been forced in at bayonet point called out a strong reaction in a large part of the clergy and faithful. Not able to celebrate the Liturgy in the Churches, these so-called stubborn ones celebrated in secret in Polish Churches. In time most of these "stubborn ones" were arrested (those who did not saved themselves by fleeing to Halychyna). In their place, about a hundred priests (Moscow-supporters) came from Halychyna. They were priests who had entered the service of the government of Moscow in the Russification of Kholmshchyna. The "stubborn" populace (about half of the faithful) never fell under the influence of Orthodoxy and when, in 1905, after the first Russian revolution a tolerant law came in which allowed anyone to belong to any church he wished, then all these "stubborn ones" (over one hundred thousand) went over to Latinism and Polonized.

In this way, the eparchy of Kholm, the last under Russian occupation, ceased to exist.

For his "merits" Popel was ordained a bishop. However, perhaps he was not trusted very much, for having assigned him the eparchy of Lublyn, Moscow subjected it to the archbishop of Warshaw, Lebedynsky.

19. The Metropoly of Halych (1808-1946) and Other Eparchies

After the foundation of the metropoly of Halych, the Uniate Church slowly began to revive and mend the wounds she had suffered as a result of great political changes and Russian intolerance. To a great extent, the ordered relations in the Austrian state were favorable to this as was the fact that Austria was not interested in Latinizing the Ukrainian Church as the Poles had attempted to do for several centuries. The early years of this metropoly fell in stormy warring times. The wars of Napoleon indirectly touched Halychyna as well. The first metropolitan, about whom there will still be more said, was unable to expand his efforts but even in the short time of his metropolitanate, he improved the inter-eparchial relations, improved the education of priests and brought order to the church properties. As has already been mentioned, the Ukrainain Church now took the name of "Greek-Catholic" and this name, with few exceptions, has been retained to this day. At this time, three eparchies belonged to the metropoly of Halych: Lviv, Peremyshl and Kholm. The latter remained until it was forcibly taken over into Orthodoxy. Ten years later the eparchy of Stanyslaviv was founded (in 1885). Better standards of living and a supportive attitude of state activists soon became evident in the life of the Church. Now the clergy could obtain,

Metropolitan Ierakly Lisowsky
(1806-1809)

205

without great difficulty, its education either at home, at the university of Lviv, or in other universities, Austrian or foreign. Thanks to this, the Church became the key mover in the spreading of a national awareness in the development of schooling and the maintaining of the native language. She also had definite service in economic relations.

Fraternities of Sobriety

One of the chief plagues which was destroying Ukrainian villages was the plague of taverns. The Church began a courageous battle against this evil. In the 1860's, hundreds of fraternities of sobriety appeared and realized a dual purpose - they saved many families from public auction and besides that, joined them to an organized Ukrainian society.

Worry about the native language in schools and university (the lectures of theology were at the university of Lviv) always weighed heavily on the hearts of Ukrainian church activists. This movement of national awakening gave the Ukraine Markian Shashkewych, a graduate of the seminary of Lviv, who entered history as one of the finest sons of the Ukrainian Church.

Michael Lewytsky became the successor of Anhelowych on the metropolitan's throne. During his rule there sprang up in Lviv the Halych-Rus Motherhood (in 1848) a foundation caring for the educational and literary movement in the nation, the schooling in the native language, the publishing of popular books and the defending of those rights which the newly-proclaimed constitution guaranteed.

The Church rid herself of foreign ritual influences and during Gregory Yakhymovych's rule (1860-1863), slowly returned to the old Ukrainian ritual forms. This movement spread still farther during the reign of his successor, Metropolitan Lytvynovych (1863-1869), a sincere Ukrainian patriot. This did not come easily, for ritual forms are not changed by one or another regulation. The same situation existed here: the clergy was divided into the supporters of the ancient Ukrainian practices and those who looked to Moscow for guidance. The reason for such an orientation (of the supports of Moscow) was the further efforts of the Poles, even in the circumstances of their lack of a state, to harm the Ukrainian Church and nation by any means. Nevertheless a healthy intellect, the raising of the national awareness, the political activeness, the growth of the class of the intelligentsia, the enlivening of literary activity, the press, and finally the reading movement paralyzed these unhealthy Moscow-oriented theories and did not give them any opportunity to take root in the Ukrainian Church.

For the reordering of Church relations, both ritual and administrative, Metropolitan Sembratovych called the General Council in Lviv (in 1891). This was the first council of the Province of Lviv.

The Greek-Catholic Church experienced her greatest growth and complete Ukrainianization during the metropolitanate of Andrew Sheptytsky, who was perhaps the greatest metropolitan which the Ukrainian Church had after her union with Rome. This Good Shepherd, who returned to the nation of his ancestors, a nation oppressed for ages, robbed, weakened and even

Metropolitan Gregory Kochanovych
(1809-1814)

Metropolitan Josaphat Bulhak
(1817-1838)

now subjected to unceasing attacks from the side of her western Catholic neighbor, this Hierarch brought in a new life, a breath of fresh air, a brilliant sun - both into the life of the Church, and that of the nation. He raised the spiritual and cultural life of the Church, freshened the monastic spirit, educated a new type of priest and taught Ukrainians the Christian wisdom - love and patience.

In 1928, the metropolitan founded the Theological Academy in Lviv, which was comprised of two faculties - the philosophical and the theological and set up Joseph Slipyj as its first rector. The Academy, thanks to the efforts of its founder and her rector, did not have many equals among higher schools of that type in the whole Catholic world. This was a great achievement considering the conditions in which the Ukrainian Church was forced to live and act.

The State of the Metropoly

The whole metropoly was comprised of three eparchies: archeparchy of Lviv and the eparchies of Peremyshl and Stanyslaviv.

The administrative archeparchy of Lviv was divided into five proto-archpriestates: Halych, Zolochiw, Lviv, Stryj and Ternopil. These proto-archpriestates were subdivided into deaconates shortly before the second world war. There were fifty-four archpriestates in the whole archeparchy, 874 priests and about a million and a half faithful.

The metropolitan, as has been mentioned, was an ardent champion of the monastic life. After the reform of the Basilian order in 1883 monastic life significantly improved and the metropolitan paid special attention to the development of monasticism. There were 44 monasteries within the territory of the archeparchy - Basilian, Studite, Redemptorist and others, in which there lived 271 monks and 419 nuns.

The eparchy of Peremyshl was divided into 45 deaconates with 574 parishes (and 61 of independent collaboration), 695 priests and about one million, two hundred thousand faithful. There were 8 monasteries within the territory of the eparchy and over forty Congregational Houses.

The eparchy of Stanyslaviv had twelve deaconates, 419 parishes, 503 priests and about one million faithful, 8 monasteries and about 30 Congregational Houses.

In 1934, the Apostolic Administration of Lemkiwshchyna was created which, although it did not come under the jurisdiction of the metropolitan of Halych, nevertheless in spirit and later in fact it was dependent on the metropoly (the renewed metropoly of Halych had its see in Lviv). The Administration was divided into 9 deaconates with 111 parishes and 11 independent collaborators. There were 130 priests, 127,000 faithful and 2 monasteries.

There was also a second Administration of Volynia, assigned for the Greek-Catholics of Volynia.

The Eparchies in Carpathian Ukraine

In Carpathian Ukraine, beside the previously mentioned eparchy of Mukachiw, a second eparchy sprang up in 1818 with its see in Pryashiv. The

Metropolitan Michael Lewytsky
(1816-1858)

situation of the Ukrainian Church in Carpathian Ukraine significantly worsened after the Hungarians began to institute repressions against the
Ukrainians and began to Hungarianize the Church. A separate vicariate was
taken away from the eparchy of Mukachiw in Haydudorog and the Hungarian liturgical language was instituted. The Hungarianization in Mukachiw
continued until 1918. The reaction against Hungarianization (similar to that
against Latinization in Poland) was the spreading of Orthodoxy and when, in
1919, Carpathian Ukraine separated from Hungary, about one-third of the
Greek-Catholic faithful left. The patriarch of Serbia had jurisdiction over
them and he assigned here two bishops, that of Uzhorod and that of
Mukachiw.

The Greek-Catholic Church in Bukovina

In former times, the Orthodox Ukrainians of Bukovina belonged under
the jurisdiction of the metropolitan of Halych (in the 14th century). Later,
several hierarchs held the jurisdiction here - the Okhrydian archbishop, later
the metropolitan of Suchav, and from 1402 Bukovina had its own bishop,
dependent upon the metropolitan of Moldavia, until 1772. In that year
Bukovina was joined to Austria and in 1783 the episcopal cathedral was
transferred from Radovets to Chernivtsi. For some time, the bishop of
Bukovina was subject to the metropolitan of Serbia. In 1873, an autocephalous Dalmatian metropoly was founded with its capitol in Chernivtsi. The
Bukovinian Church had always been under a strong influence from the
Rumanians and only during the First World War was a Ukrainian, Titus
Tyminsky, ordained there as bishop; he was pensioned off by the Rumanians
after the war (in 1918).

From the mid-12th century there also existed in Bukovina the Greek-
Catholic Church; however this church never had more than 10-15 parishes.
Especially dedicated to the expansion of the Greek-Catholic Church in
Bukovina was Metropolitan Lewytsky. From 1919 this church had a vicar-
general, appointed from Rome, who was subject to the bishop in Mar-
marosh. Earlier the churches of Bukovina belonged to the eparchy of Stanyslaviv (until 1919).

The Eparchy of Kridgevtsi

In Yugoslavia before the war there lived about 40,000 Ukrainian Greek-
Catholics who belonged to the eparchy of Kridgevtsi. Pope Pius IV had
founded this eparchy in 1777 and had joined to it the Ukrainians who were
emigrants from Carpathian Ukraine. After the First World War Ukrainians
in Bosnia were added to this eparchy. The largest center of Ukrainians in this
eparchy was Kerestur. The first Ukrainian Bishop of this eparchy, Dionysius
Nyardi, (1915-1940) came from this area. After Bishop Naryadi's death,
Bishop Gabriel Bukatko ruled the eparchy, at first as an administrator and
from 1952 as the ordinary. In 1962, Rome appointed Bishop Bukatko to be
the primate of the Catholic Church in Yugoslavia and in his place, a new
bishop, Joakim Segedy, came to the eparchy of Kridgevtsi.

20. The Greek-Catholic Metropolitans of Halych, 1807-1946

Anthony Angelovych (1808-1814)

Angelovych, the first metropolitan of the renewed metropoly of Halych, was born in 1756 in the village of Hrynev in the country of Bibrka, where his father, Jakiw, was a priest. He studied at the Barbareum and after completing his theological studies, he was rector of a spiritual seminary in Lviv and a professor of dogmatics at the university of Lviv. He lectured in Ukrainian. In 1795 he was ordained bishop of Peremyshl and in 1798, after the death of Bishop Bilansky, he also administrated the eparchy of Lviv. He brought in discipline among the clergy and forbade the clerics from wandering among various Latin places for retreats. He also began the battle against the taverns, which later continued throughout almost the whole century. When in 1798 the Austrian rulers wanted to bring in the Gregorian calendar, Angelovych opposed this, standing by the Church's right to decide on her own what calendar was to be used. In 1803, the Latin bishop reordered church matters and proposed the suggestion to the tsar that he subjugate the Greek-Catholic bishop to them and when these bishops died off he not appoint new ones. A Ukrainian proverb says that "a Pole is intelligent after schooling" but this is not true. What misfortune had arisen in both the Church and in the Polish state because of the stupidity of the clergy was certainly apparent to them, yet this did not help. The Poles had influences in the royal court and for this reason Angelovych did not take the matter lightly. With the choirmaster, Harasevych, he foiled this Polish plan. On the 17th of April, 1807, Rome renewed the metropoly of Halych and on the 11th of August, 1808, the Austrian emperor ratified this. Angelowych was set up as metropolitan. In 1809, Napoleon occupied Vienna and ten days later, the Polish armies, which were Napoleon's allies, occupied Lviv. The metropolitan was forced to flee. While fleeing, he fell into the hands of the Poles and no one knows how it would have ended had it not been for the fact that after a day or two the Austrian armies recaptured Lviv and the Poles, like it or not, decided to let the metropolitan go (in Strey City).

Metropolitan Anhelovych's greatest service was that he defended the right to use the Ukrainian language in the schools and in the university. Being himself still a professor, he lectured on dogma, strictly in Ukrainian, (at the theological faculty of the university of Lviv). He also cared for the ordering of Church properties, but in this he had less luck. Doubtless, Anhelovych was an Austrian patriot; however that patriotism did not interfere with his defense of the rights of his native Ukrainian nation.

Michael Lewytsky (1816-1858)

After Anhelovych's death the metropoly was without a leader for two years. In 1815, Emperor Franz I nominated Michael Lewytsky to be metropolitan and in the following year (in March, 1816), Rome confirmed this

Metropolitan Gregory Yakhymovych
(1860-1863)

nomination. Up to now, Lewytsky had been the bishop of Peremyshl (1813-1815). He remained on the metropolitan's throne for 42 years and his metropolitanate constitutes an important period in the life of the Greek-Catholic Church. During his rule the "spring of nations" took place in 1848) as well as important changes in Ukrainian social and political life. In 1848, the "Halych-Rus Motherhood" was formed, in which Lewytsky's services cannot be ignored. But he concerned himself most zealously perhaps with matters of schooling. He had unceasing troubles and disagreements over schooling with the Poles who, having influences in local Austrian governments, did not want to allow the organization of Ukrainian schools. Nevertheless, the metropolitan was successful in that, by a decree of 1818, the use of the Ukrainian language was permitted in those schools in which there was a majority of Ukrainian children. He cared for the material safeguarding of priests and obtained pensions for them from a "religious fund" (a fund set up after the abolishment of monastic properties by Joseph II). In Peremyshl, together with bishop Snihursky, he funded a Deacon's institute where deacon-teachers were trained.

In 1850, the metropolitan began his efforts to have the episcopate of Stanyslaviv established. This matter stretched on until 1885, however. During Lewytsky's rule, the work of enlightenment in villages continued, especially the movement for sobriety, which reached great proportions.

Evaluating Lewytsky's merits, the Austrian emperor nominated him primate of Halychyna in 1848, while Pope Pius IX made him a cardinal in 1856. This was the second cardinal in the Ukrainian Church since her union with Rome.

Metropolitan Lewytsky had good co-workers. At that time, the bishops of Peremyshl were Snihursky (1818-1847) and H. Yakhymovych (1847-1858).

Snihursky was an uncommon person. Deeply religious, a dedicated pastor and a sincere patriot, he set up many foundations, built the library of the Capitol and gathered a multitude of manuscripts, old printings, documents and other treasures of old. Yakhymovych, who came after Snihursky, was the actual leader of the national movement of that time, the organizer and leader of the Motherhood of Rus and for a time the leader of the parliamentary club in the Viennese parliament. It is not surprising that the era of Metropolitan Lewytsky is recorded in Ukrainian histories as a turning-point towards the complete Ukrainianization of the Ukrainian Church. Metropolitan Lewytsky died in a monastery at Uniw where he had lived since 1852 while his helper, Bishop Lytvynovych, ruled the metropoly.

Gregory Yakhymovych (1860-1863)

Gregory Yakhymovych was born in 1792. At first he was a professor at the University of Lviv and rector at the Spiritual Seminary. In the years 1849 to 1859, as has already been mentioned previously, he was the bishop of Peremyshl and at the same time the leader of the Ukrainian renewal in

СПІРІДОН ЛИТВИНОВИЧ Го митр. 1864-1869.

Metropolitan Spyrydon Lytvynovych
(1864-1869)

Halych. After Lewytsky's death he became metropolitan. In Kholmshchyna at that time, after the unsuccessful Polish rebellion which also involved the Greek-Catholic clergy of the eparchy, oppressions and repressions by the Russian government began (the matter of Kalynsky). As has been mentioned, the Polonization of the eparchy of Kholm had made great advances. For this reason, the un-Polonization of the Uniate Church in Kholmshchyna received sympathies among the supporters of the orientation towards Moscow in Halych. The so-called ritual movement began, which brought along with itself a somewhat greater purification of the rite. So as to decide this matter with authority, the metropolitan called a council in Lviv in 1863, yet he himself did not live to see this council. The greatest services of Yakhymovych were in the area of enlightenment of the nation in its national individuality. He died in April, 1863.

Spiridon Lytvynovych (1864-1869)

Spiridin Lytvynovych came from a priestly family. He sutdied in Vienna, was later a preacher in Lviv, a religion teacher in Chernivtsi, the pastor of the Church of St. Barbara in Vienna and in 1857 he was ordained bishop, as an aide to the metropolitan of Lviv. After the death of Yakhymovych, he became metropolitan. During his rule the seemingly important agreement, the so-called "concordia", was reached with the Poles. By this concordia, matters regarding the changing over from one rite to another were decided. Henceforth, no one could change rites without permission from the pope and those who had already changed over could return to their old rite within six months. Engaged couples in which one person was Greek-Catholic and the other Roman-Catholic rite were to be married by the pastor of the bride. The children of such "mixed" marriages were to be educated as follows: daughters in the rite of the mother and sons in the rite of the father. Both the pope and the emperor confirmed this concordat and it was in effect (at least on paper) until the Second World War. In practice it is doubtful whether Latin priests of the latter times even knew of this concordia, while before the war they ignored it. One more important event took place during Lytvynovych's life - the canonization of St. Josaphat by Pope Pius IX in 1896. The metropolitan liked going to Vienna often. In December 1868, during such a journey, he caught a very bad cold and after his return to Lviv, he fell ill and died a few months later, on the 4th of June 1896.

Joseph Sembratovych (1870-1882)

Sembratovych came from Lemkiwshchyna, from a priestly family. He did his theological studies in Vienna and was later a professor in Lviv. He was ordained a bishop in 1865. For some time, he worked in Rome and from 1867 he was an aide to the aged bishop of Peremyshl, Thomas Polansky. After Lytvynovych's death, Michael Malynowsky, a canonist of St. George Cathedral and a famous Ukrainian Church activist and historian of the Church, controlled the metropoly for one year. In June 1870, Rome con-

Metropolitan Joseph Sembratovych
(1870-1882)

firmed Sembratovych's election as metropolitan. The metropolitan had Sylvester Sembratovych as an aide. Joseph Sembratovych was a very dedicated pastor. A decisive supporter of the Ukrainianization of the Church, he himself gave his sermons in Ukrainian and ordered his priests to do the same. As former metropolitans had done, he continued the battle against drinking. After the abolishment of serfdom (in 1848), people began to change their minds gladly and notwithstanding the campaign of opposition by the Church, taverns prospered well. Thus Sembratovych personally devoted himself to this matter and gave it a church or religious character. He even issued a separate statute for the brotherhoods of sobriety. This was one of the reasons why he was so despised by the Polish nobility, which did not pass up any opportunity to trip him up.

A second important matter which he took care of was the reform of the Basilians. Monasticism had declined sharply in the Ukraine during Austrian rule; monasteries had emptied and some had collapsed. during Sembratovych's rule, there were 14 such deserted monasteries. At the request of Rome, the Jesuits took the Basilians into their own hands for re-education (in 1882). They established a novitiate in Dobromyl and brought in discipline. This reform proved beneficial and from the ranks of the reformed Basilians there came many wonderful priests, learned theologians, and Church or social activists. These reformed Basilians set up a printing press in Ghovkva which published hundreds of thousands of books beneficial to the nation.

The fall of Metropolitan Sembratovych was dramatic. After the liquidation of the eparchy of Kholm, the movement for orientation towards Moscow continued in Halychyna (Hnylychky). When its famous pastor, Ivan Naumovych, a social and church activist, an author and former legate, went over to Orthodoxy, the blame was placed on the metropolitan. After plotting by the Poles and at the request of the Austrian government, Rome relieved Sembratovych of his duties as metropolitan and gave control of the eparchy to his aide, Sylvester Sembratovych, in 1882. The metropoplitan lived for 18 more years and outlived his successor on the throne. He died in 1900.

Sylvester Sembratovych (1885-1898)

Sylvester Sembratovych was a professor of dogmatics in the University of Lviv and later the aide of the former metropolitan. At first, after the removal of Metropolitan Joseph, he ruled the metropoly for three years and for three years as administrator and only in 1885 did he become metropolitan. In that year, the episcopate of Stanyslaviv was finally established encompassing part of Podilya and Pokutya. Aware of the threat of an orientation to Moscow, Sembratovych applied himself to social action and favored the nationalistic movement and such parties. The most important event of his metropolitanate was the Council of Lviv in 1891. There were many matters, primarily of a ritual nature, which held up the work and the development of the Church and for this reason, his predecessor had already entertained the thought of holding just such a council. One matter which was a subject of

Metropolitan Sylvester Sembratovych
(1885-1898)

Metropolitan Julian Sas-Kuilowsky
(1899-1900)

heated discussion was the matter of the establishment of celibacy, the unmarried state of clergy, in the Ukrainian Church. Although only bishops had a deciding vote at the council (Sembratovych, Pelesh and Kuyilowsky), nevertheless the representatives of the priesthood who took part in an advisory capacity (and to whom the bishops had to pay special heed) came out decisively against such an innovation. In 1895, the pope nominated Metropolitan Sylvester a cardinal. But he did not enjoy cardinalate long, for he died in 1898.

Julian Kuyilowsky (1899-1900)

Julian Sas-Kuyilowsky was a little-known figure. He came from a priestly family from the village of Konushky (near Komarno). Earlier he had been the bishop of Stanyslaviv, (1891-1899) after the first bishop of Stanyslaviv, Julian Pelesh, a noted activist and historian of the Church, was transferred to the vacant eparchy of Peremyshl. In general, he was a good pastor and rendered indisputable service towards the beginnings of the organization of the eparchy. He remained all of one year in the metropoly and died on August the 4th, 1900.

Andrew Sheptytsky (1901-1944)

The Sheptytsky family gave the Church her greatest sons - abbots, bishops, and three metropolitans. This was an ancient noble family which played a key role in the Ukrainian national and church life. From it came: Varlaam, the bishop of Lviv (1710-1715), Athanasius, the bishop of Lviv (1715-1746) and the metropolitan of Kiev (1727-1746), Leo, the bishop of Lviv (1749-1779), Athanasius, the bishop of Peremyshl (1762-1779), Clement, the archimandrite of the Studite order and Andrew, at first the bishop of Stanyslaviv (1889-1900). The activity of Metropolitan Andrew was so widespread that he entered the ranks of the most notable figures of Ukrainian Church history during his own lifetime. During his metropolitanite, he achieved a complete renewal of church life, an improvement in the education and training of clergy, a reform and expansion of monasticism, a return to eastern church traditions, and a unification of Church and national interests in such a way that the hierarchs became to a large extent the spiritual leaders of the Ukrainian political and cultural effort.

The future metropolitan, for whom his social ancestry created the finest opportunity for a wordly career, decided not to take advantage off this opportunity. And thus this young count, having received the finest education in the best universities abroad, entered the monastery.

After the transfer of Bishop Kuyilowsky to Lviv, the emperor nominated Hieromonk Andrew as bishop of Stanyslaviv. Although this does not belong strictly to history, nevertheless it is worthwhile to note how he conducted himself among the pastorate entrusted to him and how he understood his pastoral function. Thus it became known to the bishop that one spiritual father, instead of celebrating Vespers on Sunday, liked to travel to the neighboring

221

parish for recreation. On one such Sunday, the physically large bishop came to the parish, went to the bell-tower, rang the bells, obtained the keys to the Church while the people gathered, celebrated Vespers, conducted the catechisation, blessed the congregation and left on the return trip. Meanwhile, the priest (whom the people had informed) ran up to ask forgiveness. The bishop answered, "Next time, at least let me know". But this was not-necessary, for the pastor had already received his finest lesson.

On the Metropolitan's Throne

After Kuyilowsky's death, the emperor appointed Bishop Andrew metropolitan of Halych on the 31st of October, 1900, with the enthronement taking place on the 17th of January, 1901. The metropolitan also held the following offices: he was a member of the Austrian parliament (the house of Lords), the vice-marshal of the local parliament of Halych, a member of the Ukrainian National Assembly (from the 19th of October, 1918) the honorary president of the National Assembly in Lviv in 1941, an active member of NTSH, an honorary member of the "Prosvita" society, an honorary member of the "Native School Board" and a member of a multitude of other institutions. He was the founder and funder of the Ukrainian National Museum in Lviv, the founder of the Theological Academy, a benefactor in various charitable organizations, the National Hospital, dormitories, schools and orphanages. Where his hand reached is hardly known, or not at all. It was only known in 1939 that out of his own treasury he gave two million in Polish gold currency annually for national causes. Besides that he went about in a patched cassock. He funded tens of students in universities abroad, helped writers, artists, students in local higher schools, invalids, and everyone who came to him. During the Bolshevik occupation, the metropolitan had no resources to live off. Good people brought him flour, bread and milk from the villages.

At the beginning of the First World War, the Russian occupational military leadership arrested the metropolitan in Lviv on the 19th of September, 1914 and sent him to a monastic prison in Suzdalia and later one in Kursk. On his journey to banishment (on the 21st of November, 1914), he ordained M. Botsan in Kiev as bishop for the episcopate of Lutsk. However, after the war, the Poles opposed having Bishop Botsan take control of the episcopate of Lutsk, for this would hinder the process of changing over to Roman Catholicism. Sheptytsky remained in prison for three years and returned to Lviv on the 10th of September, 1917. In 1921, the metropolitan went to visit the Greek-Catholic Churches in Canada, U.S.A., Brazil and Argentina. Along with that he visited the major cities of the western world and tried to unite the political leaders of Europe in the matter of a Ukrainian state. At his return to his fatherland, the Polish leaders imprisoned him and the metropolitan remained in prison in Poznan for a time.

When the metropolitan had first taken the throne of Halych, a significant portion of the Ukrainian intelligentsia speculated as to what sort of policies the new metropolitan would implement. The speculations and doubts were

Metropolitan Andrew Sheptytsky
(1900-1944)

readily resolved when the metropolitan showed himself to be a patriot, a dedicated and wise pastor and an apostle of unity - both religious and national. He did not wish to "capture" souls to expand his Church, instead, he approached Orthodox Ukrainians with the greatest tolerance and respect and a few Orthodox bishops even lived with him at one time or other in his metropolitan's palace and celebrated the holy Liturgy in the metropolitan's chapel. But not only this happened. When Metropolitan Anthony (Khrapowytsky), the last metropolitan of Kiev, who sought to destory the Ukraine and who was the main force behind the imprisonment of Metropolitan Andrew, came to Lviv, Andrew paid him back with bread for his stone: he gave him shelter in his place and later arranged his journey to the border. No comment is necessary.

"Polish Christianity"

In the 1930's the destructive course of Polish policy in relation to Ukrainians, progressed to such an extent that it seemed the times of the persecutions of the first Christians by the Roman Nero had returned. In Kholmshchyna, hundreds of churches were destroyed or changed to Roman Catholic Churches. In the 20th century, in view of the civlized world, graveyards were plowed up, stone crosses were broken and even the bodily remains of the Orthodox bishops were not spared. Polish Christian bishops kept silent and only one metropolitan of Halych protested to the pope in a letter, standing in the defense of his persecuted brothers, the Orthodox Christians, and called on the whole Ukrainian populace to "prayer and works of penance to obtain God's mercy for them from heaven".

About Metropolitan Andrew, tens of books and hundreds of essays have been written. It would be impossible to describe his many-sided activity in a short paragraph. What has been said before characterized him as a person and a pastor, a Christian and an apostle of truth. Everything went into the program of his work - service to God and to the nation. While caring for the eternal, he did not forget that he had real people to deal with; thus he cared for the temporal, for the education of the young, for national culture, for art, for Ukrainian enlightenment and for social institutions. By his Pastoral letters Andrew Sheptytsky, like Moses, taught, admonished, and advised.

One of the more important problems in the internal Ukrainian social life of the 1930's was the indifferent attitude of Ukrainian youth towards nationalism. About this matter, the metropolitan regarded it his duty to speak, and he spoke in the letter "to Ukrainian Youth". How great a pastoral love, understanding, and respect for the impulses of youth is shown here. But there is also a warning here, a warning founded on a great insight and a deep understanding of people's souls and situations.

In 1931 he ordained N. Charnetsky as bishop of Volynia and Kholmshchyna. A separate part of his pastoral work was his apostolic work towards church union of the East and the West. From his very enthronement as metropolitan until the last day of his life he taught by word and writing, by wise advice and tolerant behaviour, how one was to work and what was to be done to obtain from heaven that grace of God that would make "all one".

Of the literary inheritance from Metropolitan Andrew there remain his Epistles, Pastoral letters, ascetic and theological works, political speeches, translations of the holy Fathers, and his works about art, about rites, about social matters and about the union of the Churches.

The metropolitan lived through four foreign occupations: Russian, Polish, German and Soviet. He did not survive the fifth and final occupation of the Bolsheviks and he died on the 1st of November, 1944, a symbol of the sufferings of the nation to which he had given his whole heart, all his talent and knowledge, and all his efforts. He never left his flock and in the darkest days in the history of the Ukraine, he shared its troubles - the sadness of war, the terror, the persecutions and the degradations. The nation repayed him with love and boundless trust.

The Funeral

The metropolitan's funeral took place on Sunday, November the 5th, in the presence of tens of thousands of faithful from the farthest corners of Halychyna. He was laid to eternal rest by the new metropolitan, Joseph Slipyj, with the participation of the Ukrainian episcopate and the bishops of other Churches, the Polish Catholic, the Armenian, and the Orthodox. Altogether, 30 bishops and hundreds of priests took part in the funeral. This was the first time in the whole history of the Church that the official representatives of four Churches buried a Greek-Catholic archbishop. The body of the blessed metropolitan rested in the crypts of the Church of St. George, built by one of his ancestors.

The Catholic Church, aware of the righteous life he had lived, began the process of beautification shortly after the metropolitan's death.

The successor of Metropolitan Andrew, hitherto his archbishop-aide, was Joseph Slipyj, the greatest co-worker of the deceased and the rector of the Theological Academy for many years.

21. The Ukrainian Orthodox Church after the Revolution of 1917

With the destruction of the Russian Empire in 1917, the national movement which sprang up in the Ukraine also encompassed the Church. Two and a half centuries of Russification, destruction, and uprooting of anything which indicated the independence of the Ukrainian Church from that of Moscow, the prohibition of the use of the native language in sermons and the erasing of all trace of the ancient Ukrainian traditions and cultural memories -all this was unable to destroy the living soul and it manifested itself at the first opportunity.

In 1917, the Pan-Ukrainian Church Council, composed of clergy and laity, was founded in Kiev. It set itself the task of obtaining independence for the Ukrainian Church from that of the Russian. But the action did not prove easy. Almost the whole hierarchy (with the exception of perhaps, two bishops), whose origins were in Moscow, adopted an opposing position. This church movement was seen, above all, as an attempt at the sacramental unity of the imperial-group. For this reason, this hierarchy applied all efforts so as not to allow the ecclesiastical and spiritual renewal of the millions of faithful who trusted it.

U.A.O.C.

In 1918, by the efforts of the Council, a Pan-Ukrainian Church Council was called in Kiev. Through this Council, the clergy indicated the wishes of the lower clergy and faithful. Nevertheless the episcopate, which in matters of Ukrainian statehood enjoyed complete freedom, decided to ignore these wishes. The statements of Hetman Skoropadsky, as well as those of the Directorate later, defined the matter, requesting from the hierarchy an agreement for the autocephaly of the Church. Not having obtained this agreement, the Directorate, the leading body of government in the Ukraine, issued a law (on the 1st of January, 1919) in which it recognized the Ukrainian Autocephalous Orthodox Church as a Church separate from and independent of that of Moscow.

Now efforts were begun to obtain the support of the patriarch of Constantinople and to obtain his agreement to the proclaimed autocephaly. In all likelihood, these efforts would have been successful if not for the fact that the Bolshevik horde descended on the Ukraine and the young Ukrainian state found itself in mortal danger. The destruction of the Ukrainian state finally cancelled all efforts for autocephaly in Constantinople.

Under the conditions of the Bolshevik occupation, it was not easy to organize a fight for church independence. But neither the Ukrainian clergy nor the laity retreated from their position and when the hierarchy of Moscow decisively refused to set up even one Ukrainian bishop, they decided to act independently.

In October 1921, a Council took place in Kiev and since it was impossible to arrange the canonical establishment of a Ukrainian episcopate, the clergy decided to conduct an episcopal ordination in a manner unusual in the Church, by the laying on of hands by priests. The ordination of a bishop by priests is regarded, according to the canons of the Church, as anti-canonical and thus invalid. These first hierarchs, ordained by priests, were the archpriest, Basil Lypkiwsky, who accepted the office of metropolitan of the U.A.O.C. and the archpriest, Nestor Sharayewsky. They later ordained bishops, 27 in all. The autocephalous Church obtained a large number of followers. In 1927, still at the relative time of the Bolshevik terror, this Church had 10.657 priests and obviously, several thousand parishes.

Basil Lypkiwsky (1921-1927)

Yet this action of self-ordination, as it was called, gave the enemy good ammunition. The Moscow hierarchy in the Ukraine conducted a strong campaign against the autocephalists, explaining to the nation that it was a sin to belong to such a Church. This campaign, understandably, began to create ferment, uneasiness, and disorganization in the church, and it severely weakened the Autocephalous Church. In this way, the faithful were divided and there existed in the Ukraine the patriarchal Orthodox Church (during the Bolshevik regime, the patriarchate had been restored and Patriarch Tykhon then ruled), or that of Tykhon and the Autocephalous - a Ukrainian Church which was in turn divided into several factions. In addition, a new blessing came from Moscow in the form of the so-called Living Church, that is, a new church organization which had sprung up in Moscow under the inspiration of the Bolshevik regime and which bowed to this regime in all things. The Bolshevik policy was aimed at creating the greatest possible disharmony in the Church and to create completely impossible conditions for all types of church life. Accusations, investigations, and arrests began. In 1927, Metropolitan Lypkiwsky was relieved of his office and in the following several years, a vicious Bolshevik terror swept in and the U.A.O.C. ceased to exist. At the outbreak of the Second World War, there was not one bishop in the Ukraine. Those who had not saved themselves by fleeing the country died in the snows of Siberia. Perhaps the only one who remained alive was Metropolitan Ivan Theodorovych who in 1925 came to the west and later led the Ukrainian Orthodox Church in the U.S.A.

The Second World War (1939-1945)

At the final division of Poland (in 1939), the western Ukrainian lands were joined to the Soviet Union and together with this a part of the Autocephalous Orthodox Church in Poland, that is, the eparchies in the northern Ukrainian lands and those Orthodox islands which were distributed in Halychyna and in Lemkiwshchyna. Metropolitan Nicholas immediately came here from Moscow. He made himself a center in Lutsk and began the action for "union". To help him, two newly-ordained bishops were sent from Moscow: Damascene Maluta and Panteleymon Rudik - the latter as bishop of Lviv. Those bishops who had earlier been under the jurisdiction of the metropolitan of the metropoly of Warsaw in Poland - Dionysius, Alexis and Policarp - found themselves under Moscovite rule and were forced by this rule to break their ties with their former hierarch and recognize the supremacy of the patriarch of Moscow. In this manner, without much difficulty, the patriarchate of Moscow again extended her boundaries and influences.

In 1941 war broke out between the Bolsheviks and the Germans and soon great reaches of the Ukraine were under the new Hitlerian terror. Now, two Churches sprang up in the northwestern and central Ukrainian lands. One, led by Archbishop Alexis (Hromadsky), who regarded himself as bound to the patriarch of Moscow by oath (although earlier he had not regarded himself as "bound" by his oath to Metropolitan Dionysius) was called "Autonomous" and the other one was the "Orthodox Autocephalous Church". Bishop Policarp joined the latter, refusing to recognize the patriarch any longer. After Archbishop Alexis' death, control was taken by Bishop Rudik who had earlier been ordained bishop of Lviv.

U.A.O.C. in 1942

The renewed Ukrainain Autocephalous Church (in 1942) differed greatly from that of the U.A.O.C. of 1921. She had an ordained hierarchy, all her bishops were canonically established and for this reason, her position was much stronger. Ordained in Pinsk, Kiev, and Lutsk by the hierarchs Alexander, the archbishop of Polisia and Pinsk, and Policarp of Lutsk, were the following bishops: Nikanor, Ihor, Michael, Volodimir, Platon, Gregory, Genady, Vyacheslav, Mstyslav, and Sylvester Thus the hierarchy of the U.A.O.C. now numbered twelve bishops. Metropolitan Alexis, who headed the Autonomous Church, realized his mistake and by a decree on the 8th October, 1942, joined the U.A.O.C. Nevertheless, other bishops of the Autonomous Church (Simon, Panteleymon, Venyamin and Anthony) remained autonomists and with the help of the Germans, did not permit the complete union of these two Churches to occur.

The Germans took an inimical attitude towards the Ukrainian Church and for this reason they encouraged ecclesiastical disagreements. At the end of 1942 or at the beginning of 1943 they issued a law by which they subjected the eparchial bishops to authority of the local German commissars. Now the bishop constituted a church unto himself and could not bow to any authority save that of the German administrative rule. What the Ukrainian Church endured! But the German invasion ended as well. In 1944 and 1945, the defeated and tired German army retreated from the Ukraine under pressure from the Soviets, aided by the western Allies. The majority of the autocephalous clergy and the entire hierarchy fled to the west. In the new postwar conditions, the clergy was forced to organize the Ukrainian Orthodox Church in the diaspora. The Church in the Ukraine again fell under Moscow rule.

22. The Orthodox Autocephalous Church in Poland

After the agreement at Riga between Poland and Soviet Russia (on the 18th of March, 1921), an agreement ratified by the Council of Ambassadors in Paris (in 1923), within the boundaries of the Polish state there were over four million Orthodox and in this about two and a half million Ukrainians. In 1922, the Polish government issued a temporary decree by which it determined the organization of the Orthodox Church in Poland. The first metropolitan of this Church was a Ukrainian, George Yaroshevsky, who was killed a year later by Smaragd, a hater of Ukrainianism, a Moscovite, and a former archimandrite. The Polish government assigned a Russian,Dionysius Valedynsky, as the new metropolitan. The patriarch of Constantinople took a favorable attitude towards this Church and by a "tomos" (decree) on the 13th of November, 1924, this patriarch, Gergory VII, granted this Church autocephaly and by this he brought her into a prayerful union with all the Orthodox Churches of the East. From this time on, this Church became independent of the pretensions of Moscow.

Dependence upon the State

The head of the Church was the metropolitan and the general authority lay with the council of bishops. In reality, the Polish government left the council of bishops, the holy Synod, little freedom. All their activity had to pass through the censorship of the ministry of the faith and education. The government for example, did not allow the metropolitan to call a council although the metropolitan attempted this for years. By an order of 1930 (a decree of the president) and an order of the Council of ministers (in 1933), the Church was given a "Statute of the Polish Autocephalous Orthodox Church. The official language was Polish and the priests were to conduct even the teaching of religion and sermons in Polish. The same applied to the theological schools, the Spiritual Seminary of Kremyanets, and the Theological faculty at the university of Warsaw. The government did what it pleased with Church property (although the Church had not been deprived of any rights of ownership by any decree) and all the church lands in Kholmshchyna (20.000 hectares) were given over to Polish colonists. The assignment and discharging of Orthodox priests depended on the government. Priests received their pay not from the metropolitan but from local leaders, political representatives of the government.

The Destruction of Churches

In the 1930's, the Polish government began systematically and unscrupulously to destroy Orthodox Churches in Kholmshchyna in order to completely destroy in this manner the Ukrainian character of this land and to pave the road for complete assimilation. Churches were sealed up and by order of the government, the police and the army, disregarding all the pleas of the faithful, later destroyed those Churches, blew them up with dynamite or simply burned them. Such barbarianism, perhaps, had not been seen in any country in the world. The remainder, which they did not level, they turned into Roman Catholic Churches. Such Churches taken away from the Orthodox Ukrainians and changed into Roman Catholic Churches numbered 169 in 1938. This happened with only a few Orthodox Churches in Kholmshchyna. Thus by "fire and sword" the Catholic Poland spread her civilization and her own brand of Christianity.

The Administrative Division

Administratively, the Church was divided into five eparchies: Warsaw - with Metropolitan Dionysius, Volynia - with Archbishop Alexis (Hromadsky), Polisia - with Archbishop Alexander (Inozemtsev), Vilenia - with Archbishop Theodosius (a Russian), Hrodnenia - with Bishop Sava (Sovietov). In all, the Church had about one and a half thousand parishes and daughter churches. The largest was the eparchy of Volynia which had 680 parishes and 7 monasteries.

With the destruction of Poland, this Church was again divided. The eparchies which were added to the Soviet Union went back under the rule of the patriarchate of Moscow.

23. The Organization of the Church.
   Educational and Monastic Life

a) The Orthodox Church

In accordance with the ancient tradition of the Eastern Church, the Ukrainian Orthodox Church is founded and governed in a way similar to that of other Churches of the East, with the dependence of the Church on the Holy Scriptures, Church tradition (or practices or customs which the Church had gathered in the course of the years), the canons of the first seven Ecumenical Councils, the Rules of the Church Fathers, the resolutions of general councils and separate Statutes of a competent authority of a current significance. Perceptible organizational changes came about between the Orthodox and the Uniate Churches after the union of Berestya.

The head of the Ukrainian Orthodox Church is still the metropolitan, at first with a nominal dependence on the partriarch of Constantinople. At first he was elected by bishops with the considerable influence of the rulers of the hetmanate. During the times of the Ukraine's dependence on Poland, the king actually had the deciding vote. After the joining to the patriarchate of Moscow, the government of Moscow nominated the metropolitan of Kiev and he was ordained by the partiarch. The bishops had no say in the election of their hierarchial primate. The same occurred with the bishops: formerly the council of bishops had elected them, sometimes the metropolitan, had done it, also with the participation of the faithful, and later, after the loss of ecclesiastical independence, the government of Moscow appointed them.

The metropoly was divided into eparchies of which there was a number at different times. The eparchies were ruled by bishops with the help of the "Kryloses", that is, an assistant council which was comprised of the spiritual leaders of the eparchial capitol. The eparchies were subdivided further into archpriestates (deaconates). The lowest administrative rung was the parish.

The metropolitan was the highest pastor, teacher and judge in his metropoly. Only in a few cases did his resolutions of judgemental decisions go to a higher ecclesiastical court, the patriarch of Constantinople, for consideration. During the time of the dependence on the patriarch of Moscow, the metropolitan of Kiev gradually lost his rights, so that even in the most trivial matters (for example, permission to print books) he had to ask the permission of the secular and spiritual authorities of Moscow. The bishops had similar rights, each in his own eparchy. The bishop educated, judged, and disposed of priests as was needed, granted offices, conducted visitations, cared for the purity of the faith and cared about the rightful discharging of priestly duties and the spiritual life of the flock entrusted to him.

Spiritual Education

In this third historical era, religious education, schools, printing houses, authorship, theological education, and the publishing of theological books expanded greatly and became important factors in the life of the Church. At the beginning of the 17th century, new schools sprang up, the most important of these being the Mohylian College which was a first class higher school in all of Eastern Europe for a long time. In the 18th century, the College of Kharkiw was also founded (in 1727), along with the Spiritual Seminary of Pereyaslav (in 1738), a Seminary in the Novhorod of Siversk (in 1785) and later the Seminary of Poltava as well (the eparchy of Poltava was formed in 1803). At the beginning of the 20th century, the following spiritual schools existed in the Ukraine: the Spiritual Academy of Kiev and spiritual seminaries in Kiev, Kharkiw, Poltava, Chernyhiw, Kholm, Odessa, Kamyanets, Podilsky, and Katerynoslav. Nevertheless, Moscovite priests, superiors, or rectors controlled all these schools and their spirit, with few exceptions, was Russian.

Before the joining of the metropoly to the Church of Moscow, many Ukrainian students, theologians, and laity conducted their studies in the foreign schools of Prague, Olomonets, Vienna, Rome, Kracow, Braunsberg, Paris and in other famous centers of learning.

The literary production of that era was mainly in the 17th century, polemic literature and writings on theological, canonical or ritual themes in which the authors showed the truth of the teaching, organization, or ritual traditions of the Orthodox Church. This literature is often characterized by very sharp, rigorous tones, blame for error in faith or ritual, and so on. Understandably, the Uniates replied in approximately the same form.

A valuable addition to the Ukrainian ecclesiastical literature was preaching, which in the 17th century was on a very high level. In Moscovy at that time, preaching was a monstrosity and for this reason the Ukrainian preachers were in such demand in the north. Ukrainian preachers took a lively interest in the life and achievements of the western world and for this reason, in preaching as well, a strong influence of the so-called scholastic sermon was left in the Ukraine. The finest preachers of that time were Daniel Tuptalenko (St. Demitrius in the Orthodox Church) of Kiev (1651-1709), Joanicius Galatowsky (died in 1688), Anthony Radyvyliwsky (died in 1688), Lazarus Baranowych (1593-1694) and many others. In later times, preaching declined as did ecclesiastical education because of the prohibition of the use of the native language and the publishing of books (in 1863).

Monasteries and Monastic Life

The monasteries in the metropoly of Kiev were very spread out. They constituted a famous tradition beginning as early as the princely era and became

231

the most important centers of spiritual life and asceticism. The religious battle severely weakened monastic life and monastic discipline and education and made the monasteries a part of the battle for monastic possessions. It is not known exactly how many monasteries existed in the metropoly of Kiev at any time but there were over two hundred of them. Some of these, such as the Monastery of the Caves, the holy Trinity (in Vilna), the Holy Cross Monastery, that of Mychayliw, of Vydubytsky, Trakhtemyriwsky and the Monastery of Pochayiw were key centers not only of the religious and cultural movement but also played an important role in political life. Matters stood differently in the Left Bank monasteries of Hustynsk, Lubensk, and others. Earlier, influences had reached here from Moscow and for that reason the hieromonks of those monasteries were avantguardists in the uniting of the Ukrainian Church with that of Moscow.

Metropolitan Mohyla rendered a great service in the reorganization of monastic life. Having taken control of the metropoly, Mohyla, as the chronicler says, stopped that comfortable (drunken and sated) life which had begun to hold sway in monasteries, placed them under his supervision, and brought in order and discipline. From that time onward, monasteries played an important part both in the field of polemic battle and in the field of culture, translation of ecclesiastical and theological books from foreign languages, the publishing of their own preachings, and often in politics. The most important place here belongs to the Monastery of the Caves, which brought up hundreds of notable people and published thousands of books. The tsar of Moscow very gladly visited the Monastery of the Caves. Elizabeth, having visited it (in 1747), brought back fifty-four books, the Great Tsar twenty-four and the bride of the Great tsar the same number out from there. These were rare editions of theological and ecclesiastical books in costly bindings, which Moscovites today show to foreigners as achievements of their culture. Given the conditions during the tsarist regime in the Ukraine, monastic life in the Ukraine sharply declined. Nevertheless, the Monastery of the Caves had been able to preserve, at least in part, its famous tradition and from it came many activists who applied themselves to the rebirth of the Church after the revolution.

The monasteries worked for the most part under the rule of St. Theodore the Studite. They elected themselves an abbot or an archimandrite and other offices as well. Each monastery was independent of any other. The eparchial bishops had a certain control over the monasteries unless the monastery had obtained independence for itself, in which case the bishop's authority did not apply.

b) The Greek-Catholic Church

Differences

At the Council of Berestya (in 1596), the union of the Ukrainian Church with Rome was completed and since that time, this Church has been called by various names: Uniate, Rus-Catholic, United and so on. The main organizational change was that the Church recognized the primacy of the Roman pontiff in the whole Church of Christ, recognizing him as the highest pastor and teacher. It is obvious that all the articles of faith which the Catholic Church professed were professed by the Uniate Church as well. The Ukrainian Church preserved for herself her ancient rite, eastern ecclesiastical law, the Julian calendar, the old-church Slavonic language in services, a separate liturgical-ecclesiastical year, and various other practices different from those of the Latin Church, which had become accepted before the completion of the union.

When Austria took over Halychyna, the Ukrainian Church received a new name: Greek-Catholic. This is not a very good name because there is not much in common with the Greeks here, but nevertheless this name entered the Ukrainian history, literature and documents, became accepted in the understanding of the nation and thus it is not feasible to change it. It can only be changed by the highest government in the Ukrainian Church, that is, the Council of bishops.

Organization

In accordance with the resolutions of the Council of Berestya, the head of the Greek-Catholic Church is the metropolitan, who is elected by the bishops. In practice, however, this was often not the case. The metropolitan directs the metropoly as its pastor, teacher and judge in Church matters. The metropolitan's higher court is Rome. The eparchial bishops are subject to the metropolitan and discharge their authority in the eparchies entrusted to them; they teach, preach, and judge and generally care for the religious and moral life of their flock. Their higher court is the metropolitan. In the course of time, the Ukrainian metropolitans lost some of their former power and bishops became more independent. For help in the administration of the Church, the metropolitan has, as do the bishops in the eparchies, Chapters, which in administrative matters have an important, often deciding, vote. An important right of the metropolitan is the assigning of bishops. This is the law, but in practice it is not always the case. During the time of the Austrian monarchy, the emperor reserved this right for himself: he appointed the metropolitan and bishops and Rome confirmed them.

The helping executive-administrative organ of the metropolitan or bishop is the Consistory, under the leadership of a bishop-aide or a vicar general.

The entire Greek-Catholic Church (before the last war) was composed of three eparchies and two Apostolic administrations (Volynia with a capitol in Kovel and Lemkiwshchyna), as well as eparchies in Yugoslavia and churches in Bukovina and in countries across the ocean.

Spiritual Enlightenment

Metropolitan Rutsky founded the first seminary for Uniate theologians in Minsk (in White Rus). Besides that, Uniate theologians conducted their studies in Latin colleges or universities - which was not always to their benefit. After the joining of Halychyna to Austria, the Austrian government had set up the Barbareum in Vienna, where theologians lived and received part of their education. Somewhat later (in 1783) a Spiritual Seminary was founded in Lviv and in 1787 the so-called Stadium Romanum. From 1804 to 1918, a theological faculty existed at the university of Lviv for both the Greek-Catholic and the Roman-Catholic rites at once. Only certain disciplines took place separately. Besides that, as in former so in later times, many theologians studied abroad in Vienna, Rome, Innsbruck, Prague, and Freiburg. There were spiritual schools in other centers as well: seminaries in Peremyshl (in 1912), in Stanislaviv (in 1907) and in Oryashiv, and the college of St. Josaphan in Rome (in 1897). In 1928, the most important theological school, the Theological Academy in Lviv, was founded. This Academy graduated a whole generation of highly-educated priests and also a few tens of volumes of valuable scholarly publications applying to different areas of learning and knowledge: theological, canonical, ritual, pedagogical, pastoral, pastoral literature and so on. The Theological Academy ceased to exist with the coming of the Bolsheviks. After the war, by the efforts of the former deacon of the Theological Faculty of the Academy, Archpriest B. Laba, a Seminary was founded in Germany (in Hirschberg in Bavaria) which was later transferred to Holland. A few tens of priests graduated from there.

The clergy of the Greek-Catholic Church, especially from the mid-19th century applied itself vigorously to the spreading of education in the nation and to the enlivening of the Ukrainian literary movement in general.

Monasteries and Monastic Life

Monastic life again began to develop in the Uniate Church after the reform of Rutsky (in 1617). Up until this time, monasteries were like independent republics with their own government. Now the metropolitan centralized all these monasteries, gave them a new rule, established one protoarchimandrite, and stopped their former liberties. The new Rule, based on the rule of St. Basil the Great, gave the order its name. The main task of the monks now became the work of upbringing and education. Until 1675, the metropolitan of the time was the protoarchimandrite of the order. Between the metropolitan and the monasteries there was not always agreement and good-will. The reasons for this have been mentioned before. From the year 1780, the monasteries in the eparchies under Austrian rule constituted a second province. In the 18th century several new monasteries were founded which had a significant influence on ecclesiastical life. Here belong primarily the monasteries in Buchach (in 1712) and in Christinople (in 1763). By a papal decree of 1744, it was ordered that several monasteries be abolished and others joined to larger ones. Of 122 monasteries, 25 were completely shut down and 59 were joined to others, thus only 38 monasteries remained in the mid 18th century. After the first division of Poland, as the sources indicate, there were 40 under Austrian rule and 73 Basilian monasteries under the Russian part of the Church (in the so-called Lithuanian province). In the former there lived 645 monks and in the latter 599 (some sources indicate that there was a significantly greater number of monasteries, 69 under Austrian rule). In the era of the greatest expansion of monasticism, there were 235 monasteries in the entire Uniate Church. By a decree of the emperor of 1783, many monasteries were closed so that at the end of the 19th century there existed twenty-odd (24?) monasteries in all.

An important event in the life of the order was the Synod of Zamosk (of 1720) which, along with other matters, guaranteed the Basilians individual rights. This became the source of long-standing disagreements between the hierarchy and the Basilians. In the second half of the 19th century, the Basilian monasteries had become largely deserted and the monastic movement declined. In 1882, the Jesuits instituted a reform of the Order and that time dates the beginning of growth and development of monastic life in Basilian monasteries.

In 1908, Metropolitan Andrew renewed the order of the Studite Discipline with monasteries in Uhniw, Kryvchytsi (near Lviv), and Ternopil. In 1913 the order of Redemptorists was established in the Ukraine, mostly for missionary work. Besides the male orders, female orders developed as well: the Basilian sisters, the sister Auxiliaries, the Holy Family sisters, and others. In all, in the territory of the ecclesiastical province of Halych before the war there were: 67 monasteries, 64 (?) Congregational Houses and about one and a half thousand monks and nuns. Many of these had their own schools. Some concerned themselves with pedagogical work in Ukrainian high schools, institutes, and professional schools, and the Basilian sisters had their own high school in Lviv.

24. An Overview of the Era

The third era in the history of the Church in the Ukraine was an era of great decisions and changes. Until this time, the Ukrainian Church had only once decided on a major step, that is, the acceptance of the union of Florence (in 1438), but the conditions at that time had not been favorable to the consolidation of this idea in the metropoly. The following events, of internal and external (political) order, severely weakened both the spiritual life of the Church and the Church as an organization. At the end of the 16th century, the metropolitan and most of the bishops of the metropoly of Kiev decided to seek aid in union with Rome. Perhaps they were aware that this action would not be easy and that they were taking upon themselves a great responsibility before the nation and history, yet they decided on this step after a preparation of a few years.

The 17th century was a period of battle between the Uniate Church and the Orthodox, led by an able and dedicated hierarchy. This battle sapped the new energy on one side and on the other forced the leading activists into eager work for the safeguarding of those truths in which they doubtless strongly believed. This era brought in varying successes to each side alternately. In Kiev, under the guidance and protection of the Church, an important scholarly center sprang up which was a brilliant page in the history of the Ukraine. The Uniate Church was able to repel the unceasing advances of Latinism and finally proved her right to be called a Church of the Ukrainian nation.

The growth of the northern power, that of Moscow - both ecclesiastical and sovereign - led to an expansion to the south-west, into Ukrainian lands. After Pereyaslav, after the political agreement with Hetman Khmelnytsky, the Orthodox Church of Moscow went on a campaign against the hitherto independent metropoly of Kiev and finally incorporated it. From that time there began a gradual decline and a planned Russification of the Ukrainian Orthodox Church.

Historical events of the end of the 18th century changed the map of Europe. The formerly great Polish state ceased to exist. A completely new status was created for the Ukrainian Churches. The achievements of the Uniate Church in the territories held by Russia were lost, not to the benefit of the Russian Church. A part of the Uniate Church under Austrian rule, having received a better chance for development, consolidated its powers, conquered other dangers and fortified a clear position for itself in the whole Ukrainian Church.

THE FOURTH ERA

1. "Council of Lviv" of 1946 and the Liquidation of the Greek-Catholic Church in the Ukraine

The effects of the Second World War

The Second World War (1939-1945), which, to a large extent, took place on Ukrainian lands, brought the Ukraine great losses in people and property. In four years the fronts changed three times and whatever one enemy did not succeed in destroying, the next destroyed.

After the collapse of Poland in 1939, the western Ukrainian lands, with the exception of Kholmshchyna, Pidlasha and Lemkiwshchyna were occupied by the Bolsheviks in accordance with an earlier agreement with Hitlerian Germany. The remaining western Ukrainian lands stayed under German occupation.

Soon after this noisy "liberation", the Bolsheviks began a campaign against the Church, against the priesthood, and against religion in general. Yet in two years the successes of their propaganda were minimal. The communist movement in Halychyna had always been very weak and most of the populace took a hostile attitude towards it even then. No scares, arrests, terrors, or banishments to Siberia helped - the Church continued to exist and after the liquidation of all other organizations, social, educational, and political, the Church remained the only port of the independent Ukrainian life. The Bolsheviks knew this well but they did not dare to take this final fortress by assault. Metropolitan Andrew was still alive then. His authority was so great, both at home and abroad, that if these "liberators" had applied brutal force against him and the Church, then they would have induced mass disturbances. This the Bolsheviks did not want and for this reason they left the Church in relative peace.

In June, 1941 war broke out between the Germans and Bolsheviks. In the course of a few months, not only the western Ukrainian lands but the entire Ukraine found itself under the no less vicious German occupation. All the present hopes for indulgences from western civilization soon dispersed and, in those extremely difficult conditions of war and mass terror, the Ukrainian nation began to organize its own powers for its defense against two apocalyptic beasts, the Germans and the Bolsheviks. This movemet cost the nation great sacrifices but in this way its character and awareness was shown, since only by great sacrifices could great deeds be completed.

In July, 1944, the western lands of the Ukraine again found themselves under Bolshevik rule. Less than a year later, the Second World War ended. Now almost all the Ukrainian lands fell under the direct Moscovite-Bolshevik sphere of influence, with the exception of the so-called beyond Over-Khersonian lands, that is, the lands to the west of the river Syan and part of Kholmshchyna and Pidlasha which found themselves under Communist Poland. Here not only the Church was destroyed but most of the populace was killed off as well, with the remainder transferred very far to the north and west, in lands formerly German, which had come under Polish rule after the war. By such an action the entire Lemkiwshchyna became depopulated. What the aristocratic Poland had not been able to destroy in many long years was destroyed by the "national" Communist Poland.

A few months after the second coming of the Bolsheviks to Halychyna, Metropolitan Andrew, the greatest of metropolitans which the Greek Catholic Church had ever had, died on the 1st of November, 1944. This was a heavy blow for the Church and he seemingly predicted the Good Friday of her further fate.

Joseph Slipyj Kobernytskyj Dychkowsky

After the death of Metropolitan Andrew, Archbishop Joseph Slipyj Kobernytsky Dychkowsky took the helm of the Church. Doubtless, a better candidate for metropolitan could not be imagined. Metropolitan Slipyj, during all the time of his earlier activity, both ecclesiastical and social, proved himself a person of such great form, of such strong character and ability that only he himself could take the helm of the church in such terrible times. He did not betray the Church's hopes. He created one of the most brilliant pages of Ukrainian Church history. In the period of his activity as rector of the only higher Ukrainian theological school in the world, the Theological Academy, he raised its standards, making it one of the finest institutions of that type in the whole Catholic Church. He educated a whole generation of priests of a new type and he set the theological education of the Ukrainian Church on a par with the education of the western European countries. A follower of Metropolitan Joseph was able to unite the eastern type of Christianity, true to the oriental Church, with the Ukrainian Church's organic belonging to the West, to the Catholic Church and her culture.

At the beginning of 1945, the Bolsheviks decided to destroy the Greek-Catholic Church by force since neither the persecution of priests nor that of the laity nor the enforced terror and mass arrests had had the success desired. For this reason, at the beginning of this year (1945), all the bishops were imprisoned and this was a heavy blow to the very foundation of her organization. A Church cannot survive very long without her hierarchy. After such a preparation, a "council" could be called which was to seal her fate.

The So-called Council of Lviv, 1946

It must be noted here that, notwithstanding all the foreseen persecutions, all the bishops of the Greek Catholic Church had remained in their places, ready to suffer death for their faith. This shows the great moral strength of the Church. In the same way that the Church had grown and gained strength by the sacrifice of the first Christians in the era of bloody persecutions, so the Ukrainian Church will grow by the blood of these saintly men.

Thus, having arrested the Ukrainian bishops, members of the eparchial chapters, and other influential priests, the Bolsheviks forcibly brought about

Patriarch Joseph Slipyj Kobernytskyj Dychkowsky

a hundred terrorized priests and approximately the same number of faithful to Lviv and between the 8th and the 10th of March 1946, the so-called "council" took place which has no equal in the entire long history of Christianity. The council decided to reject the resolutions of the Union of Berestya (in 1596), to break canonical ties with the Catholic Church, and to "unite" with the Orthodox Church of Moscow. Such "unions" had occurred earlier as well. The Uniate eparchies had "united" after the divisions of Poland; hitherto entire eparchies had "united" in 1839. The eparchy of Kholm had "united" in 1875 and now another "union" came in 1946. All these "unions" followed the bayonets of Moscow like a shadow. This was the "goodwill" which the patriarchs of Moscow had pushed so stubbornly onto the Ukrainian Church since the mid-17th century. In this way the metropoly of Kiev had been "united" in 1686, and how this goodwill proved itself has already been seen. For a while yet Ukrainian metropolitans had remained at the metropoly of Kiev but slowly their powers diminished, their authority was undermined by enemy hands, the disobedient found themselves in prisons (of which Moscovy always had plenty) and finally Moscovite natives took the throne of the metropoly of Kiev. In Halychyna, in the Greek-Catholic Church, the matter was simpler - here a Moscovite native came at once. The basic principle of the "faith" of the Orthodoxy of Moscow, "that the tsardom of Moscow expand by Orthodoxy" thus found itself yet another reaffirmation.

In this way, the Greek-Catholic Church ceased to exist in its native land. It ceased to exist as a visible organization, as a real ecclesiastical province, but it did not cease to exist in the light of canonical law, whether of the Catholic or the Orthodox Church. This is important and it should be kept always in mind. The basic foundation of Greek-Catholicism is the fatherland where the bodily remains of the great Ukrainian Church activists are resting, where thousands of faithful and hundreds of priests laid down their lives in the defense of their faith and where even today, just like the early Christians in the catacombs, the faithful gather for prayer.

The Canonical Validity of the Council

What canonical validity did this council have? None! Regarding this, there is no difference either from the Catholic or the Orthodox Church's point-of-view. From the earliest beginnings of the Church organization, the only ones who had the right (by God's institution) to take part in the councils and make decisions during these councils were always the bishops. For this reason, any council which takes place against the wishes of the rightful hierarchical primate and without the participation of bishops, is no council at all. Its decisions have no canonical significance whatsoever. This is recognized (in theory) by the Russian Orthodox Church as well. When a council had gathered in Moscow (in 1660) on the "wishes of the local leader" and not those of the patriarch, then the patriarch of that time, Nicon, immediately observed that the "council, not having been called according to the holy rules, was no council but a parody". Such councils, which occurred by an encroachment on the norms set up by the Church, he called a "Judaic synagogue, a beastly parody and an unlawful gathering". The contemporary priests of the Church of Moscow had proved more progressive and did not take the teachings of their patriarch very much to heart.

Unfortunately, the other eastern Churches did not protest this blatant illegality either. It should be noted that eastern churches, in the sphere of church law had always manifested a great sensitivity and any infringement of the canons accepted by the Ecumenical Councils were strictly condemned.

The Liquidation of the Church in Carpathian Ukraine in 1947

A similar fate to that of the ecclesiastical province of Halychyna awaited the eparchies in Carpathian Ukraine as well. The eparchy of Mukachiw was included within the boundaries of the U.S.S.R., "united" Church in 1947. The last bishop, Theodore Romgha, died a martyr's death on the 31st of October, 1947. In the eparchy of Pryashiw, which entered into the composition of Czechoslovakia, the liquidation was conducted a few years later. In April, 1950, Bishop Paul Goydych and his aide Basil Hopko, were imprisoned, the seminary was disbanded, and the priests arrested.

In Berlin, there was still an Apostolic visitor for the Greek-Catholic Ukrainians in Germany. Here also the hand of Moscow reached him. He was arrested and sent to Siberia.

Having begun a definite vendetta against the Ukrainian Church, the Bolsheviks of Moscow destroyed her entire hierarchy. Of all the arrested bishops, only Metropolitan Joseph, now Cardinal Slipyj Kobernytsky Dychkowsky, miraculously survived. The following bishops died martyrs' deaths: Gregory Khomyshyn, the bishop of Stanyslaviv and his aide, Bishop Ivan Latyshevsky, Josaphat Kotsylovsky, the bishop of Peremyshl and his aide, Bishop Gregory Lakota, Bishop Mykyta Budka, Bishop Mykola Charnetsky, the Apostolic visitor in Volynia, Paul Goydych, the bishop of Pryashiw and his aide. Bishop Basil Hopko, Theodore Romgha, the bishop of Mukachiw and Peter Verhun, the Apostolic visitor in Germany. Besides bishops, hundreds of priests, monks, and nuns and thousands of faithful died martyrs' deaths in the concentration camps of Siberia. How many of them, these confessors and martyrs for the faith, died there only the good Lord Himself knows.

This was the fate of the Ukrainian Church in the Ukraine for both the Orthodox and the Greek-Catholic, in the final process of "union". Ukrainians had to pay very dearly for the aggressive, intrusive, unnecessary, and unwanted "goodwill" of Moscow.

This "goodwill" and its result will never be forgotten by future generations and nothing will erase it from Ukrainian history. It will remain for centuries a grave warning against the misleading Orthodoxy of Moscow and against the type of Christianity which is willing to serve any government, even a godless one, to achieve its mission: the expansion of the boundaries of the empire of Moscow and the enslavement of foreign nations

2. The Greek-Catholic Church in the Diaspora

A) In the European Countries

Austria
One of the oldest branches of the Greek-Catholic Church beyond the native land was the parish of the church of St. Barbara in Vienna. When Maria Theresa founded a seminary for Greek-Catholic clerics in 1774, this Church became a main center of Greek-Catholicism in the capital of the Austrian Empire of that time. When the seminary was disbanded (in 1784), this seminarial church of St. Barbara was changed into a parish Church to serve the spiritual needs of Ukrainian Greek-Catholics who lived in Vienna. This parish has survived all the tempestuous times up until today.

After the Second World War, in Austria there lived a few tens of thousands of Ukrainian refugees and in the years 1945-1955, they had developed a network of church groups, mainly in western Austria. With the tide of emigration to the countries beyond the ocean, there remained only a few thousand Ukrainian Greek-Catholics in Austria; thus the parish of St. Barbara remained almost the only representative of the Ukrainian Church in that country. The pastor of the church of St. Barbara is under the jurisdiction of the metropolitan of Halych at any given time and the archbishop of Vienna at any time is also Apostolic delegate to the Greek-Catholics in Austria.

Germany:
For Ukrainians who lived in Germany after the First World War, Metropolitan Andrew had created in 1927, with the permission of Rome, a spiritual capitol which during the Second World War, in 1940, was changed to an Apostolic Visitorate. Peter Verhun was Apostolic visitor administrator until his arrest by the Bolsheviks. After the end of the war, Berlin, the capitol of the Administration fell under Bolshevik rule and by the same token the fate of the Administration was determined. The Administrator, Father Verhun died in exile, having shared the fate of other Ukrainian bishops and hundreds of priests.

After the Second World War a large number of Ukrainian refugees, both Greek-Catholic and Orthodox, came to the territories of Germany and temporarily settled in occupied zones of the western Allies in western Germany.

Almost two hundred Greek-Catholic priests were found here as well and church life slowly began to mend itself. Over one hundred houses of prayer or churches were organized here, church fraternities, schools, charitable institutions were founded there was even a spiritual seminary (Hirschberg in Bavaria) under the leadership of a former dean of the Theological faculty of the Academy, Archpriest Basil Laba. This seminary was somewhat later transferred to Holland (to Kulemborg near Utrecht, in 1948) and, during its almost five years existence, it graduated about 60 candidates to spiritual positions.

The jurisdiction over the churches in Germany, in other western European countries where there were Greek-Catholic church groups, was held by Archbishop Ivan Buchko, with his permanent capitol being Rome. The vicar general of Archbishop Buchko until 1959 was Father Peter Holynsky, a former high school catechist in Peremyshl. In 1959, Rome assigned Platon Kornylak as bishop for the Ukrainians in Germany. Today there remain not more than twenty thousand Ukrainian Greek-Catholics in Germany. The ecclesiastical and the cultural-social life of the Ukrainians in general is concentrated in Munich along with the capitol of the exarchbishop, Platon Kornylak.

Yugoslavia:
The first Ukrainian colonists appeared in Yugoslavia in the mid-18th century. In 1751, a Greek Catholic parish already existed in Kerestur. Notwithstanding the fact that these colonists had little contact with the Mother Church, they nevertheless were able to sustain their ritual distinctness. The contact with the Mother Church became stronger during Metropolitan Andrew's rule. In 1908 Metropolitan Andrew Sheptytsky had taken a sincere interest in this community of faithful and founded the Studite monastery (in Kamiants), the so-called Studite Lavra, which existed here until 1945.

In 1909, Rome established a separate vicariate for Bosnia, dependent upon the metropolitan of Halych, and in 1915 Dionysius Nyaradi (the Ukrainian ecclesiastical author of Bachka,) who had ruled the eparchy of Krighevci for twenty-five years (1915-1940), was ordained bishop for the Greek-Catholic Ukrainians in Yugoslavia.

During his episcopate, a livelier ecclesiastical and cultural movement began among the local Ukrainians. The "Prosvita" society was founded, publishing houses were set up, and popular books were printed for the people.

After the war, during the Communist regime, the Ukrainian Church suffered in Yugoslavia as well. Bishop Y. Shimrak (by origin a Croatian) died a martyr's death, the Studite Lavra was disbanded, and church property was confiscated. After Bishop Shimrak's death, Rome appointed Father Gabriel Bukatko the administrator for the Ukrainian Greek-Catholics and in 1952 he was ordained bishop. In time, the persecution of the Church in Yugoslavia quietened and thanks to the dedicated work of the bishop, monastic life was renewed, convents of Basilian Sisters and sister Auxiliaries were established, and even the spiritual seminary was restored.

Today Archbishop Bukatko is the primate of the Roman Catholic Church in Yugoslavia while Joakim Segedi was ordained bishop for the Greek-Catholics in 1963. According to the statistics (of 1949), over thirty-seven thousand Ukrainian Greek-Catholics live in Yugoslavia. They have 29 parishes, a spiritual seminary in Zagreb and over 40 priests.

Poland:

The history of eastern Christianity in Poland is old and interesting. Some historians are convinced that already as early as 900 there existed a Church of the eastern rite in Kracow. On its ruins, in 1390 a Bernardian monastery was built along with the Church of the Holy Cross, where services were held in old Slavonic language as well (alongside the Latin). But this belongs to ancient history.

After the division of the Ukraine at Andrusiw, a large portion of the lands of the Ukrainian fatherland found itself under Polish rule and for this reason, there was a significant increase in the influx of young students to the Academy of Kracow, which stood at a very high level at that time. Just at that time (at the end of the 17th century) the beginnings of the Ukrainian Uniate Church occurred. Nevertheless there is no exact information about the nature or location of this Church. Exact historical facts are known only from the end of the 18th century. In 1788 the former Bernardian monastery, the so-called "Dglubek", along with the church of the Blessed Virgin Mary on St. John Street, was granted to the Basilians for the spiritual needs of the Ukrainians at Kracow. Yet after almost ten years the civil government sold both the church and the monastery at an auction (in 1797) for non-payment of taxes. From that time until 1808, the parish of Kracow did not have permanent lodgings and only then (in 1808) did the Austrian government grant it ownership of the church of St. Norbert. This was a much smaller property than the former one sold at an auction. The tax was 27 gold sovereigns and the Church and monastery had been sold for twenty thousand gold sovereigns - the remainder, obviously, went into the national treasury. Obviously the pastor of that time did not care overly much for his Church if he let matters come to such an end. After his death, this Pastor Kudrevych left over five thousand florins in a private cash box.

The Church of St. Norbert existed throughout this period and before the war it served quite a large community of Ukrainian faithful which resided in Kracow. It survived until 1947, in which year the Polish Communist government gave it over to the Roman Catholics.

There also exist Ukrainian Churches in Warsaw and in other areas colonized by Ukrainians. However, there is meager information about the organization of their ecclesiastical life, and the number of parishes, priests and faithful.

France:

The Ukrainian emigration to France dates after the First World War. In France, the emigrant government of the Ukrainian National Republic established many political military activists and gradually the working-class emigration began to flow in from the western Ukrainian lands. The numerical quantity of Ukrainian emigrants in France fluctuated, sometimes almost reaching fifty thousand.

The organizer of the Ukrainian Church in France was Father Yakiw Perridon, a Hollander by origin and a sincere friend of Ukrainians. After the war he represented Archbishop Ivan Buchko as vicar general in France. In1961, Rome named Volodimir Malanchuk, a monk of the order of Redemptorists, exarch-bishop of Greek-Catholic Ukrainians in this country. It is not a large community, but quite well organized. The exarch-bishop resides in Paris and 18 priests serve the faithful.

England:
Approximately the same number of Ukrainians as live in France also live in Great Britain (about forty thousand) as a result of wartime movements. Ecclesiastical life was organized here by Father Josaphat Jean of the Basilians in 1947, by order of Archbishop Ivan Buchko. Father J. Jean was a Canadian priest of French descent who accepted the Ukrainian rite and worked much for the good of the Ukrainian Church and nation. The first priests came to England together with military divisions such as the Ukrainian Division "Halychyna" and the Polish corps of Anders, and also from camps for displaced persons in Germany. The successor of Fr. Jean was Fr. Alexander Malynowsky, the former administrator of Lemkiwshchyna and before the war, a long-term and highly meritorious deputy of the rector of the Spiritual Seminary in Lviv. He deserves merit above all, for this Church is perhaps the best-organized one of all the Eastern European Ukrainian Church Communities. After the death of Archpriest Malynowsky, the vicariate general in England was taken over by the Redemptorist father Paul Maluga and after him, the Basilian, Augustine Horniak, came in as exarch-bishop.

In 1960, the Greek-Catholic Church community in England numbered about twenty-six thousand faithful. The exarch-bishop's see is in London. Seventeen priests serve the faithful.

The Archpastor of the Refugees:
The former bishop-aide, Archbishop Ivan Buchko rendered great service in the organization of the Ukrainian Church in the western countries in the post-war period. Archbishop Buchko had gone to the countries of South America on a visitation in the name of Metropolitan Andrew in 1939, shortly before the outbreak of war. After the war and the imprisonment of all the bishops of the Greek-Catholic Church in the fatherland, Archbishop Buchko remained the only representative of the Church in the free world. This pastor applied all efforts and did not spare any labors to consolidate Ukrainian ecclesiastical life in the countries of the new settlements in the difficult post-war conditions. To this end, in 1945, the pope appointed Archbishop Buchko as exarch and Apostolic Visitor for all the Ukrainians in western Europe and a few years later (in 1951), for his activity and service in the or-

245

ganization of the Church, he bestowed upon him the dignity of assistant to the papal throne and the title of Roman count.

The Ukrainian Division of Halychyna owes its thanks to Archbishop Ivan Buchko for the fact that the western Allies held its members after the war (although in prisoner of war camps) in the face of the forcible removal by the Bolsheviks. Many civilian people owe their rescue to him as well, for the Bolshevik mission was to compel them to return to "the family". This archpastor of the refugees sincerely and dedicatedly concerned himself with emigration in all the countries of Wesern Europe. In each country he appointed a vicar general who represented the Greek-Catholic faithful in his name.

B. In the Countries beyond the Ocean

The emigration of Ukrainians to the countries of North and South America began in the last quarter of the 19th century. Difficult political, social and economic conditions in the fatherland forced tens of thousands of people into the world to seek a better life and fate. These were mostly emigrants from western lands under Austrian rule and also from Carpathian Ukraine, Bukovina, Kholmshchyna and Volynia. The life of these emigrant-pioneers in the countries of the new settlement was unusually severe. These were mostly poor people, barely literate or completely illiterate, whom life had hit hard in the old country and who were not spared a bitter fate in the new country either. Nevertheless, they were able to overcome all the severe difficulties and discomforts of a new emigration, were able to organize themselves, to preserve (and pass on to their children) their language, customs, and practices and lay strong foundations with their blistered hands for the future development of Ukrainian life in these countries. For this they deserve honor and respect. These half-literate or completely illiterate Ukrainian ancestors showed such an attachment for their native land, its life, fate, culture, Church and rite that they may boldly be set up as an example for any so-called intellectual of today.

Obviously, in these difficult conditions among which the first settlers set up their households it was impossible to expect a sudden normalization of ecclesiastical or social life. Years passed before this ecclesiastical or social life gained somewhat normal appearance. There were also misunderstandings (and where do these not exist!), rebellions, and an unceasing barrage of foreign, inimical propaganda which misled the Ukrainian people. Nevertheless, that which was healthy in the Ukrainian nation survived. The Ukrainian nation preserved its national substance and finally took on healthy organizational forms.

Canada:

The emigration of Ukrainians to Canada began in the 1890's. Most of these emigrants were recruited from among the people from Halychyna, Carpathian Ukraine and Bukovina. In Canada they settled mostly in the western provinces: Manitoba, Saskatchewan and Alberta. These were economically undeveloped provinces and these Ukrainian ancestors were forced to clear the land to make arable land from the forests. They felt the lack of Churches, priests, spiritual aid, and protection very acutely. In 1899, the first priest came to Canada. This was Fr. Damascene Polywka of Carpathian Ukraine. Soon after two more priests from Halychyna arrived: Ivan Zaklynsky and Basil Dgoldak.

In 1900 the first Ukrainian Church was built in Canada, the Church of St. Volodimir in Manitoba. It was a tiny church which held barely 50 people; only in 1926 was it enlarged and adapted to current needs. From that time on, new churches began to spring up on the prairies of Manitoba, Saskatchewan, and Alberta, and somewhat later in other provinces.

The first Bishop:

In 1910, the good pastor, Metropolitan Andrew, visited the Ukrainian people in Canada. He saw how difficult it was for the Ukrainians to live without stable ecclesiastical care and already in 1912 he obtained from Rome an agreement to establish a separate ecclesiastical leadership for the Ukrainian faithful. In that same year, Mykyta Budka, the first bishop, appointed to Canada, came here, a possible martyr for the holy faith. At that time in Canada there were already 17 priests which served about one hundred ecclesiastical stations spread hundreds of miles from each other. In 1914 Budka called the first council at which the basic decisions with regards to the governing of and work in the Church were made. These decisions were published in a separate booklet under the title of "Rules of the Church". The work of Bishop Budka is even now not fully evaluated, but his services in the building and development of Ukrainian ecclesiastical and social life were very great.

Along with purely ecclesiastical activity, visitations, catechisations, publishing of theological booklets, catechisms, pastoral letters, teachings and sermons, the bishop also lent a hand to educational and social life. He set up schools affiliated with churches so that children could be taught their native language and he arranged accommodations for poor children. He also started a newspaper for older people ("The Rus Canadian") and he founded hospitals which he gave over to the care of the sister-auxiliaries. Secular societies and organizations found their houses and lodgings in church halls.

With Bishop Budka's leadership of the Church, the Ukrainian emigration to Canada grew greatly. In 1901, according to the statistics in Canada there were 5,682 Ukrainians in all; in 1911, there were 75,432 and shortly after his departure, in 1931, there were already 225,113. Most Ukrainians were Greek-Catholic. Some of them fell under various foreign influences and propaganda, left their Church, and converted to Orthodoxy and different Protestant sects.

The Ukrainian Church was forced to defend her rights even against Canadian Latins. It is a known fact that there are no married priests in the Catholic

Church while in the Ukrainian Church in Canada there were some married priests. The Roman Catholic priests, and mainly several bishops, looked at this in askance. Perhaps they knew or perhaps they didn't know the rights which the Ukrainian Church had preserved for herself according to the union of Berestya. They were afraid that their priests would demand for themselves the same rights which the Ukrainian priests had. For this reason there sprang up many misunderstandings and suspicions which, obviously, made the Ukrainian Church leadership's work much more difficult. It cannot be denied that there were also Latin bishops who were very sympathetic to the Ukrainian Church, favored it, and helped to obtain from Rome a Greek-Catholic bishop for the Ukrainians. Among these was Archbishop A. Langevin.

Reorganization:

In 1928, Bishop Budka took the office of aide to Metropolitan Andrew in Lviv and in his place Rome appointed a Basilian, Basil Ladyka, as bishop for the Greek-Catholics in Canada. Bishop Niles Savaryn, also a Basilian, was assigned to him as an aide in 1942. After the war, in 1948, Rome conducted a reorganization of the Ukrainian Church in Canada. Three exarchates were formed: the Central with its see in Winnipeg, presided over by Archbishop Ladyka, the Western with its see in Edmonton, headed by Bishop Savaryn and the Eastern or Torontonian, ruled by Bishop Isidore Boretsky. In that same year, besides Bishop Boretsky, another bishop, Andrew Roboretsky, was also ordained and assigned as an aide to Archbishop Ladyka. In 1951 a new-exarchate was formed, that of Saskatchewan, and Bishop Roboretsky was appointed here.

As an aide to Archbishop Ladyka, a hieromonk of the Redemptorist order, Maxim Hermaniuk, was ordained. In 1956, Archbishop Ladyka died and in his place Rome assigned Maxim Hermaniuk, first as archbishop and later as metropolitan. This was an important date in the history of the Ukrainian Church in Canada. Those who had been exarchs to this date became normal bishops or eparchial bishops. The bishops of these eparchies gained the same rights which the ordinary bishops of the Latin rite had.

A short summary of the development of the Ukrainian Church in Canada is as follows: Bishop Budka left behind him in 1947 about 150,000 faithful, 47 parish priests, 256 parishes and local stations, 35 evening schools, two dormitories for the education of school-age youth and five shelters for orphaned children which he gave over to the care of the sister-auxiliaries. Besides charitable work, the sister-auxiliaries concerned themselves with education and teaching in evening schools, catechisation and helping work in the churches. During Bishop Budka's rule there were over 80 of them.

Today the Greek-Catholic Church in Canada has a metropolitan, four bishops, about 140 parish priests, about 450 churches and houses of prayer and 15 monasteries. The statistics of 1961 show 189,653 faithful. Important work among the faithful is being done by the sister-auxiliaries, which number 224 in Canada today. They conduct 7 schools, 2 hospitals, 3 homes for orphaned children and other charitable institutions.

U.S.A.

The emigration to the United States of America began somewhat earlier than that to Canada. As to the faith of the Ukrainians, almost 90% were faithful to the Greek-Catholic Church. A large number of them converted to Orthodoxy or joined other local denominations. One of the reasons for the desertion was that here - as in Canada - the married Ukrainian Priests were viewed very skeptically by the Catholic priests and bishops.. The Latins reached the point where they completely prohibited the Ukrainian priests from discharging their ecclesiastical work. The Polish Catholic priests personally applied themselves to this, having transferred their hatred to the Greek-Catholic Church to the U.S.A. as well. The married priests, unable to fulfil their priestly duties, were forced to return to their native lands. Such a treatment of Ukrainian priests called up a great disorder among the faithful and threw them into the embrace of various sects which were innumerable here. A large number sought positions in the Orthodox Church which was dependent on the holy Synod in Moscovy.

Besides these troubles, within the Greek-Catholic Church itself disagreements sprang up between priests from Carpathian Ukraine and priests from Halychyna. The Carpathian element, mostly Hungarianized or Slovacized, could not find any common language with the priests of Halychyna, who felt themselves Ukrainian and wished in this spirit to work and develop the Church.

The Church Hierarchy:

In 1902, Rome assigned as visitor of the Greek-Catholic Church in U.S.A. the Krylosian of Pryashiw, A. Hodobay, yet he pleased neither group. Neither the Halychanians nor the Carpathians accepted him. Having remained for a few years, Hodobay himself resigned (in 1905).

Only in 1907, by the efforts of Metropolitan Andrew, did Rome agree (disregarding the opposition of the Latin bishops) to ordain a separate bishop for the Greek-Catholic Church in the U.S.A. Soter Ortynsky became the first Ukrainian bishop in America. Yet he did not have full jurisdiction but was subject to the Latin bishop-ordinary who was considered the vicar general. Such a subjection had no benefit for the Ukrainian Church; it interfered with her development, contaminated the Ukrainian rite and brought out dissatisfaction among the faithful. Thanks to the efforts of Metropolitan Sheptytsky, Rome finally made Bishop Ortynsky independent (in 1913) and removed him from under the jurisdiction of the Catholic bishop but Bishop Ortynsky was even able to repair somewhat the ties with the Carpathians but his death broke off this good deed, (1916).

After the death of Bishop Ortynsky, the old internal misunderstandings again surfaced. Rome assigned two administrators: for the Halychanians Fr.

249

P. Poniatyshyn and for the Carpathians Fr. H. Martiak.

This condition continued to exist after the First World War until 1924. In that year, as if confirming this division, Constantine Bohachewsky was ordained bishop for the Halychanians while Basil Takach was ordained bishop for the Carpathians. Nevertheless, this solution proved unsatisfactory for it did not help the Church at all while bringing out even greater divisions among the faithful. Again there was trouble over the matter of married clergy which the Catholic priests could not tolerate. Matters became so thorny that in the end Rome forbade, at the beginning of the 1930's, the sending of married priests to serve the Greek-Catholic Church in the U.S.A. From that time on, this celibacy trouble died down and the bishop was able to apply himself more fully to the development of the internal life of the Church.

Bishop Bohachewsky, with his see in Philadelphia, received an aide in the person of the Basilian Ambrody Senyshyn (in 1942). The latter was assigned the see of Stamford. A few years later (in 1946) Takach, the bishop of the Carpathians, who had his see in Pittsburgh, also received an aide. This was Bishop Daniel Ivancho, who after the death of Bishop Takach (in 1947) took control of the eparchy of Pittsburgh. For some reason Bishop Ivancho resigned in 1950 and his place was taken by Bishop Nicholas Elko. In his turn, Bishop Elko also received an aide in the person of Bishop S. Kotsisko (in 1956). In this way the Greek-Catholic Church in the U.S.A. was divided in two; seemingly one Church and one rite, in reality there were two hierarchies and two ecclesiastical organizations. This was an unhealthy phenomenon in the Ukrainian Church, insofar as the Church is not a political institution. Such a state does not contribute to the spiritual growth of the faithful.

In that same year, 1956, the exarchate of Philadelphia was divided into two. The exarchate of Stamford was created with Exarch Ambrosy Senyshyn and that of Philadelphia with Archbishop Constantine Bohachewsky, to whom Bishop Joseph Shmondiuk was given as an aide. In August, 1958, the exarchate of Chicago was formed with Bishop Yaroslav Gabro and at the same time the Greek-Catholic church in the U.S.A. was raised to the status of having three eparchies. Archbishop Bohachewsky became the first metropolitan in the U.S.A. and after his death (in 1956), Ambrosy Senyshyn took his place.

The Condition Today:

Today the Greek-Catholics in the U.S.A. number about 330 thousand faithful, about 200 parishes and local stations, and over 270 priests-pastors of souls. In 1958 the exarchate of Pittsburgh was also divided in half and two eparchies were formed: that of Pittsburgh with Bishop Elko and about 100 priests and that of Passaic with Bishop Kotsisko with his see in Passaic and about 50 priests.

There are also several male and female monasteries in the metropoly. During the war, the Basilians revived their activity here, founding monasteries in Chicago and in New York and also a novitiate at Glen Grove near

New York. The Redemptorists have their monastery in Newark and the spiritual Seminary in Washington serves the U.S.A. by training candidates for the spiritual state. In 1961 it had over ten students who were preparing in the seminary for the spiritual life while obtaining their theological education at the Theological faculty of the University of Washington. The Carpathian bishops have their own separate spiritual seminary in Pittsburgh.

The Basilian sisters have developed a wide circle of activity in the U.S.A. They work in both eparchies, in that of Philadelphia and that of Pittsburgh. They conduct 41 evening parish schools, two girls' high schools, one college with the powers of a university, a publishing house, and a home for orphaned children.

The sister Auxiliaries take part in educational work, teach in fulltime and parish schools, prepare children for their First Holy Communion and conduct charitable work. In all, there are 93 sister Auxiliaries in the U.S.A.

Argentina:

The Ukrainian emigration to Argentina dates from 1897. These first emigrants settled mainly in the Missiones province, in the area of the city of Apostoles. Before the First World War, Ukrainians numbered about ten thousand here. After the war, between 1925 and 1930, a new wave of emigration enlarged this number to approximately fifty thousand. These were mostly emigrants from Halychyna, Volynia, Polisia, Carpathian Ukraine and also a small group (of about a thousand) from Bukovina. After the last war, again about six thousand new emigrants came here. Today Ukrainians number about 100 thousand in Argentina. The Ukrainian element is concentrated mostly in the province of Missiones (30 thousand) and in Buenos Aires and Berisso (30 thousand), with the remainder living in other cities, industrial centers, plantations, farms, and so on . . .

Two-thirds of this number are Greek-Catholic in faith, the remainder is mostly Orthodox. The first priests, K. Bdgukhowsky and Y. Karpiak, came here in 1908. Three years later, two more, O. Ananevych and I.Senyshyn arrived. The lack of priests was always felt in Argentina and is felt even today. By jurisdiction, the Ukrainian priests there were subject to the local Catholic hierarchs until 1961. The Apostolic See created an Apostolic exarchate in 1961 and named Andrew Sapelak, a Ukrainian priest of the Greek-Catholic branch of Salezian Order, as exarch-bishop with his see in Buenos Aires. Sapelak, who fully devoted dedication, is organizing ecclesiastical life.

Brazil:

The first emigrations from Halychyna appeared in Brazil in 1876 and by the end of the 19th century there were already 15 thousand of them there. Today there are about 120 thousand Ukrainians in Brazil. The first Ukrainian priests came here in 1897. The life of the Ukrainian settlers in Brazil was perhaps the hardest of all the areas of a new settlement. The government usually sent them to colonies in very unfavorable forrested terrains in the state of

Parana, among primeval forrests, to a climate to which the Ukrainian settlers were not accustomed. Therefore mortality rate was very great.

Just as it was in Canada and in the U.S.A., the attitude of the Catholic clergy to the Ukrainian married priests was inimical and for this reason in time the Basilian fathers took control of all the spiritual care over the faithful. Until 1951, the Ukrainian Brazilian priests were subjected to the Latin bishops. Only in this year did Rome remove the Greek-Catholic Church from under the direct jurisdiction of the Roman Catholic bishops and create a separate vicariate. This was the first step towards the creation of an exarchate in 1958. The first exarch-bishop here was Joseph Martynets with his see in the city of Kuritiba.

The exarchate embraces large tracts of the entire Brazil and is divided into 10 parishes with 17 priestly stations where over 40 priests work, among them 33 of the Basilian order. The pastors serve about 70 thousand faithful.

In Brazil there are about 110 Greek-Catholic churches and houses of prayer. The main spiritual work is conducted by the Basilian fathers here. In Prudentopolis the Basilians have a separate base of their order; they conduct a four year high school, they have a novitiate, they publish the religious monthly, the "Ukrainian Missionary", the weekly, "Work" and many booklets of a religious or general educational character.

Very dedicated work has also been done here since 1911 by the sister Auxiliaries, who arrived from Halychyna. They also have their base, the Assembly at Prudentopolis, they maintain two hospitals, two homes for orphaned children and conduct about 30 primary schools. In comparison with Argentina, the Ukrainian Church in Brazil is somewhat better organized. Probably the external conditions are more favorable for this.

Australia:
The emigration of Ukrainians to Australia began after the last war. Formerly there had been very few Ukrainians here. In 1950 Ukrainians numbered about 20 thousand on this continent and of this 18 thousand were Greek-Catholics. At first Archbishop Buchko took care of the Ukrainian Church in Australia, sending the first priests here. In 1958, Rome established a separate exarchate for Australia and set up Ivan Prashko as exarchbishop, by origin from the district of Ternopil. The exarch's see is in Melbourne, in the province of Victoria. The bishop proved a very dedicated pastor and the results of his work soon showed up. Although the number of faithful was small, in a few years they were able to build a cathedral and a bishop's residence where religious and social life is concentrated. Bishop Prashko even proved "aggressive" to the Latins, corrupting one Latin priest and bringing him over (by permission from Rome) to Greek-Catholicism. The Ukrainians came to love him very much. His name is John Bowden but the Ukrainians call him Bowdenko. This compensation for the Ukrainian losses to the Latin's benefit is not very great but Ukrainians are thankful even for this.

This Church numbered, as has been mentioned, about 18 thousand faithful and has 10 priests who serve their faithful scattered across the wide horizons with modern means of communication - by plane. These are very dedicated people, these flying priests, and, as can be seen, God blesses their dedicated work.

C. The General State of the Greek-Catholic Church in the Diaspora

After the great losses which the Greek-Catholic Church sustained in the fatherland after the war, it seemed that the prospects of her branches in the wide world were very dim. Of all the Greek-Catholic bishops in Europe, only two remained alive and free: Archbishop Ivan Buchko, the only archpastor of Ukrainians in Western Europe and Archbishop Gabriel Bukatko in Yugoslavia. The churches in the countries beyond the ocean were not sufficiently strong or prepared to take over the spiritual inheritance, traditions and missions which God's Grace had placed upon the Ukrainian Church.

For this reason many began to doubt whether the Ukrainian Church could survive in the diaspora at all without a Mother Church. These doubts were completely well-grounded and if not for the fact that the Apostolic See hastened to help, the future of the Ukrainian Church would truly have been in great peril. In view of the situation which existed in the native lands, Rome directed its attention to the development of the Greek-Catholic Church in the diaspora. Fifteen years after the war, this Church completely shaped herself organizationally, obtained new pastors in various places with her own jurisdiction, a new influx of priests and a great chance for further development.

Metropolitans were nominated in Canada and in the U.S.A., the Ukrainian Church was removed from under the jurisdiction of the Roman Catholic bishops in Brazil, exarchates were formed in Australia, England, Argentina, France and Germany and the costs of Ukrainian schooling in Rome were deferred. All this was a strong stimulus to Ukrainian church life.

In 1963 at the beginning of February, thanks to the efforts of the late saintly Pope John XXIII and by God's Grace, there appeared in the free world the metropolitan-confessor, hierarch primate of the Greek-Catholic Church, Joseph Slipyj Kobernytsky Dychkowsky, after 18 years of Bolshevik imprisonment. This event flashed like lightening across the world and called up so much joy and hope, so much faith in the victory of God's truth, and such uplifting that the problem of the Ukrainian Church came to the fore. The Ukrainian Church received in the person of the hierarch-primate a central focus for her organizational development. The future will show whether she will be able to take advantage of this.

Today the Greek-Catholic Church in the diaspora has her own hierarch primate, the Major Archbishop and Metropolitan Joseph, two metropolitans and 18 bishops, altogether 21 archpastors who represent about one million faithful in the free world.

The most numerous and the largest monastic order is doubtless the order of Basilian fathers, with ten monasteries in countries across the ocean: Canada. U.S.A., Brazil, and Argentina. The numerical status of this order stands at about 140 monks in the diaspora.

Metropolitan Joseph, after his return, engaged himself in the renewal of a second ancient Ukrainian order, the Studites. This order has two monasteries with twenty-odd monks to date.

The Assembly of Redemptorist fathers, which centered its activity mainly in Canada, has four monasteries and conducts educational and publishing work. Four monasteries in Canada and one in U.S.A. encompass 34 monks and in Meadowvale (Canada) the Redemptorists maintain a spiritual seminary with 7 students.

The women's monasteries cannot be overlooked.There is the order of Basilian sisters with monasteries in Argentina, Brazil and U.S.A. and the Assembly of sister Auxiliaries, who also have their monasteries in Brazil, U.S.A. and Canada and who conduct educational and charitable work. There are about 300 sister Auxiliaries in Brazil, about 100 in U.S.A. and over 220 in Canada who, like the Basilian sisters, apply themselves to the brilliant traditions of the monastic orders in the fatherland.

In summary the Ukrainian Church in the diaspora numbers:

a confessor of the faith, the Major Archbishop, Metropolitan Joseph, two metropolitans,
eighteen bishops,
about 900 parish priests,
about 200 hieromonks,
about 1300 nuns,
about 20 monasteries,
about 150 homes and
about 2 million faithful.

All these gains do not compensate for the great losses of the Ukrainian Church which she sustained after the war. Nevertheless they show her openness, her dedication, the devotion of her faithful, her power of opposition in a strange environment, and a guarantee of a good future.

Although in some areas in the Ukrainian ecclesiastical horizon dark clouds are emerging, it must be believed that these are but temporary phenomena which have occurred many times in the Ukrainian Church and which she was able to successfully absorb. In the end her fate rests with people only in part and the remainder is in the hands of God's Providence. The ways of God are unfathomable.

3. The Ukrainian Orthodox Church in the Diaspora

The Orthodox Church in Poland:

As has been mentioned before, the Orthodox Church in Poland was established after the First World War. She received autocephaly from the patriarch of Constantinople, Gregory VII (by the Tomos of November 13th, 1924) and numbered over four million faithful, including about two and a half million Ukrainians.

After the Second World War and the changing of the boundaries of the Polish nation, the Orthodox Church underwent great changes as well. Today she has four eparchies (formerly five): Warsaw, Bilistoch-Gdansk, Lodz-Poznan, and Vrotslav-Shchetsin and twenty deans offices altogether, but nevertheless her numerical status has greatly diminished. In approximately 195 parishes, she embraces about 150 thousand faithful, mostly Ukrainians and White Rus. For the education of the clergy, there exists in Warsaw a Spiritual Seminary and an Orthodox Division at the Christian Theological Academy in the same place.

The Bolsheviks arrested Metropolitan Dionysius after the war (at St. Pelten in Germany) and imprisoned him in Warsaw. In 1948, the Polish government, in a separate ruling of its president, relieved him of all the rights of a hierarch primate and ceased to recognize him as the metropolitan of the Orthodox Church in Poland. Bishop Timothy (Shretter) took the helm of the metropoly. There was the danger that this Church would also fall sacrifice to the patriarchate of Moscow. However, possibly in Moscow, they feared to enter into conflict with the patriarch of Constantinople from whom the Orthodox Church had received her autocephaly (in 1924) and they decided differently. Under pressure from the patriarch of Moscow, the Orthodox Church in Poland rejected the authocephaly of 1924 and accepted the "blessing" from the patriarch of Moscow. Metropolitan Dionysius, who still remained under arrest, by his own will or by force confirmed this autocephalous change and affirmed it as canonical.

In 1951, the council of bishops "unanimously" turned to the patriarch of Moscow, Alexei, with a request that he send this Church a metropolitan from the U.S.S.R. Obviously it was not necessary to ask twice. The patriarch proclaimed that the new metropolitan of the Orthodox Church in Poland would be the archbishop of Lviv, Makary (Oksiuk).

In this way, seemingly respecting canonical procedure, the patriarchate of Moscow came in through the back door into a Church independent and doubtless autocephalously important as of 1924. Unable to incorporate her unscrupulously, not only because of possible complications with the Orthodox Churches of the East but also because the Church existed in a foreign (although communist) state, the hierarchy of Moscow made sure that it obtained if not a complete, then a partial influence over this Church.

Although there was a forceful pressure on the Church from the side of the patriarchate of Moscow, nevertheless she was enjoying somewhat autocephalous rights which underlined her spiritual submission not to the Orthodoxy of Moscow but to the metropoly of Kiev as the primary metropoly of Eastern European Christianity. To this date, this has been accepted from her without penalty.

255

The Orthodox Churches in the
Countries of the Emigrational Settlement:

With the end of the Second World War, many thousands of Orthodox Ukrainians, both faithful and priests, left the western European countries for those across the ocean. In the emigration many bishops were also found from both the autocephalous and the autonomous Ukrainian Churches.

The bishop of the Autonomous Church joined the Russian "cut away" Church which was led by Metropolitan Anastasy Hrybanowsky with his see in Karlovytchi (Yugoslavia) and later in Munich. From Germany, the autonomists slowly spread across the world: Archimandrite Krydganowsky - to Chile, the former bishop of Zhytomyr, Leonty - to Paraguay, the former bishop of Rivno, Theodore - to Australia, the bishop of Kiev, Panteleymon - to Argentina and the bishop of Dnipropetrowsk, Dimitrius - to the U.S.A. (Boston).

Immediately after the war (in May, 1946), a council of bishops of the Russian cut-away Church occurred in Munich under the leadership of Metropolitan Athanasius, together with the autonomous bishops. This council declared the Ukrainian Autocephalous Church uncanonical and denied her clergy (as well as the clergy of the Church of Lypkiwsky) any canonical validity. In this way the rift which sprang up between the Autonomous Church in the Ukraine and the U.A.O.C. deepened and was transferred to the countries of its new settlement. With what intolerance the Russian cut-away Church treated Orthodox Ukrainians is shown also by the fact that it even condemned Metropolitan Dionysius and the bishops under his jurisdiction - Ilarion, Palladius and Alexander - for the fact that they supported the U.A.O.C. and remained in prayerful union with her. The resolutions of this council of Munich were recognized by 25 Russian (and autonomous) bishops, hierarchs in the free world.

The dispute between the U.A.O.C. and the supporters of the Autonomous Church transferred itself to individual communities, camps, and parishes and created very difficult conditions for the ordering of Ukrainian ecclesiastical life in the emigration. And its ordering became an urgent need. In the emigration to Germany, there appeared a numerous hierarchy of three different directions or jurisdictions. The most numerous, with the largest number of faithful, was the hierarchy of the U.A.O.C., renewed in 1942. The second hierarchy was the group of bishops of the Autonomous Church in the Ukraine, who recognized, during the war, the jurisdiction of Sergius, the patriarch of Moscow, and who after the war joined the aforementioned Russian Church (cut-away), which did not recognize the patriarch of Moscow. Finally there was the hierarchy of Metropolitan Dionysius whose jurisdiction was in Warsaw, over the bishops of the Orthodox Church in Poland.

In such a situation, to normalize the ecclesiastical life in a foreign country, in unusually difficult conditions, was not an easy matter. Goodwilled and dedicated people were not wanting both in the hierarchy and among the faithful, yet ecclesiastical antagonism, mutual flamings and accusations about uncanonicity complicated the life of the Orthodox Church to such an extent that it is felt painfully even today. In addition, from before the war there existed yet another Orthodox Church in the free world, led by Metropolitan Ivan Theodorovych, to whom the churches in the U.S.A. and in Canada were subject. Metropolitan Theodorovych belonged to the U.A.O.C. of first creation, that is, to the Church of Metropolitan Lypkiwsky, whose canonicity was not recognized by any Eastern Orthodox Church.

As a result of such a system of relations, in the emigration there were formed several independent Orthodox Churches, with their own separate hierarchy, separate metropolitans and a separate ecclesiastical policy.

The Ukrainian Autocephalous Orthodox Church in foreign lands is a Church led by a hierarchy of valid canonical establishment of the renewed U.A.O.C. (of 1942). This hierarchy was headed by the former administrator of the U.A.O.C. in the Ukraine, Metropolitan Policarp, with a see in Hannover, Germany at first. Metropolitan Policarp was one of the main organizers of the Ukrainianization of the Orthodox Church in Poland. While bishop of Lutsk (in 1932), he also played an important role in the renewal of ecclesiastical life in the Ukraine during the war and in the organization of the U.A.O.C. (of 1942). Now a somewhat more difficult matter was fated for him - the matter of the battle against the autonomists and also against the internal disorders in the U.A.O.C. in foreign lands.

A difficulty for the U.A.O.C. in foreign lands was, among other things, the fact that many priests ordained by Lypkiwsky were included in her structure, that is, priests whom the canonical Orthodox bishops did not regard as validly ordained. They did not recognize as canonical the ordinations of Metropolitan Theodorovych in the U.S.A. either. This was the reason for the first blow in the U.A.O.C.

In August 1947 Bishop Gregory Ohiychuk, a canonically ordained bishop (on May 17th, 1942), gathered a conference of his supporters, both clergy and faithful, at Aschaffenburg and condemned the hierarchy of the U.O.A.C. for her attitude towards Metropolitan Theodorovych. Metropolitan Policarp reacted to this. He called a council of bishops of the O.U.C.C., also in Aschaffenburg, condemned Bishop Gregory and the participants of the aforementioned conference, relieved them of their offices and excommunicated them from the Church. At the same time, the council delegated Archbishop Mstyslav (Skrypnyk) to the U.S.A. to convince Metropolitan Theodorovych to again accept a canonically valid ordination as bishop.

Theodorovych was now the only hierarch ordained by Lypkiwsky and he had already made advances to the patriarch of Constantinople earlier (in 1932) through Dionysius, metropolitan of Warsaw. These efforts were unsuccessful because Metropolitan Theodorovych had then met with the strong opposition of his clergy. In the process of these negotiations, the exarch of the patriarch of Constantinople in the U.S.A. Athenagoras, had ordained (in 1936) as bishop for the Orthodox Ukrainians in the U.S.A. by order of the patriarch, Bohdan Shpylka, who, from that time on, represented a separate branch of the Ukrainian Orthodox Church in the U.S.A. in canonical union with the patriarch of Constantinople and the other Orthodox Churches of the East.

Now Archbishop Mstyslav was able to convince Metropolitan Theodorovych to renew his ordination, which occured on the 27th of August, 1949. This doubtless, was a very significant success for the hierarchy of the U.A.O.C. in foreign lands, for this important impediment to the union of all the Orthodox Churches and the consolidation of their strengths had now been removed. Unfortunately, this has not happened yet.

The U.A.O.C. in the foreign lands, with Metropolitan Nicanor, united the Orthodox communities in western Europe and Australia (Archbishop Sylvester Hayevsky and Bishop Donat Varlaam). At first there was also a small community of U.A.O.C. faithful in the U.S.A. (Archbishop Ihor Huba). Later, however, Ihor had a disagreement with the hierarchy of the U.A.O.C. and created a new jurisdiction (Utica and Cleveland) out of several communities and also found his supporters in Argentina.

The U.A.O.C. Church does beneficial work for the Ukrainian nation, both Christian and social, and she doubtless earns for herself the sincere acceptance and aid of all Ukrainians, regardless of faith. She has a validly ordained (from the point-of-view of canon law) hierarchy and if she could obtain recognition of autocephaly from the patriarch of Constantinople, it would be an important historical success in the direction of normalization of church life. The deficiencies do not have to be blamed on anyone, for deficiencies may be found in any Church. The dedicated work of her bishops and clergy must be valued and she must be aided to be able to return to that glory which the Ukrainian Orthodox Church enjoyed during the times of Mohyla, Kosiw, and her other great hierarchs.

The Council-True U.O.A.C.

This Church, led by Archbishop Gregory (Ohiychuk), sprang up as a result of the aforementioned internal misunderstanding of the U.A.O.C. as to the validity of the ordinations of the U.O.A.C. in 1921, and mainly because of the non-recognition of the ordination of Metropolitan Theodorovych. By 1955 this ecclesiastical community, small in number of faithful and clergy, was separated from the other Ukrainian Orthodox Churches. In September, 1955, by a decision of Metrooplitan Nicanor, the hierarch primate of the Council of bishops of the U.A.O.C., the resolution of the Council of Ascheffenburg (of 1947) to relieve Archbishop Gregory for his episcopal office and the excommuication of him and his priest and faithful from the Church was reversed, his rights were restored to him and a prayerful union was instituted with the Church led by him. It was proposed to Archbishop Gregory that he join one of the larger Ukrainian Orthodox Churches in the diaspora and in this way stop the fragmentation in U.A.O.C. Archbishop Gregory in turn made efforts to place the Council-True U.A.O.C. under the jurisdiction of the patriarch of Constantinople. However, his good intentions have not yet been successful.

The U.O.C. in the U.S.A.

Until 1918, the Orthodox Ukrainians in the U.S.A. were under the jurisdiction of Russian bishops who were assigned by the patriarch of Moscow. Obviously, the policies of these bishops were approximately the same as those of the Russian bishops in the Ukraine. they considered the Church a good means to the Russification of the Ukrainian populace. In 1918 (on the 19th of August), a separate ecclesiastical unit was created in Saskatoon (Canada) which gathered together the Orthodox Ukrainians of three of the western provinces of Canada. The first bishop of this Church was the Syrian Metropolitan German. When the U.O.A.C. was founded in the Ukraine, Lypkiwsky immediately began to make efforts to organize the spiritual care of the Ukrainians in North America. In 1923 he delegated the bishop of Vynnytsia, Ivan Theodorovych, to the task of heading the Ukrainian Orthodox Church on the North American continent. With the title of metropolitan, Theodorovych made his see in Brown Brook (U.S.A.), founding at the same time a Consistory for Canada in Winnipeg. With these beginnings, the church numbered about 300 parishes and missionary stations and approximately 60 priests.

No one doubted his canonical ordination and only at the beginning of the 1930's, when the problem of the so-called self-ordination became the subject of heated debate, did Metropolitan Theodorovych make all efforts to rid himself of this irregularity and receive by permission of the patriarch of Constantinople, a second ordination. As has been mentioned, because of the opposition of a number of his priests, he was unable to do this. In 1936, the patriarch of Constantinople ordered Bohdan Shpylka to function as ordained bishop for the faithful of the Ukrainian Orthodox Church in U.S.A. Shpylka, obviously, was not subject to Metropolitan Theodorovych, but directly to the patriarch of Constantinople or his exarch in the U.S.A. In this way, beginning in 1936, there were two Ukrainian Orthodox Churches on the North American continent, one under jurisdiction of Metropolitan Theodorovych and the other subject to Bishop Bohdan Shpylka.

When in 1948 Archbishop Mstyslav (Skrypnyk) came to Canada, a number of the churches, until now subject to Bishop Bohdan, separated from him and took Archbishop Mstyslav as their hierarch. In this way, a third Church or a third jurisdiction was founded. In August, 1949, Metropolitan Theodorovych received his second ordination at the hands of Archbishop of Alexandria, and in this way he created the possibility of union with Archbishop Mstyslav. The union of these two Churches occurred at a Council in New York on the 15th of October, 1960. At the beginning of 1951, Archbishop Mstyslav came from Canada to the U.S.A. and enlivened the work of the development of the U.O.C. (Ukrainian Orthodox Church), becoming the head of her Consistory. Yet another bishop came here, Archbishop Genady (Sheprykevych), earlier the bishop of Dnipropetrovsky, and the ecclesiastical life of the U.O.C. began to gain new impetus. In the early 1950's the U.O.C. numbered about 100 parishes. The U.O.C. in the U.S.A. took a large step forward after the war. In this, the undeniable merit belongs primarily to Archbishop Mstyslav, a highly-talented, wise and far-seeing person and a sincere Ukrainian patriot. Today this Church also has jurisdiction over the Ukrainian Orthodox faithful in Brazil.

The U.G.O.C. in Canada:

After Archbishop Mstyslav's passing over to the U.S.A. from Canada, Metropolitan Ilarion (Ohienko), formerly the archbishop of Kholm and Pidlasha, who was ordained bishop on the 20th of October, 1940, came to Canada from Switzerland, took control of the care and leadership of the Ukrainian Orthodox Community. Archbishop Michael (Khoroshy), formerly the bishop of Mykolayiw (in 1942), became the second bishop in the U.G.O.C. in Canada.

Today the U.G.O.C. (Ukrainian Greek-Orthodox Church) in Canada is divided into four eparchies: Winnipeg, led by Metropolitan Ilarion, metropolitan of Winnipeg and all of Canada, Toronto and eastern Canada with Archbishop Michael, Edmonton and Western Canada with Archbishop Andrew (Mytiuk) and Saskatchewan with Bishop Borys. The see of the metropoly is in Winnipeg where exists the College of St. Andrew (associated with the University of Manitoba), that is, a school for the rearing of candidates to the spiritual state.

From about the beginning of the 1950's, between the U.O.C. in the U.S.A. and the U.G.O.C. in Canada there have been conferences for the purpose of entering some sort of union. To date however, nothing has been achieved, though already the second conference declared that:

"beyond the boundaries of the Ukraine there exists but one Ukrainian Orthodox Church, which spiritually forms and unites the entire Ukrainian nation in the free world. In the United States of America and in Canada there exist two spiritually indivisible parts of this Ukrainian Orthodox Church: The Ukrainian Orthodox Church in U.S.A. and the Ukrainian Greek-Orthodox Church in Canada, which live an independent, autocephalous life in accordance with their statutes and in accordance with the state structure of their countries".

Thus these two Churches recognize themselves as one although they have two different names, two different hierarchies, independent one from the other and also live their separate lives in accordance with their statutes.

There was also an attempt on the part of the patriarch of Constantinople, by the method of examining the canonicity of the ordinations in the eparchy, to somehow normalize the status of those Churches in accordance with the canon law of the Eastern Church, yet niether the U.O.C. nor the U.G.O.C. would agree to such solution, believing that their union was satisfactory and as for canonical normalization, that no repair was necessary here.

However, the Eastern Orthodox Churches believe differently and for this reason between the U.O.C. and the U.G.O.C. on the one hand and the Orthodox Churches of the Christian East on the other there is no prayerful union.

The U.O.C. in the U.S.A. in Canonical Subjection to the Patriarch

Besides the U.O.C. in the jurisdiction of Metropolitan Theodorovych there exists in U.S.A. yet another Ukrainian Orthodox Church with the same name (U.O.C.) but under a canonical subjection to Athanagoras, the patriarch of Constantinople. This is the Church which Archpriest Bohdan Shpylka ruled from 1936. After his death (in 1965), Archbishop Pallady took control of this Church.

Summarizing all that has been mentioned above, in the free world there exist four independent Ukrainian Orthodox Churches: 1) U.A.O.C., which includes the Orthodox communities of Europe and Australia, 2) U.G.O.C. in Canada, 3) U.O.C. with Metropolitan Theodorovych in U.S.A. and 4) U.O.C. in U.S.A. with Archbishop Pallady, subject canonically to the patriarch of Constantinople.

It cannot be thought otherwise but that it would be far more beneficial if those Churches or jurisdictions which do not have a prayerful union with the other Orthodox Churches of the East could somehow structure themselves canonically in this way and unite themselves in such a way that their unity would be not merely declarative but factual as well. Then such a Ukrainian Orthodox Church, with one leading authority, could develop far better, would save herself unnecessary internal misunderstandings, would gain the support of the other Orthodox Churches and could also become an important partner in the ecumenical movememt of today. This would also have a beneficial influence on the faithful, which the Church would not divide by jurisdiction but would unite in the spirit of the Christ of the Holy Scriptures.

4. What does the History of the Ukrainian Church teach?

It is said that history is a teacher of life, that historically one can recognize the mistakes and good deeds, the virtues and the faults of a nation. If this is true, then the history of the Church of a given nation supplies abundant material for self-recognition. Perhaps even more than secular history, church history underlines the deep sufferings of a nation, its passions, its agitations, its fierceness in battle and even its fanaticism. From church history one can see, no less than from secular history, one's faults and one's virtues, one can recognize what has contributed to good and to national culture and what has brought misfortune and decline, in a word, what was good and what evil.

Church history should be studied without prejudice, without passion and without condemnation of one's ancestors for they will be judged by the Righteous Judge. It must be studied in such a way that intelligent and logical conclusions can be drawn from it.

There is one more important precognition to the study of church history. Because this history is concerned with matters of the Church as a visible institution of God but also often speaks about matters of faith, that is, matters which cannot always be easily explained by one's intellect, one must be very careful with one's judgement and be as humble as possible. Above all, the first say in matters of faith should be left to those who, by God's institution are called to decide on matters of faith. And to decide in matters of faith, according to the will of the Founder of the Church, Jesus Christ the Lord, the bishops have the right.

What does the history of the Church of Christ in the Ukraine teach? It teaches that with the coming of the light of the Holy Scriptures to the Ukrainian lands in the mid-9th century, the Church played an important role in the life of the Ukrainian nation and the daybreak of its life. It can be said that the Church changed the course of the nation's history and brought the Ukrainian nation into the circle of cultured nations of the world of that time. Notwithstanding the misunderstandings between Rome and Byzantium, the Ukrainian Church grew and strengthened spiritually and culturally. Then a break came in the Church, and although the metropoly of Kiev remained on the side of the Byzantine Church, nevertheless there was no religious intolerance in the Ukraine as can be seen in other Churches. The Ukrainian bishops of that time paid much more attention to the moral fulfilment of the pastorale entrusted to them than they did to accusations for erring in faith.

From the mid-13th century, with the decline of the principate, the Church also underwent visible decline. Her center was transferred to the north and slowly fell under the secular influence of the newly-arisen state, inimical to the Ukrainian nation. From that time, the metropoly of Kiev lost the significance which it had had until then. In time it fell under the exclusive influence of secular powers which made impossible the free expression of spiritual life and the longings of the ecclesiastical hierarchy and faithful.

From the mid-15th century, the Ukrainian Church yearned for Christian unity in accordance with the will of Jesus Christ "that all be one".

The structure of the political relations of that time did not favor these noble aims. At the end of the 16th century the Ukrainian Church, which was then already separated from that of Moscow, decided to direct her paths to the West. Her road was difficult and thorny. Having overcome many difficulties, this Church, at first called the Uniate and later the Greek-Catholic, did not lose her national visage or her eastern tradition either. She became a true Ukrainian Church.

However, a considerable portion of the clergy and faithful did not wish to follow the Ukrainian hierarchy at the end of the 16th century. At the beginning of the 17th century the hierarchy of the Ukrainian Orthodox Church was renewed. It must be acknowledged that in the whirlpool of this battle there were many events which harmed both Churches; energy was expended for mutual vanquishing, destruction and accusation. Nevertheless, the Orthodox Ukrainian Church created in time an ecclesiastical culture and was able to maintain it until she was swallowed up by a Church which stood in the service of secular powers. From the end of the 17th century there began a slow decline of Ukrainian Orthodoxy, a decline caused by a foreign, inimical force. This same foreign power had undermined for ages and finally (in 1946) physically buried the other Ukrainian Church, the Greek-Catholic.

Ukrainians, both Greek-Catholics and Orthodox, need to keep this well in mind. It is not necessary to see one another as enemies, as so often happened among Ukrainians. Ukrainians have other enemies in common. First of all, any Christian should fight against any evil in the world and stand for the truth of Christ, for the holiness of life and for the rightful order of God. It must be remembered that the best weapon in this battle is the love of one's neighbor according to the will of Christ. Ukrainians still have enemies who are attacking the Ukrainian Church and Ukrainian Spirit. Against these enemies, Ukrainians must unite their powers under the banner of Christ, forgetting that which separates them and seeing that which unites them.

Ukrainian history is rich in examples showing that mutual respect and agreement lead to Ukraine's growth, while conflicts often end in catastrophe.

We should leave it to those who, by God's will, have the right to "bind and unbind", to solve that which unbinds Ukrainians. One must give them the obedience and respect that is their due. One must not condemn others but leave all to the judgement of the Lord. Although in God's Providence, Ukrainians do not have one Ukrainian Church, nevertheless they have one Christ and under His flag there is enough room for all.

Bibliography

Abraham W. - Powstanie Organizacji Kosciola Katolickiego na Rusi, Lw'ow 1904.

Amman A. - Storia della chiesa russa, Toronto, 1948.

Antonowych B. - An Outline of the Position of the Orthodox Church in Ukraine from the mid-17th to the end of the 18th centuries, Lviv, 1900.

Askochensky B. - Kiev with its Teaching Institution, the Academy, Kiev, 1856, 2 vls.

Baran S. - Metropolitan Andrew Sheptytsky, Munich, 1947.

Batashkov I. - The Rus of Kholm, SPB, 1887.

Bedrov B. - The Orthodox Church in Poland and Latvia, Ecatherinoslav, 1078.

Bidnov B. - Researches of Church History in Orthodox Countries, Kreminets 1931.

Blazejowski D. - De potestate metropolitarium Kieviensium catholicorum inclerum regulatem, Roma 1943.

Bobrowsky P. - The Rus, Greek-Catholic Church in the tsarate of Alexander I, SPB, 1890.

Bozhyk P. - Church of Ukrainians in Canada, Winnipeg, 1927.

Bozhyk S. - Ukrainian Catholic Parish and Church of St. Norbert in Kracow, 1959.

Buchynsky B. - Studies in the History of Church Union (Notes of the NTsh) (vols. 85-87).

Chodynicki K. - Kosciol prawoslawny a Rzeczpospolita polska 1370-1632, Warszawa, 1934.

Chotkiewicz W. - W. Dzieje zniszczenia sw.unji na Bialorusi i Litwie w swietle pamientnikow Siemaszki, Krar'ow, 1898.

Chotkowski W. - Hostoria polityczna kosciola w Galicji za rzadow Maryi Teresy Krak'ow, 1909.

Chotkowski W. - Dokumenta Pontificum Romanorum historiam Ukrainae ilustrantia, Roma 1953-4, 2 vol.

Chystovych J. - Sketches of History of the Western Rus Church, SPB. 1882-4.

Chubaty M. - Western Ukraine and Rome in the XIIth Century, Lviv 1917. - The History of Christianity in Rus-Ukraine, Rome 1965 2 vls.

Dobryansky A. - The History of the Bishops of three uniate Eparchies: Peremyshl, Sambir and Sanik, Lviv 1893.

Doroshenko D. - The Orthodox Church in the Past and Current life of the Ukrainian Nation, Berlin 1940.

Harasewicz M. - Annales Ecclesiae Ruthenae, Leopoli 1863.

Heyer Fr. - Die orthodoxe Kirche in der Ukraine von 1917 bis 1947, Kölin, 1953.

Holubev S. - The Metropolitan of Kiev, Peter Mohyla and his Fellow-Champions Kiev 1883-1898, 2 vls.

Holubynsky E. - History of the Church of Rus, Moscow 1900-1

Hrushevsky M. - The History of Rus-Ukraine, Lviv-Kiev 1898-1937, 10 vols. - From the History of Religious thought in Ukraine, Lviv, 1925.

Ishchak A. - Uniate and Autocephalous efforts in Ukrainain Lands from Daniel to Isidore, Lviv 1923-4 (in "Bohoslovia" vols. I-II).

Kharlampovych K. - The Little Russian Influence on the life of the Church of Great Russia, Kazan 1914.

Korolevskij C. - Metropolite Andre Szeptyckyj, Roma 1964.

Kostruba T. - Outlines of the Church History of Ukraine, X-XII centuries 2 ed., Toronto; 1955.

Koyalowych M. - The History of the Junction of the Uniates of the Ancient Times to the Times, SPB, 1873.

Kulczynski J. - Specimen Ecclesiae Ruthenicae, Roma, 1733.

Lewicki A. - Unia Florencka w Polsce, Krak'ow 1899.

Levyrsky O. - The Internal Status of the Western-Rus Church at the end of the 16th century and the Union, Lviv 1900, (Rus Historical Library, Vo. 6).

Likowski E. - Dzieje Kosciola Unickiego na Litwie i Rusi, XVII-XIX w. Poznan 1880. 2 vol.

Lypkiwsky B. - The Rebirth of the Church in Ukraine, 1917-1930, Toronto 1959.

Lypynsky V. - Religion and the Church in the History of Ukraine, Philadelphia, 1925.

Luzhnytsky H. - The Ukrainian Church between West and East, Philadelphia 1954.

Makary - The History of the Church of Rus, vols. I-XII, St. Petersburg, 1857-1883.

Malinowski M. - Die Kirchen und - Staatssatzungen bez. griechisch-kath. Ritus der Ruthenen in Galizien, Leopoli, 1864.

Nahayewsky I. - Rome and Byzantium, Toronto, 1956.

Pelesh J. - Geschichte der Union der Ruthenischen Kirche mit Rom, Wien 1870-1880, 2 vol.

Petrov A. - Ancient Documents in the History of the Carpatho-Rus Church and Hierarchy, Prague, 1930.

Petrushevych A. - A short Historical summary from the Introduction of Christianity in the Carpathian Areas until the times of St.'s Cyril and Methodius, Lviv 1882. - On the Sobornal Church of the Mother of God in the City of Halych, Lviv 1899. - A Summary Chronicle of Halych-Rus from 1600-1700, Lviv, 1874.

Pryselkov M. - A sketch of the Ecclesiastical-Political History of Kievan Rus X-XVth centuries, SPb., 1913.

Slipyj J. - A Historical overview of the Education of Clergy in the Catholic Church in general, in particular in Ukraine, Lviv 1935 (Works of the Greek Catholic Theological Academy, vols. I-II.

Stebletsky S. - The Persecution of the Ukrainian and White Rus Catholic Church by the Russian Tsars, Munich, 1954.

Susza J. - Saulus et Paulus Ruthenae unionis, Brussels, 1864.

Szaraniewicz I. - Patryarchat wschodni wobec kosciola ruskiego i Rzec-zypospolitej polskiej, Krak'ow, 1879.

Theiner A. - Monumenta Poloniae et Lithuaniae, Romae, 1861-1864, 5 vol.

Tomashiwsky S. - A surface History of the Kiev-Rus Church, Zhovkva, 1932 (Records of the Order of St. Basil, of St. Basil the Great, vols. I-IV).

Wasilewski J. - Arcybiskupi i administratorwie archidiecezji mohilewskiej, Pinsk, 1930.

Wasilweski J. - Sacra Congregatione per la Chiesa Orientale Cattilico Cenni storici e statistiche, Citta del Vaticano, 1962.

Zhukovych P. - The Civil Government's Battle of the Orthodox Nobility Subject to Russia against the Church Union 1609-1632. SPb. 1910.

Text References

273